IFIP Advances in Information and Communication Technology **585**

Editor-in-Chief

Kai Rannenberg, Goethe University Frankfurt, Germany

Editorial Board Members

IFIP – The International Federation for Information Processing

IFIP was founded in 1960 under the auspices of UNESCO, following the first World Computer Congress held in Paris the previous year. A federation for societies working in information processing, IFIP's aim is two-fold: to support information processing in the countries of its members and to encourage technology transfer to developing nations. As its mission statement clearly states:

IFIP is the global non-profit federation of societies of ICT professionals that aims at achieving a worldwide professional and socially responsible development and application of information and communication technologies.

IFIP is a non-profit-making organization, run almost solely by 2500 volunteers. It operates through a number of technical committees and working groups, which organize events and publications. IFIP's events range from large international open conferences to working conferences and local seminars.

The flagship event is the IFIP World Computer Congress, at which both invited and contributed papers are presented. Contributed papers are rigorously refereed and the rejection rate is high.

As with the Congress, participation in the open conferences is open to all and papers may be invited or submitted. Again, submitted papers are stringently refereed.

The working conferences are structured differently. They are usually run by a working group and attendance is generally smaller and occasionally by invitation only. Their purpose is to create an atmosphere conducive to innovation and development. Refereeing is also rigorous and papers are subjected to extensive group discussion.

Publications arising from IFIP events vary. The papers presented at the IFIP World Computer Congress and at open conferences are published as conference proceedings, while the results of the working conferences are often published as collections of selected and edited papers.

IFIP distinguishes three types of institutional membership: Country Representative Members, Members at Large, and Associate Members. The type of organization that can apply for membership is a wide variety and includes national or international societies of individual computer scientists/ICT professionals, associations or federations of such societies, government institutions/government related organizations, national or international research institutes or consortia, universities, academies of sciences, companies, national or international associations or federations of companies.

More information about this series at http://www.springer.com/series/6102

Ilias Maglogiannis · Lazaros Iliadis ·
Elias Pimenidis (Eds.)

Artificial Intelligence Applications and Innovations

AIAI 2020 IFIP WG 12.5 International Workshops

MHDW 2020 and 5G-PINE 2020
Neos Marmaras, Greece, June 5–7, 2020
Proceedings

 Springer

Editors
Ilias Maglogiannis ⓘ
Department of Digital Systems
University of Piraeus
Piraeus, Greece

Lazaros Iliadis ⓘ
Department of Civil Engineering, Lab of
Mathematics and Informatics (ISCE)
Democritus University of Thrace
Xanthi, Greece

Elias Pimenidis ⓘ
Department of Computer Science and
Creative Technologies
University of the West of England
Bristol, UK

ISSN 1868-4238   ISSN 1868-422X (electronic)
IFIP Advances in Information and Communication Technology
ISBN 978-3-030-49192-5   ISBN 978-3-030-49190-1 (eBook)
https://doi.org/10.1007/978-3-030-49190-1

This Springer imprint is published by the registered company Springer Nature Switzerland AG
The registered company address is: Gewerbestrasse 11, 6330 Cham, Switzerland

Preface

AIAI 2020 Workshops

Artificial Intelligence (AI) is already affordable through a large number of applications that offer good services to our post-modern societies. Image-face recognition and speech translation are already a reality. File sharing via Dropbox, Uber transportations, social interaction through Twitter, and shopping from eBay are employing Google's TensorFlow platform. AI has already developed high levels of reasoning. Respective applications like AlphaGo (released by Google DeepMind) have managed to defeat human experts in highly sophisticated demanding games, like *Go*. This is a great step forward, if we realize that in the *Go* game the number of potential moves is higher than the number of atoms in the entire Universe. *AlphaGo Zero* is a recent and impressive advance which is using Reinforcement Learning to teach itself. It started with no knowledge at all and in three days it bypassed the capabilities of *AlphaGo Lee*, which is the version that defeated one of the best *Go* human players in four out of five games in 2016. In 21 days, it evolved even further and it reached Master level. More specifically, it defeated 60 top professional *Go* players online and the world champion himself.

Deep Learning has significantly contributed to the progress made during the last decades. Meta-Learning and intuitive intelligence are on the way, and soon they will enable machines to understand what learning is all about. The concept of Generative Adversarial Neural Networks will try to fuse "imagination" to AI. However historic challenges for the future of mankind will be faced. Potential unethical use of AI may violate democratic human rights and may alter the character of western societies.

The 16th conference on Artificial Intelligence Applications and Innovations (AIAI 2020) offers an insight to all timely challenges related to technical, legal, and ethical aspects of AI systems and their applications. New algorithms and potential prototypes employed in diverse domains are introduced. AIAI is a mature international scientific conference held in Europe and well established in the scientific area of AI. Its history is long and very successful, following and spreading the evolution of Intelligent Systems.

The first event, was organized in Toulouse, France, in 2004. Since then, it had a continuous and dynamic presence as a major global, but mainly European, scientific event. More specifically, it has been organized in China, Greece, Cyprus, Australia, and France. It has always been technically supported by the International Federation for Information Processing (IFIP) and more specifically by the Working Group 12.5 which is interested in AI applications.

Following a long-standing tradition, this Springer volume belongs to the IFIP AICT Springer Series. It contains the papers that were accepted to be presented orally at the following workshops, held as parallel events of the AIAI 2020 conference which was held during June 5–7, 2020, as a remote live event with presentations, a lot of interaction, and Q&A sessions. There was no potential for physical attendance due to the COVID-19 global pandemic.

The following scientific workshops on timely AI subjects were organized under the framework of AIAI 2020:

9th Mining Humanistic Data Workshop (MHDW 2020)

We would like to thank the Steering Committee of MHDW 2020, Professors Ioannis Karydis and Katia Lida Kermanidis from Ionian University, Greece, and Professor Spyros Sioutas from the University of Patras, Greece, for their important contribution towards the organization of this high-quality and mature event. Also, we would like to thank Professor Christos Makris and Dr. Andreas Kanavos from the University of Patras, Greece, and Professor Phivos Mylonas Ionian University, Greece, for doing an excellent job as Senior Members of the Program Committee. MHDW is an annual event that attracts an increasing amount of high-quality research papers, under the framework of the AIAI conference.

MHDW 2020 accepted 6 full papers (12-pages long) out of 16 submissions. Due to the high quality of the submissions, the Program Committee decided additionally to accept three more papers to be published as short papers (10-pages long).

5th Workshop on 5G-Putting Intelligence to the Network Edge (5G-PINE 2020)

We would like to thank Dr. Ioannis P. Chochliouros, Research Programs Section, Research and Development Department, Fixed & Mobile, Hellenic Telecommunications Organization (OTE). We really appreciate his great efforts in organizing this high-quality 5th 5G-PINE workshop, which is a well-established annual event. It presents timely and significant results from state-of-the-art research in the 4th industrial revolution area. This workshop connects the conference with the latest AI applications in the telecommunication industry.

5G-PINE 2020 accepted 11 Full papers out of 22 submissions. Due to the high quality of the submissions, the Program Committee decided additionally to accept one more paper to be published as a short paper (10-pages long).

June 2020

Ilias Maglogiannis
Plamen Angelov
John Macintyre
Lazaros Iliadis
Stefanos Kolias
Elias Pimenidis

Organization AIAI 2020

Executive Committee

General Chairs

Ilias Maglogiannis — University of Piraeus, Greece (President of the IFIP WG12.5)

Plamen Angelov — University of Lancaster, UK

John Macintyre — University of Sunderland, UK (Dean of the Faculty of Applied Sciences and Pro Vice Chancellor of the University of Sunderland)

Program Chairs

Lazaros Iliadis — Democritus University of Thrace, Greece

Stefanos Kolias — University of Lincoln, UK

Advisory Chairs

Andreas Stafylopatis — Technical University of Athens, Greece

Vincenzo Piuri — University of Milan, Italy (IEEE Fellow (2001), IEEE Society/Council Active Memberships/Services: CIS, ComSoc, CS, CSS, EMBS, IMS, PES, PHOS, RAS, SMCS, SPS, BIOMC, SYSC, WIE)

Honorary Chair

Robert Kozma — University of Memphis, USA

Liaison Co-chairs

Ioannis Kompatsiaris — IPTIL Research Institute, Greece

Ioannis Chochliouros — Hellenic Telecommunications Organization, Greece

Workshop Chairs

Christos Makris — University of Patras, Greece

Phivos Mylonas — Ionian University, Greece

Spyros Sioutas — University of Patras, Greece

Katia Kermanidou — Ionian University, Greece

Publication and Publicity Chairs

Antonis Papaleonidas — Democritus University of Thrace, Greece

Konstantinos Demertzis — Democritus University of Thrace, Greece

George Tsekouras — University of the Aegean, Greece

Special Sessions Chairs

Panagiotis Papapetrou	Stockholm University, Sweeden
Georgios Paliouras	National Center for Scientific Research NSCR Demokritos, Greece

Steering Committee Chairs

Ilias Maglogiannis	University of Piraeus, Greece
Plamen Angelov	University of Lancaster, UK
Lazaros Iliadis	Democritus University of Thrace, Greece

Program Committee

Michel Aldanondo	Toulouse University, IMT Mines Albi, France
Georgios Alexandridis	University of the Aegean, Greece
Serafín Alonso Castro	University of Leon, Spain
Ioannis Anagnostopoulos	University of Thessaly, Greece
Costin Badica	University of Craiova, Romania
Giacomo Boracchi	Politecnico di Milano, Italy
Ivo Bukovsky	Czech Technical University in Prague, Czech Republic
George Caridakis	University of the Aegean, Greece
Francisco Carvalho	Polytechnic Institute of Tomar, Portugal
Ioannis Chamodrakas	National and Kapodistrian University of Athens, Greece
Adriana Coroiu	Babeş-Bolyai University, Romania
Kostantinos Delibasis	University of Thessaly, Greece
Konstantinos Demertzis	Democritus University of Thrace, Greece
Sergey Dolenko	Lomonosov Moscow State University, Russia
Georgios Drakopoulos	Ionian University, Greece
Mauro Gaggero	National Research Council of Italy, Italy
Ignazio Gallo	University of Insubria, Italy
Angelo Genovese	Università degli Studi di Milano, Italy
Spiros Georgakopoulos	University of Thessaly, Greece
Eleonora Giunchiglia	Oxford University, UK
Foteini Grivokostopoulou	University of Patras, Greece
Peter Hajek	University of Pardubice, Czech Republic
Giannis Haralabopoulos	University of Nottingham, UK
Ioannis Hatzilygeroudis	University of Patras, Greece
Nantia Iakovidou	King's College London, UK
Lazaros Iliadis	Democritus University of Thrace, Greece
Zhu Jin	University of Cambridge, UK
Jacek Kabziński	Lodz University of Technology, Poland
Andreas Kanavos	University of Patras, Greece
Stelios Kapetanakis	University of Brighton, UK
Petros Kefalas	CITY College, International Faculty of the University of Sheffield, Greece

Katia Kermanidis	Ionio University, Greece
Niki Kiriakidou	University of Patras, Greece
Giannis Kokkinos	University of Macedonia, Greece
Petia Koprinkova-Hristova	Bulgarian Academy of Sciences, Bulgaria
Athanasios Koutras	Technical Educational Institute of Western Greece, Greece
Paul Krause	University of Surrey, UK
Florin Leon	Technical University of Iasi, Romania
Aristidis Likas	University of Ioannina, Greece
Ioannis Livieris	University of Patras, Greece
Doina Logofătu	Frankfurt University of Applied Sciences, Germany
Ilias Maglogiannis	University of Piraeus, Greece
Goerge Magoulas	Birkbeck College, University of London, UK
Christos Makris	University of Patras, Greece
Mario Malcangi	University of Milan, Italy
Francesco Marceloni	University of Pisa, Italy
Giovanna Maria Dimitri	University of Cambridge, UK and University of Siena, Italy
Nikolaos Mitianoudis	Democritus University of Thrace, Greece
Antonio Moran	University of Leon, Spain
Konstantinos Moutselos	University of Piraeus, Greece
Phivos Mylonas	Ionio University, Greece
Stefanos Nikiforos	Ionio University, Greece
Stavros Ntalampiras	University of Milan, Italy
Mihaela Oprea	Petroleum-Gas University of Ploieşti, Romania
Ioannis P. Chochliouros	Hellenic Telecommunications Organization, Greece
Basil Papadopoulos	Democritus University of Thrace, Greece
Vaios Papaioannou	University of Patras, Greece
Antonis Papaleonidas	Democritus University of Thrace, Greece
Daniel Pérez López	University of Leon, Spain
Isidoros Perikos	University of Patras, Greece
Elias Pimenidis	University of the West of England, UK
Panagiotis Pintelas	University of Patras, Greece
Nikolaos Polatidis	University of Brighton, UK
Bernardete Ribeiro	University of Coimbra, Portugal
Leonardo Rundo	University of Cambridge, UK
Alexander Ryjov	Lomonosov Moscow State University, Russia
Simone Scardapane	Sapienza University, Italy
Evaggelos Spyrou	National Center for Scientific Research – Demokritos, Greece
Antonio Staiano	University of Naples Parthenope, Italy
Andrea Tangherloni	University of Cambridge, UK
Azevedo Tiago	University of Cambridge, UK

Francesco Trovò	Polytecnico di Milano, Italy
Nicolas Tsapatsoulis	Cyprus University of Technology, Cyprus
Petra Vidnerová	Czech Academy of Sciences, Czech Republic
Paulo Vitor de Campos Souza	CEFET-MG, Brazil
Gerasimos Vonitsanos	University of Patras, Greece

Preface

5G-PINE 2020

The 5th Workshop on 5G-Putting Intelligence to the Network Edge (5G-PINE 2020) followed the great success and wider impact of its predecessors, established to disseminate knowledge obtained from actual 5G EU-funded projects, as well as from any other action of research, in the wider thematic area of 5G innovative activies and with the main focus on Artificial Intelligence (AI) in modern 5G telecommunications infrastructures.

5G-PINE 2020 had a strong impact in the broader context of the AIAI 2020 conference. The preparatory work was mainly driven by the hard organizational effort and the dynamic coordination of Dr. Ioannis P. Chochliouros (Hellenic Telecommunications Organization - OTE, Greece) who is also the coordinator of the relevant EU-funded 5G-PPP project "5G-ESSENCE", with the support of Dr. Latif Ladid (President of IPv6 Forum and Researcher of SnT and University of Luxembourg, Luxembourg); Professor Ramjee Prasad (University of Aarhus, Denmark) who is also the coordinator of the H2020-MCSA-ITN "MOTOR-5G" project; Professor Pavlos Lazaridis (University of Huddersfield, UK); Dr. Zaharias Zaharis (Aristotle University of Thessaloniki, Greece); Mr. Uwe Herzog (EURESCOM GmbH, Germany) who is also the coordinator of the 5G-PPP project "5G-DRIVE"; Professors Oriol Sallent and Jordi Pérez-Romero (Universitat Politècnica de Catalunya, Spain); Dr. Tao Chen (VTT Technical Research Center of Finland, Finland); Dr. Slawomir Kukliński and Dr. Lechosław Tomaszewski (Orange Polska, Poland); Mr. Athanassios Dardamanis (SmartNet S.A., Greece); Dr. Ioannis Neokosmidis (inCITES Consulting SARL, Luxembourg); Mr. Stelios Pantelopoulos (Singular Logic Systems Ltd., Greece); Professor Fidel Liberal (Universidad del Pais Vasco and Euskal Herriko Unibertsitatea, Spain); and Dr. Monique Calisti and Mrs. Kai Zhang (Martel Innovate GmbH, Switzerland).

Apart from the above members of the Workshop Organizing Committee, the entire process was also supported by more than 90 European experts, several of who came from the relevant EU-funded H2020/5G-PPP projects "5G-ESSENCE" and "5G-DRIVE" as well as from the H2020-MCSA-ITN "MOTOR-5G" project, that forms the core of the corresponding effort for realizing a joint 5G-PINE 2020 workshop, purely 5G-oriented. Among the originally submitted 23 proposed papers, 11 were accepted as full papers (acceptance ratio of 50%). The acceptance of papers was based on the high quality of the works and, most importantly, due to their strong relevance to ongoing EU-funded research activities, especially in the scope of the H2020/5G-PPP framework for promoting important innovations from current-and applied-5G research activities and incentives for growth. Due to the high quality of the submissions, the Program Committee decided additionally to accept one more paper to be published as a short paper (10-pages long).

5G-PINE promotes, *inter-alia*, the context of modern 5G network infrastructures and of related innovative services in a complex and highly heterogeneous underlying Radio Access Network (RAN) ecosystem, strongly enhanced by the inclusion of cognitive capabilities and intelligence features, with the aim of improving the network management. Furthermore, based upon the well-known Self-Organizing Network (SON) functionalities, the 5G-PINE promotes network planning and optimization processes through AI based tools, able to smartly process input data from the environment and come up with knowledge that can be formalized in terms of models and/or structured metrics, able to represent the network behavior. This allows for the gaining of in-depth and detailed knowledge about the whole underlying 5G ecosystem, understanding hidden patterns, data structures, and relationships, and using them for a more efficient network management.

5G-PINE supports delivery of intelligence directly to network's edge, by exploiting the emerging paradigms of Network Functions Virtualisation (NFV), Software Defined Networking (SDN), Network Slicing, and Edge Cloud Computing. Moreover, it supports the promotion of rich virtualization and multi-tenant capabilities, optimally deployed close to the user. It emphasizes the Small Cell (SC) concept, so as to support improved cellular coverage, capacity, and applications in a fully dynamic and flexible manner with strong emphasis on vertical applications, based on well-defined scenaria and/or selective use cases as promoted by the detailed 5G ESSENCE context. Another one among the important areas of interest has been around the original scope of the "5G-DRIVE" project promoting cooperation between EU and China, especially by discussing the proposed context for trials according to the corresponding European policy for realizing tests and trials, as well as by promoting the context for enhanced Mobile Broadband (eMBB) applications and "Vehicle-to-Everything" (V2X) communications. Last but not least, among the pillars of the 5G-PINE workshop there has also been the framework promoted by the ongoing H2020-MCSA-ITN "MOTOR-5G" project focusing on embedding AI into 5G communication systems for the smarter use of network-generated data, the automated enabling of network operators and service providers to adapt to changes in traffic patterns, security risks, and user behavior, thus paving the way towards safe and reliable next-generation wireless ecosystems.

The accepted papers focus on several innovative findings coming directly from modern European research in the area, that is from the 5G-PPP projects "5G-ESSENCE", "5G-DRIVE", "5G-PHOS", "5GCity", and "5G-MEDIA"; the H2020 "DataPorts" and "YAKSHA" projects; as well as from the Spanish "SONAR 5G" Grant all covering a wide variety of technical and business aspects and promoting options for growth and development in the respective market(s). One additional work also comes from the H2020-MCSA-ITN "MOTOR-5G" project. The other accepted papers cover broader aspects of current research activities in the respective domains, as briefly outlined before. All works are fully aligned to the objectives of the 5G-PINE 2020 scope and introduce innovative aspects.

Organization 5G-PINE 2020

Co-chairs

Ioannis P. Chochliouros	Hellenic Telecommunications Organization (OTE), Greece
Latif Ladid	IPv6 Forum and University of Luxembourg, Luxembourg
Ramjee Prasad	University of Aarhus, Denmark
Pavlos Lazaridis	University of Huddersfield, UK
Zaharias Zaharis	Aristotle University of Thessaloniki, Greece
Oriol Sallent	Universitat Politècnica de Catalunya, Spain
Jordi Pérez-Romero	Universitat Politècnica de Catalunya, Spain
Uwe Herzog	EURESCOM GmbH, Germany
Tao Chen	VTT Technical Research Center of Finland, Finland
Slawomir Kukliński	Orange Polska, Poland
Lechosław Tomaszewski	Orange Polska, Poland
Athanassios Dardamanis	SmartNet S.A., Greece
Ioannis Neokosmidis	inCITES Consulting SARL, Luxembourg
Stelios Pantelopoulos	Singular Logic Systems Ltd., Greece
Fidel Liberal	Universidad del Pais Vasco and Euskal Herriko Unibertsitatea, Spain
Monique Calisti	Martel Innovate, Switzerland
Kai Zhang	Martel Innovate, Switzerland

Program Committee

George Lyberopoulos	COSMOTE - Mobile Telecommunications S.A., Greece
Nancy Alonistioti	National and Kapodistrian University of Athens, Greece
Anastasios Kourtis	National Centre for Scientific Research Demokritos, Greece
Tilemachos Doukoglou	Hellenic Telecommunications Organization (OTE), Greece
Alexandros Kostopoulos	Hellenic Telecommunications Organization (OTE), Greece
Begoña Blanco	Universidad del Pais Vasco and Euskal Herriko Unibertsitatea, Spain
Anastasia Spiliopoulou	Hellenic Telecommunications Organization (OTE), Greece
Nina Mitsopoulou	Hellenic Telecommunications Organization (OTE), Greece

Ridha Soua	University of Luxembourg, Luxembourg
Oscar Carrasco	CASA Communications Technology SL, Spain
Stamatia Rizou	Singular Logic Systems Ltd., Greece
Theodoros Rokkas	inCITES Consulting SARL, Luxembourg
Roberto Riggio	Fondazione Bruno Kessler, Italy
Maria-Rita Spada	Wind Tre S.p.A., Italy
Michail-Alexandros Kourtis	ORION Innovations Private Company, Greece
Ioannis Giannoulakis	National Centre for Scientific Research Demokritos, Greece
Daniele Munaretto	Athonet S.R.L, Italy
Betty Charalampopoulou	Geosystems Hellas S.A., Spain
Juan Sánchez-González	Universitat Politècnica de Catalunya, Spain
Seyedeh Soheila Shaabanzadeh	Universitat Politècnica de Catalunya, Spain
Qasim Zeeshan Ahmed	University of Huddersfield, UK
Abdelwahab Boualouache	University of Luxembourg, Luxembourg
Cedric Crettaz	Mandat International, Switzerland
Vishanth Weerakkody	University of Bradford, UK
George Agapiou	Hellenic Telecommunications Organization (OTE), Greece
Rodoula Makri	National Technical University of Athens, Greece
Emmanouil Kafetzakis	ORION Innovations Private Company, Greece
Stephanie Oestlund	University of Luxembourg, Luxembourg
Antonino Albanese	Italtel S.p.A., Italy
Paolo-Secondo Crost	Italtel S.p.A., Italy
Mike Iosifidis	Clemic Services S.A., Greece
Claus Keuker	Smart Mobile Labs AG, Germany
Nissrine Saraireh	Smart Mobile Labs AG, Germany
Leonardo Goratti	TriaGnoSys GmbH, Germany
Tinku Rasheed	TriaGnoSys GmbH, Germany
Elisenda Temprado-Garriga	TriaGnoSys GmbH, Germany
Elisa Jimeno	ATOS Spain S.A., Spain
Vasilios Vassilakis	University of West London, UK
Irene Karapistoli	Cyberlens Ltd., UK
Manos Panaousis	University of Brighton, UK
Jose-Oscar Fajardo	Universidad del Pais Vasco and Euskal Herriko Unibertsitatea, Spain
Javier Fernandez Hidalgo	Fundació Privada i2CAT, Internet i Innovació Digital a Catalunya, Spain
Miguel Catalan-Cid	Fundació Privada i2CAT, Internet i Innovació Digital a Catalunya, Spain
Faiza Bouchmal	CASA Communications Technology SL, Spain
Estefania Coronado	Fondazione Bruno Kessler, Italy
Ehsan Ebrahimi Khaleghi	Thales SIX GTS France SAS, France
Hicham Khalifé	Thales SIX GTS France SAS, France
Paul Hirst	BAPCO LBG, UK

Adam Flizikowski	IS-Wireless Pietrzyk Slawomir, Poland
Olga Segou	ORION Innovations Private Company, Greece
Elina Theodoropoulou	COSMOTE - Mobile Telecommunications S.A., Greece
Ioanna Mesogiti	COSMOTE - Mobile Telecommunications S.A., Greece
Juha Jidbeck	VTT Technical Research Center of Finland, Finland
Octavian Fratu	Politehnica University of Bucharest, Romania
Maria Belesioti	Hellenic Telecommunications Organization (OTE), Greece
Evangelos Sfakianakis	Hellenic Telecommunications Organization (OTE), Greece
Eirini Vasilaki	Hellenic Telecommunications Organization (OTE), Greece
Jason Sioutis	Eight Bells Ltd., Cyprus
Kelly Georgiadou	Hellenic Telecommunications Organization (OTE), Greece
Konstantinos Helidonis	Hellenic Telecommunications Organization (OTE), Greece
Christos Mizikakis	Hellenic Telecommunications Organization (OTE), Greece
Ioanna Papafili	Hellenic Telecommunications Organization (OTE), Greece
Velissarios Gezerlis	Hellenic Telecommunications Organization (OTE), Greece
Christos-Antonios Gizelis	Hellenic Telecommunications Organization (OTE), Greece
Theodoros Mavroeidakos	Hellenic Telecommunications Organization (OTE), Greece
Konstantinos Filis	COSMOTE - Mobile Telecommunications S.A., Greece
Fotini Setaki	COSMOTE - Mobile Telecommunications S.A., Greece
Dimitrios Tzempelikos	Municipality of Egaleo, Greece
Evridiki Pavlidi	Municipality of Egaleo, Greece
Kostis Kaggelides	Gnomon Informatics S.A., Greece
Vangelis Logothetis	INCITES Consulting S.A.R.L., Luxembourg
Dimitrios Kavallieros	Centre for Security Studies (KEMEA), Greece
Miltos Anastasiadis	Motivian Eood, Bulgaria
Alessandro Guarino	StagCyber, Italy
Donal Morris	RedZinc Services, Ireland
Luis Cordeiro	OneSource Consultoria Informatica, LDA, Portugal
Makis Stamatelatos	National and Kapodistrian University of Athens, Greece
Panagiotis Kontopoulos	National and Kapodistrian University of Athens, Greece
Vasilios Vlachos	Technological Educational Institute of Larisa, Greece

Andreas Drakos	Channel VAS, Greece
Srdjan Krčo	DunavNET Doo, Serbia
Nenad Gligoric	DunavNET Doo, Serbia
Luca Bolognini	Italian Institute for Privacy, Italy
Camilla Bistolfi	Italian Institute for Privacy, Italy
Christina Lessi	Hellenic Telecommunications Organization (OTE), Greece
Konstantina Katsampani	Hellenic Telecommunications Organization (OTE), Greece
George Tsiouris	Hellenic Telecommunications Organization (OTE), Greece
George Goulas	Hellenic Telecommunications Organization (OTE), Greece
Ioannis Stephanakis	Hellenic Telecommunications Organization (OTE), Greece
Antonis Georgiou	ACTA Ltd., Greece
Simos Symeonidis	ACTA Ltd., Greece
Konstantinos Patsakis	University of Piraeus, Greece
Marinos Agapiou	National and Kapodistrian University of Athens, Greece

Preface

MHDW 2020

The abundance of available data, which is retrieved from or is related to the areas of Humanities and the human condition, challenges the research community in processing and analyzing it. The aim is two-fold: on the one hand, to extract knowledge that will help to understand human behavior, creativity, way of thinking, reasoning, learning, decision making, socializing, and even biological processes; on the other hand, to exploit the extracted knowledge by incorporating it into intelligent systems that will support humans in their everyday activities.

The nature of humanistic data can be multimodal, semantically heterogeneous, dynamic, time and space-dependent, as well as highly complicated. Translating humanistic information, e.g. behavior, state of mind, artistic creation, linguistic utterance, learning, and genomic information into numerical or categorical low-level data, is considered a significant challenge on its own. New techniques, appropriate to deal with this type of data, need to be proposed whereas existing ones must be adapted to its special characteristics.

The workshop aims to bring together interdisciplinary approaches that focus on the application of innovative as well as existing data matching, fusion, and mining as well as knowledge discovery and management techniques (like decision rules, decision trees, association rules, ontologies and alignments, clustering, filtering, learning, classifier systems, neural networks, support vector machines, preprocessing, post processing, feature selection and visualization techniques) to data derived from all areas of Humanistic Sciences (e.g. linguistic, historical, behavioral, psychological, artistic, musical, educational, social, etc.) Ubiquitous Computing, as well as Bioinformatics.

Ubiquitous Computing applications (aka Pervasive Computing, Mobile Computing, Ambient Intelligence, etc.) collect large volumes of usually heterogeneous data in order to effect adaptation, learning, and in general context awareness. Data matching, fusion, and mining techniques are necessary to ensure human centered application functionality.

An important aspect of humanistic centers consists of managing, processing, and computationally analyzing biological and biomedical data. Hence, one of the main aims of this workshop was to attract researchers interested in designing, developing, and applying efficient data and text mining techniques for discovering the underlying knowledge existing in biomedical data, such as sequences, gene expressions, and pathways.

Topics of interest include but are not limited to (please see):
https://conferences.cwa.gr/mhdw2020/workshop-aim/

Organization MHDW 2020

Program Chairs

Andreas Kanavos   University of Patras, Greece
Christos Makris   University of Patras, Greece
Phivos Mylonas   Ionian University, Greece

Steering Committee

Ioannis Karydis   Ionian University, Greece
Katia-Lida Kermanidis   Ionian University, Greece
Spyros Sioutas   University of Patras, Greece

Program Committee

Ioannis Anagnostopoulos   University of Thessaly, Greece
Georgios Drakopoulos   Ionian University, Greece
Ioannis Hatzilygeroudis   University of Patras, Greece
Costas Iliopoulos   King's College London, UK
Andreas Komninos   University of Patras, Greece
Fotis Kounelis   Imperial College London, UK
Ioannis Livieris   University of Patras, Greece
Manolis Maragoudakis   University of the Aegean, Greece
Alaa Mohasseb   University of Portsmouth, UK
Iosif Mporas   University of Hertfordshire, UK
Ioannis Panagis   University of Copenhagen, Denmark
Emmanuel Pintelas   University of Patras, Greece
Panayotis Pintelas   University of Patras, Greece
Evaggelos Spyrou   University of Thessaly, Greece
Gerasimos Vonitsanos   University of Patras, Greece

Contents

5th Workshop on "5G-Putting Intelligence to the Network Edge" (5G-PINE 2020)

A Framework to Support the 5G Densification

Eleni Theodoropoulou[1]([⊠])[ID], Ioanna Mesogiti[1],
George Lyberopoulos[1], George Kalfas[2], Christos Vagionas[2],
Nikos Pleros[2], Annachiara Pagano[3], Mauro Agus[3], Luiz Anet Neto[4],
Nikos Psaromanolakis[5], and Athina Ropodi[5]

[1] COSMOTE Mobile Telecommunications S.A., 99 Kifissias Avenue,
15124 Maroussi, Athens, Greece
etheodorop@cosmote.gr
[2] Aristotle University of Thessaloniki, Thessaloniki, Greece
[3] Telecom Italia, Turin, Italy
[4] Orange Labs, Lannion, France
[5] Incelligent, Athens, Greece

Abstract. 5G networks are shaping a new ecosystem necessitating various transformations of the existing network infrastructures combined with the use of network softwarization and programmability, so as to satisfy the needs of all the involved stakeholders (telecom/service providers, infrastructure owners, tenants, vertical industries, end-users, etc.), while a wide range of issues have to be addressed spanning from technology to business domains. The 5G-PPP project 5G-PHOS [1] proposes a novel framework to allow telecom operators and service providers to overcome 5G densification issues while supporting the stringent 5G requirements in a flexible and cost efficient manner to allow for commercialization. This paper aims at providing indicative architectural instantiations of the 5G-PHOS solution, depicting the way the technology supports the 5G requirements and the stakeholders' needs along with the functionalities and the deployment feasibility of an ambitious 5G fronthaul/backhaul network solution.

Keywords: 5G · Use cases · 5G-PHOS architecture · Architectural instantiations · Fiber-wireless · Optical technologies · R-RRH · SL-RRH · Massive MIMO · Flexbox

1 Introduction

The 5G vision to support the next generation services mandates the satisfaction of very strict user experience and system performance Key Performance Indicators (KPI) imposed by the 5G-PPP, that the current networks are incapable of satisfying without being transformed; including, among others, efficient feasible and affordable fronthaul/backhaul networks and related infrastructures to support the ultra-broadband 5G New Radio (NR) requirements [2–8]. In particular, the densification which is expected to be an integral part of 5G deployment, is about 10x denser than 4G and 100x denser than 3G networks and carries a number of issues to be addressed, such as the exploitation of higher frequency bands for extreme data throughput, low latency

I. Maglogiannis et al. (Eds.): AIAI 2020 Workshops, IFIP AICT 585, pp. 3–14, 2020.
https://doi.org/10.1007/978-3-030-49190-1_1

and ubiquitous coverage to be achieved, limited real-estate in urban and hotspot areas, the need for new regulations to facilitate the costly and time-consuming deployment of Base Stations/Small Cells and fibers, not to mention the hardware equipment costs associated with the Centralized Radio Access Network (C-RAN) deployment to address the expected explosion of the fronthaul (FH) capacity. A framework to help the telecom/service provider to mitigate and overcome the densification problems and deployment costs, is currently missing from the 5G solution pool, and is offered via the 5G-PHOS 5G-PPP EU project.

More specifically, the 5G-PHOS project aims at providing Mobile Network Operators (MNOs) and possibly, verticals and/or infrastructure owners (municipalities, stadium owners, etc.) [13], with an attractive fronthaul network solution, both in terms of performance and cost, especially addressing the 5G NR densification and 5G capacity issues. By capitalizing on existing wireless and optical technologies, the 5G-PHOS transforms the current all-digital Point-to-Point (PtP) FH to a Point-to-Multi-Point (PtMP) digital and analog converged Fiber-Wireless (FiWi) FH, bridging one centralized to multiple remote locations through combined fiber and ultra-broadband wireless links, while maintaining compatibility with the standardized enhanced Common Public Radio Interface (eCPRI) –capable of combating the FH capacity explosion by supporting higher FH splits.

The paper is organized as follows: To start with, an overview of the 5G-PHOS project is presented to facilitate better understanding of the framework and the solution innovations, as well as the impact of 5G-PHOS solution on the 5G architectures. In the next section, the 5G-PHOS architecture is elaborated in the context of the three (3) Use Cases (UCs) envisioned by the project [12], to be followed by the architectural instantiations that depict the feasibility of the 5G-PHOS solution deployment so as to satisfy the needs and requirements of all the involved stakeholders, while conclusions are drawn at the end.

2   5G-PHOS Solution Overview

5G-PHOS addresses, in a flexible and efficient manner, the challenging 5G densification framework encompassing a range of urban, dense urban and hotspot environments, exhibiting different traffic density and coverage needs, that arise either under normal daily conditions or occasionally, during specific events (e.g., parades, outdoor concerts), while supporting the wide variety of 5G services, including: enhanced Mobile Broadband (eMBB), massive Machine-Type Communications (mMTC) aka Massive IoT (mIoT), Ultra-Reliable Low-Latency Communications (URLLC), and at the same time the Network Operation Services addressing the functional system requirements, including: flexible functions and capabilities, multi-tenancy, energy efficiency, interworking, security, etc. Indicative environments may span from typical residential and business areas in big European cities to highly touristic areas with seasonality based activity, and hotspots -usually small privately-owned establishments, like stadiums or concert halls hosting crowd events in a random or periodic frequency. In this context, the goal of the 5G-PHOS project is to develop novel 5G broadband architectures and evaluate them at dense, ultra-dense and hotspot areas.

The main incentive behind the 5G-PHOS architecture is to create an ultra-broadband converged FiWi PtMP fronthaul network, capable of supporting the required 5G NR fronthaul bandwidth, while at the same time alleviating the need to install fiber terminations at every MNO Base Station (BS) site. Therefore, it comprises a very appealing solution for MNOs and infrastructure owner since it exhibit a wide range of benefits, such as:

- Utilization as front-/mid-/backhaul or Fixed-Wireless Access (FWA), meeting the 5G KPIs in terms of capacity, latency, QoS, energy efficiency, etc.
- Fast 5G network deployment capability (use of wireless (PtMP) vs. fibers)
- Cost efficiency (utilization of novel optical/wireless technologies, reliable wireless technologies, energy efficient components, etc.)
- Support of a wide range of UCs/scenarios over a single architecture
- Flexibility/versatility at various levels (e.g., wireless links at 5G networks' last-mile, flexible allocation of resources planned and handled by SDN, flexible channel/sub-band allocation framework to support different UCs)
- Scalability (modularity of the MIMO antennas and network reconfigurability to up-scale in terms of capacity)
- Multi-tenancy, multi-operator, multi-domain support through slicing and infrastructure/resources sharing
- Interoperability with and smooth migration from 4G networks/solutions

The 5G-PHOS solution builds upon the prevalent enhanced eCPRI standard and creates the necessary infrastructure to interconnect eCPRI-capable equipment in a PtMP manner, that is, the centralized equipment, e.g. in the fronthaul case the Base Band Unit (BBU), can be concurrently connected to several Remote Radio Heads (RRHs), through a converged FiWi network, as depicted in Fig. 1.

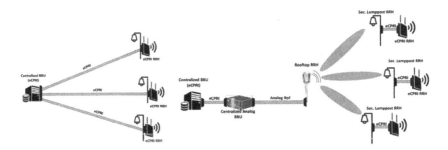

Fig. 1. 5G-PHOS transforms the PtP dedicated fiber link Fronthaul (left side) to a converged Fiber-Wireless PtMP high capacity analog Fronthaul (right side).

The 5G-PHOS aims to produce a powerful Photonic Integrated Chip (PIC) technology toolkit capitalizing on novelties in optical technologies, such as Indium Phosphide (InP) transceiver, Triplex optical beamformers and multi-bitrate optical communications into next generation fronthaul in order to migrate from CPRI-based to integrated FiWi packetized C-RAN fronthaul supporting Millimeter Wave (mmWave) massive Multiple-Input Multiple-Output (mMIMO) communications.

The novel technologies combined into one powerful suite and their associated benefits are the following:

- Analog Radio-over-Fiber (A-RoF) transmission, enabling the use of higher order modulation schemes, resulting in low complexity of Rooftop-RRHs and high spectral efficiency.
- Synergy of mmWave wireless radio and mMIMO antennas to provide increased capacity and link reliability, while reducing the need for PtP fiber deployment.
- Combination of Optical Beamforming Networks (OBFNs) and massive MIMO mmWave antennas, enabling the creation of complex Rooftop RRH antenna patterns to reach the multitude of lamppost antennas with highly-directed beams; thus enhancing the flexibility of the wireless links.
- Cutting-edge PIC technologies for a number of critical functionalities, i.e., laser arrays, Optical Beamforming Networks (OBFNs), Reconfigurable Optical Add Drop Multiplexers (ROADMs), offering high-power, low-cost, better power-coupling, high-responsivity, etc.
- Ethernet-based network processors allowing not only for connectivity/ integration with (MNO) equipment for a smooth 4G to 5G migration, but also enabling the Software Defined Networking (SDN) framework for efficient network management towards low-latency and energy-efficient reconfigurable 5G network-on-demand schemes.

In the end, 5G-PHOS expects to release a seamless, interoperable, Radio Access Technology (RAT)-agnostic and SDN-programmable high-capacity FiWi 5G C-RAN network solution for dense, ultra-dense and hotspot scenarios supporting 64x64 MIMO antennas in the V-band able to offer data rates up to 400 Gb/s, while efficiently facing the CPRI fronthaul capacity problem.

3 5G-PHOS Architecture for Representative Use Cases

The 5G-PHOS solution is versatile and can be used not only as fronthaul but also as midhaul or backhaul, by appropriate placement of the 5G-PHOS stack within 3GPP's three-way split defining the respective entities:

- the Centralized Unit (CU) located at the MNO's Central Office (backhaul)
- the Distributed Unit (DU) usually at the basement of the building containing the antennas or somewhere close-by (fronthaul) and
- the Radio Unit (RU) including the radio elements and the unit closest to the mobile users (fronthaul).

The 5G-PHOS proposes 3 variants (Fig. 2, Fig. 3, Fig. 4) of the architectural design, one for each of the 3 UCs envisioned by the project: the dense, ultra-dense and hotspot [9, 10].

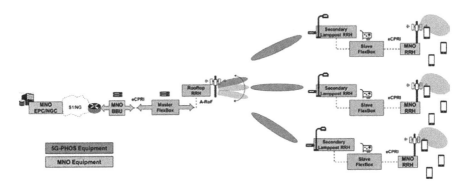

Fig. 2. The 5G-PHOS PtMP fronthaul solution for Dense Area Use Case. (Color figure online)

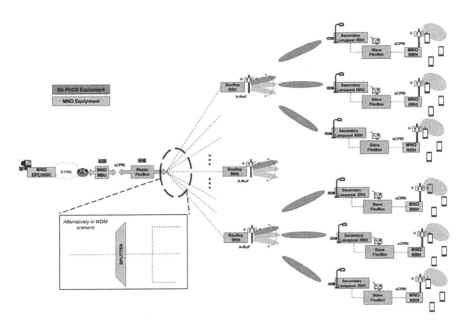

Fig. 3. The 5G-PHOS PtMP fronthaul solution in the Ultra-Dense Use Case. (Color figure online)

The 5G-PHOS architecture (as shown in Fig. 2, Fig. 3, Fig. 4) introduces a number of nodes (in orange) the functionality of which is described below:

- Master Flexbox: It receives the digital eCPRI signals generated by the BBU/CU/DU, and loads the incoming Ethernet packets onto analog carriers to traverse the converged FiWi network. It creates and transmits all FH control plane signals and hosts all higher-level operations such as SDN agents and access control, while creating the analog signals for the downlink direction. Regarding SDN functionalities, the Master Flexbox supports OpenvSwitch (OvS), a production quality, multilayer virtual switch, while OpenFlow, OVSDB and NETCONF

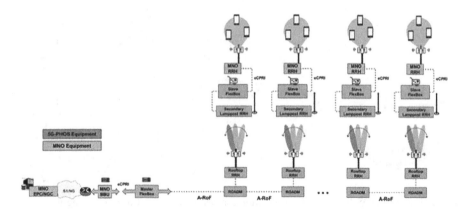

Fig. 4. The 5G-PHOS PtMP fronthaul solution in the Hotspot area Use Case. (Color figure online)

protocols support the interaction with the SDN controller [11]. In terms of hardware, the Master Flexbox contains the network controller that hosts the upper-layer functionalities and Ethernet packet processing, as well as the FPGA module that performs the Digital Signal Processing (DSP) functions and the transceivers of the actual data. The Master Flexbox is connected through an Ethernet port (provided by the network controller) to the centralized unit (BBU, CU, DU or 4G/5G core depending on the 5G-PHOS stack placement).

- Rooftop RRH (R-RRH): It receives the analog signals from the Master Flexbox and transmits them over the air in the mmWave band. In terms of hardware, it contains the OBFN module and the mmWave massive MIMO antenna. In the hotspot UC (Fig. 4), the R-RRH contains also the ROADM module to perform wavelength selection among multiple wavelengths employed.
- Secondary Lamppost RRH (SL-RRH): It comprises the mmWave antenna that receives the signals from or transmits to the R-RRH. It is simpler than the R-RRH, since it communicates to a single R-RRH only in the uplink direction and does not contain OBFNs.
- Slave Flexbox: It contains a lightweight version of the network controller and an FPGA that receives and decodes the signals belonging to the FH Control and Data planes (CP, DP). Moreover, the Slave Flexbox hosts some high-level operations such as SDN agents, while it creates the analog signals for the uplink direction for both CP and DP. It is connected through an Ethernet port (provided by the network controller) to the remote unit (RU, DU, or gNB depending on the placement of the solution). Again, the Slave Flexbox supports OpenvSwitch and hence OpenFlow, OVSDB and NETCONF.

In the variant of the ultra-dense UC architecture, the number of R-RRH (as well as MNO RRH) modules in a geographical area may increase up to 16 R-RRH connected to the Master Flexbox by either 16 fibers or alternatively by the use of 16 wavelengths in a WDM manner. In this way, MNOs or Infrastructure Owners (IOs) can multiply accordingly the offered capacity in areas with great population densities and increased capacity requirements, such as city centers.

What differentiates the hotspot architecture is the adoption of a WDM approach to increase capacity, supported by the employment of the 5G-PHOS ROADM module placed in a single fiber bus topology, recommended for internal cabling.

4 5G-PHOS Architectural Instantiations

This Section presents the architectural instantiations that fulfill the requirements of the main stakeholders of the 5G-PHOS solution (that is, MNOs, site owners, tenants) in a flexible and economically viable way, in dense, ultra-dense, hotspot areas, based on representative scenarios: multi-operator through slicing (sharing part or the entire 5G-PHOS solution), multi-tenancy to support multiple verticals concurrently, multi-domain operation (e.g., fixed and wireless belonging to the same or different operators).

Scenario #1: Multi-operator and slicing support of "local" Operator(s)
Operator A shares with Operator B (having no or limited "presence" in the area), part of or the entire 5G-PHOS solution (R-RRHs, SL-RRHs, 5G equipment) already deployed to meet Operator A own capacity, coverage and (own) customer needs. Two (2) sub-scenarios can be considered:

(a) **Operator B as Operator's A tenant sharing the same SL-RRH**

Operator B connects its antennas directly (through the Ethernet interface) to an existing SL-RRH that belongs to Operator A, as depicted in Fig. 5. The SDN framework allows for slicing functionality support and provides the Operator A with the capability of forming a "slice" for Operator B with several options based on rules, such as: (a) allocate dedicated sub-bands to Operator B either a static (pre-defined) way or dynamically with an upper limit (scaled-up or scaled-down automatically based on optimization algorithms that are running on the SDN controller) and b) allocate certain capacity within an existing sub-band, for instance share 1 Gbps out of a 2.4 Gbps sub-band. The rules are transmitted to both the Master and Slave Flexbox units by use of the OpenFlow and OVSDB protocols (based on TCP/IP).

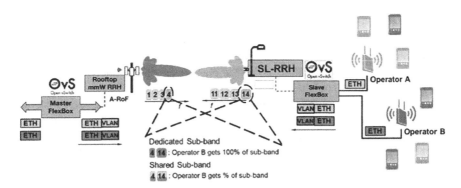

Fig. 5. 5G-PHOS multi-operator architectural instantiation using the same SL-RRH.

(b) **Operator B as Operator's A tenant sharing the same R-RRHs**

Operator B deploys own SL-RRHs and 5G RRHs (connected to its SL-RRH through the Ethernet interface provided by the Slave Flexbox unit), as depicted in Fig. 6. This new SL-RRH communicates wirelessly to the R-RRH owned by Operator A, and is added to the 5G-PHOS system. Again, Operator A forms a separate "slice" for Operator B through the SDN (assign sub-bands static or dynamic, limit traffic bandwidth, increase/decrease capacity if the contract changes, etc.)

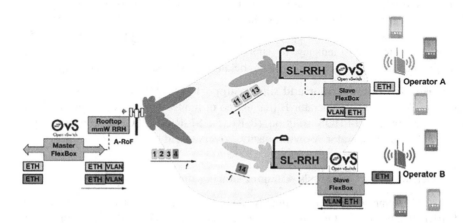

Fig. 6. 5G-PHOS multi-operator architectural instantiation using different SL-RRHs.

Scenario #2: MNO adopts 5G-PHOS solution at dense/ultra-dense areas
The Operator/MNO deploys the 5G-PHOS solution (R-RRHs, SL-RRHs, 5G equipment) to meet its own needs (mobile and fixed subscribers via fixed wireless access (FWA), tenants, excluding "local" MNOs) in a dense/ultra-dense area in a flexible and economically viable way. Two (2) sub-scenarios can be considered:

(a) **Multi-tenancy to support multiple verticals concurrently through slicing**

A vertical application, e.g., based on security cameras can be easily integrated into the 5G-PHOS system, since they are connected to the MNO's SL-RRH through the Slave Flexbox's Ethernet interface as depicted in Fig. 7. As in Scenario #1, the cameras' IP addresses are utilized for the assignment of fronthaul capacity to them through the OpenvSwitch interface. In case that more than one cameras are connected to the same SL-RRH, the SDN rules could be either port-based (the same rule for the total traffic) or IP-based depending on camera/user requirements. As described in Scenario #1, the security cameras can either get dedicated sub-bands or share sub-bands with other services, while the OpenvSwitch ensures that the traffic will not exceed the allocated capacity.

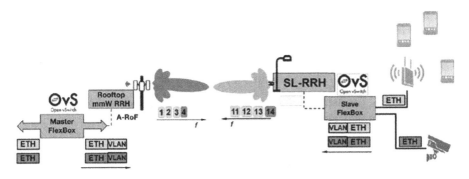

Fig. 7. 5G-PHOS multi-tenancy architectural instantiation using the same SL-RRH.

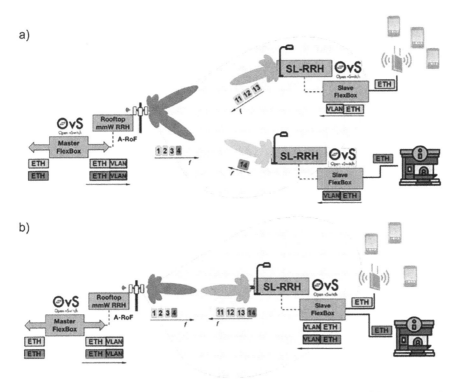

Fig. 8. 5G-PHOS multi-domain architectural instantiation a) using dedicated SL-RRHs and b) sharing the same SL-RRH.

(b) Support of multi-domain applications

The MNO uses the 5G-PHOS solution to provide fixed access to a subscriber, for instance a Tourist Information kiosk in a central square. Two alternatives can be envisaged/supported:

(i) Through a dedicated SL-RRH (that will serve the kiosk) (Fig. 8 (a)) added to the 5G-PHOS system and managed by the MNO via the SDN framework

(ii) Direct connection of the kiosk router/switch to an existing SL-RRH (Fig. 8 (b)). The kiosk becomes a tenant connected to the 5G-PHOS solution (see Multi-tenancy to support multiple tenants/verticals concurrently through slicing).

Scenario #3: 5G Infrastructure Owner (IO) serves own and tenant needs supporting Multi-tenancy and Multi-operator domain

The infrastructure owner (e.g., a stadium owner) has deployed its own 5G-PHOS solution for its own needs (own staff, fans). In addition, it offers the possibility to verticals and MNOs to deploy their own infrastructure.

The stadium owner has set up its own network consisting of a series of R-RRHs (deployed in bus topology) connecting several SL-RRHs (spread out in the fans' seating area) offering access to WiFi access points through its Slave Flexbox Ethernet interfaces. During a football match -it is necessary or a contractual obligation with third parties- to deploy extra services for various tenants, such as MNOs, TV broadcasters or first-responders. The tenant's equipment, as depicted in Fig. 9 could be installed: (i) either directly to the Ethernet interface of an already deployed SL-RRH or the IO could allow the tenant –upon agreement- to deploy its own SL-RRH(s).

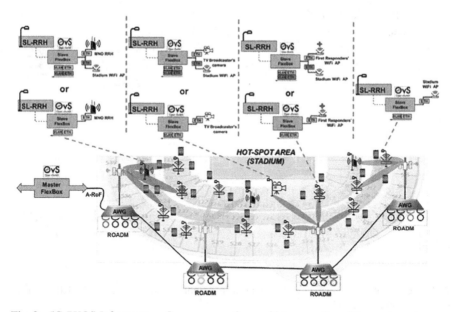

Fig. 9. 5G-PHOS Infrastructure Owner supporting multi-tenancy & multi-operator schemes.

Since the IO is the 5G-PHOS solution owner, the IO has exclusive access to the SDN framework and thus can manage the various "slices" flexibly. For instance, TV broadcaster's camera equipment connected to a dedicated or shared SL-RRH can be assigned to a static and dedicated "slice" with the necessary number of sub-bands, since the cameras produce a constant load and it is critical not to disrupt the service. The first responders' dedicated WiFi APs can either have a dedicated sub-band or guaranteed capacity within a shared sub-band, since the service is critical, not high-load and used in emergency situations only. The MNOs can also lease (static or dynamic) capacity for the duration of the football game.

5 Discussion

This paper focuses on the 5G-PHOS solution and its impact on the 5G networks architecture, especially addressing the 5G densification. The 5G-PHOS solution is a high-capacity FiWi 5G C-RAN network solution for dense, ultra-dense and hotspot scenarios supporting 64×64 MIMO antennas in the V-band able to offer data rates up to 400 Gb/s, while efficiently facing the CPRI fronthaul capacity problem. Depending on its placement in the MNO's network, the 5G-PHOS solution can be utilized as telecom bridge for fronthaul, midhaul, backhaul, or combination of them, as well as a FWA solution and WiFi hotspot solution. Focusing on the fronthaul, it comprises an attractive network solution, in terms of performance cost and supported functionalities, for the involved stakeholders (e.g., telecom operators/MNOs, vertical infrastructure owners), while alleviating the need for fiber deployment at every BS site. The paper elaborates on the 5G-PHOS through architectural instantiations, explaining how the 5G user and system requirements as well as the involved stakeholders' needs are supported by the 5G-PHOS solution.

Acknowledgements. The research leading to these results has received funding from the European Union's Framework Programme Horizon 2020 under grant agreement No. 761989 and project name "5G-PHOS: 5G integrated Fiber-Wireless networks exploiting existing photonic technologies for high-density SDN programmable network architectures".

References

1. 5G-PHOS H2020 5G-PPP Project. http://www5g-phos.eu/
2. 5G-PPP Program, European Commission, Living document on "5G-PPP use cases and performance evaluation models"
3. 5G-PPP, The 5G Infrastructure Public Private Partnership. https://5g-ppp.eu/
4. 5G Americas: 5G Services and Use Cases, White paper, November 2017. http://www. 5gamericas.org/files/6214/3569/1603/4G_Americas_Mobile_Broadband_Evolution_ Toward_5G-Rel-12_Rel-13_June_2015.pdf
5. Nokia white paper: Ultra dense networks (2016)
6. Osseiran, A., Monserrat, J., Marsch, P. (eds.): 5G Mobile and Wireless Communications Technology. Cambridge University Press, Cambridge (2016)
7. 5G-PPP View on 5G Architecture, Version 2.0 (2017). https://5g-ppp.eu/wp-content/ uploads/2018/01/5G-PPP-5G-Architecture-White-Paper-Jan-2018-v2.0.pdf
8. 3GPP, TS 23.501: System Architecture for the 5G System; Stage 2. Rel. 15
9. 5G-PHOS, Deliverable D2.1: Initial report on use cases, system requirements, KPIs and Network Architecture. http://5g-phos.eu/pdf/5G-PHOS_D2.1_Final.pdf

10. 5G-PHOS, Deliverable D2.2: Initial design of 5G-PHOS flexbox and RRH system architecture and component specifications including resource allocation and SDN functions, (Internal to the consortium)
11. 5G-PHOS, Deliverable D7.1: SDN controller and FPGA-based DSP engine implementation (Confidential)
12. Lyberopoulos, G., et al.: Fiber-wireless Fronthaul/Backhaul network architectures for 5G. In: Proceedings of the Computer Aided Modeling and Design of Communication Links and Networks (CAMAD), 2018 IEEE 20th International Workshop, Barcelona, Spain, 17–19 September 2018. https://doi.org/10.1109/camad.2018.8514991
13. Mesogiti, I., et al.: A framework to support the role of telecommunication service providers in evolving 5G business models. In: MacIntyre, J., Maglogiannis, I., Iliadis, L., Pimenidis, E. (eds.) AIAI 2019. IAICT, vol. 560, pp. 60–69. Springer, Cham (2019). https://doi.org/10. 1007/978-3-030-19909-8_5

A New Approach to 5G and MEC Integration

Lechosław Tomaszewski[1]([⊠]), Sławomir Kukliński[1,2], and Robert Kołakowski[1]

[1] Orange Polska, Warsaw, Poland
`lechoslaw.tomaszewski@orange.com`
[2] Warsaw University of Technology, Warsaw, Poland

Abstract. This paper presents a concept of integration of MEC into the 5G network slicing architecture. Three variants of the architecture have been proposed, which incorporate: individual MEP/MEPM for each slice, shared ones for multiple network slices and Distributed Autonomous Slice Management and Orchestration (DASMO) approach. Each variant is focused on efficient integration of 5G Core and MEC solutions and utilizing additional functionalities of both components, including MEC APIs and 5G Control Plane exposure capabilities. Finally, main issues of 5G-MEC implementation have been discussed, which include the aspects of MEC service APIs, MEC Apps mobility in demanding use cases, challenges of service continuity in roaming scenarios as well as the role and availability of 5G enablers.

Keywords: 5G · MEC · Network slicing · Orchestration · Management · Architecture · Scalability

1 Introduction

One of the main challenges, since the introduction of 5G network, remains meeting the requirements of latency-critical services. Initially, network slicing together with RAN enhancements were perceived as satisfactory enablers for achieving much lower delay than previous generation networks. However, due to the cloud character of networks and related time consumed by physical transmission of data, it has become clear that in order to meet the exorbitant requirements for low latency, services have to be migrated to the edge of the network.

Currently, the integration of ETSI Multi-access Edge Computing (MEC) and 5G is considered as a possible solution to the problem. Despite considerable facilitation provided by MEC, such as application deployment close to UE or mobility procedures enabling migration of applications to other hosts for maintaining low latency, the current status of MEC concept development raises significant concerns.

This work has been supported by the EU-China project 5G-DRIVE (under the Grant Agreement No. 814956) and by the EU project 5G!Drones (under the Grant Agreement No. 857031).

I. Maglogiannis et al. (Eds.): AIAI 2020 Workshops, IFIP AICT 585, pp. 15–24, 2020.
https://doi.org/10.1007/978-3-030-49190-1_2

This paper discusses the issues of MEC in terms of integration with slice-enabled, stand-alone 5G System (5GS). Such integration has already been described by ETSI; however, it seems that this approach to integration of MEC with NFV and slicing-enabled 5G network is over-complex. It is hereby proposed to use a different way, by removing duplicate functionalities of both solutions and integrating the information provided by network slice instances (NSIs) control message bus and MEC APIs. It is also proposed to integrate the approach with In-Slice Management (ISM) concept. The paper concerns not only the architectural alterations but also a discussion of mechanisms of MEC and 5G for their reciprocal integration.

The structure of the paper is as follows. Section 2 describes the current state of the art of MEC and its facilitation towards integration with 5G network. In Sect. 3 the scalable MEC-enabled network slicing architecture is proposed. In Sect. 4 implementation remarks are presented. Section 5 summarizes and concludes the paper.

2   State of the Art

Recently, an intensified research can be observed in the field of integration of the MEC framework with the 5G Core (5GC). Basic requirements concerning MEC–5GC inter-operation have been defined in [1]. The most important ones involve necessary MEC support for provisioning of traffic steering and policy control information of applications in 5GS. Specific data have to be exchanged between MEC management entities and 5G Network Exposure Function (NEF).

Following the basic requirements, a common architecture integrating MEC and NFV has been defined [2], which incorporates ETSI NFV MANO as a part of the management and orchestration domain. To prevent doubling of management functionalities, vital changes have been introduced, which include i.a. moving Life Cycle Management (LCM) of the MEC platform and MEC Apps to NFVO and VFNM. Moreover, the NFV Infrastructure (NFVI) is used for deployment of MEC Apps, MEC Platforms and MEC Platform Managers.

Two essential enhancements for integration of MEC with 5G network slicing have been introduced in [3]. According to the first one, a slice is deployed in the MEC ecosystem, meaning that MEC Platform (MEP) and MEC Platform Manager (MEPM) entities can be shared by several slices. The second one involves MEC deployment within a slice – each slice has its separate MEP and MEPM entities. Deployment of multiple slices within MEC raises fundamental questions concerning performance, isolation and slice awareness. According to [3], to enable safe operation, slice awareness of MEC Applications Orchestrator (MEAO) and virtualized MEPM (MEPM-V) as well as isolation of each slice (in case of shared MEP/MEPM approach) have to be ensured. Separation has to be provided especially in terms of MEC Apps access to UEs information.

Another important aspect of 5G–MEC integration is provisioning of mechanisms for seamless migration of applications and thus service continuity in latency-critical scenarios. Exemplary solutions have been proposed in [4], such as

MEC host pre-allocation based on UE trajectory prediction or creating *relocation groups* – sets of MEC hosts in UE's vicinity where each host is pre-configured for running desired application to reduce deployment time in case of handover.

Ksentini *et al.* have proposed the architecture of MEC-enabled 5G network [5] where MEC is defined as a separate orchestration domain but implemented on the same NFVI as VNFs and hosted by the ETSI NFV MANO stack of the VNF domain. Several aspects concerning security and data isolation in MEC APIs have been pointed out, i.a. filtering of RAN-related data before delivery to MEP in in-slice deployment scenarios. The results of exemplary MEC Apps deployment times in a laboratory environment have been presented.

An interesting view of the reasons for MEC implementation and its advantages is proposed in [6]. The additional benefits to usually accented latency reduction and UE's computational offloading, include data scalability, application scalability, intent-driven networking or partial offloading of network functions. They pertain directly to optimization of network architectures, distribution of traffic (especially in the transmission domain), network operations and – in result – both investment and operational costs, which are issues of premium importance for network operators.

3   Scalable MEC-enabled Network Slicing Architecture

3.1   Fundamentals of the Concept

Kukliński *et al.* have proposed a reference architectural framework for network slicing [7], which is based on the ETSI NFV MANO architecture [8], compliant with various communication network architectures and facilitates vertical and horizontal slice expansion due to incorporation of common/dedicated slice concepts, exposure of slice functions via slice API and slice stitching. The framework follows the paradigm of hierarchical multi-domain orchestration and supports tenant-oriented operations and interfaces based on embedded in-slice managers. In [9] the internal structure of slices has been further defined – the core part of slice, consisting of functions composing the Application (AP), Control (CP) and Data (DP) Planes (A-VNFs, C-VNFs and S-VNFs, respectively), is accompanied by two special functional blocks: Slice Manager (SM) and Slice Operation Support (SOS), both implemented as sets of VNFs (M-VNFs and S-VNFs respectively), belonging to slice template and sharing the life cycle of their slice. The architecture is called "Distributed Autonomous Slice Management and Orchestration" (DASMO) and is presented in Fig. 1.

SM is a central point of slice management plane and has links to Embedded Element Managers (EEMs) of all VNFs implemented within a slice. These EEMs follow the ETSI NFV concept of Element Manager (EM), but they are augmented with additional functionalities facilitating slice-level management support, VNF monitoring, actuating and autonomic control loop, etc. SM plays a role of slice OSS and incorporates the functions responsible for slice-level monitoring, analysis, actuating and autonomic control loop according to the Monitor-Analyze-Plan-Execute (MAPE) [10] model (real-time feedback loop).

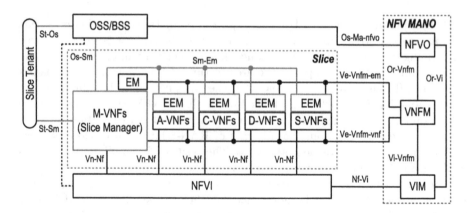

Fig. 1. DASMO framework with internal structure of network slices – ETSI NFV MANO extensions (slice management plane shown in red) (Color figure online)

Additionally, SM implements tenant-oriented functions: accounting, KPI monitoring and reporting, configuration support (following the "intent-based management" paradigm), which are exposed via the Tenant Portal functionality of SM. SM exposes also an interface to the global OSS/BSS, which is of importance especially in multi-domain slicing. SOS functions support slice-level operations as slice selection, subscription, authentication and stitching of sub-slices to provide transparent communication between NFs belonging to different domains for creation of the end-to-end slice.

The described architecture implements the ISM concept, which – due to hierarchical distribution of management tasks – is inherently scalable. The scalability of orchestration may be provided by recursive orchestration ("MANO in MANO"), and the DASMO concept is compliant with it.

3.2 Inclusion of the MEC Framework into the 5G Network Slicing Architecture

The proposed MEC-enabled 5G network slicing architecture is based on the following principles:

– MEC services, similarly as NSIs, have limited geographic scope and are focused on a specific service – this is in line with the network slicing philosophy, which emphasizes customization of NSI to its service or a group of services with similar characteristics. In more complicated use cases, like UAV or V2X, the overall service uses several NSIs of different type. Utilization of MEC as platform offers useful mechanisms to provide a specific service. Consequently, in case of network slicing, the number of MEC Apps will be limited and they will be defined during the slice creation. Therefore, orchestration of MEC Apps during the NSI run-time will be rather rare.

– Flexible architectural approach, adapted to NSI characteristics (complexity, longevity, critical deployment time, etc.), is required. As a result, coexistence of various architectural variants can be expected.
– Implementation of MEC Apps as a part of slice AP – the same NFVI is used by CP/DP and no separated MEC orchestration domain is needed. Therefore, the orchestration of MEC Apps belongs to slice-level orchestration activities.
– Tight integration on an equal basis of MEC APIs (RNIS, Localization, etc.) with information obtainable from 5GC via NEF, to extend the amount of information available for slice creation and for avoidance of duplication of 5G and MEC functions like Network Repository Function (NRF), etc.

Figure 2 shows the proposed generalized architecture of MEC and 5G integration. All VNFs are implemented in the VNF space, using common NFVI managed by VIM (omitted in the picture for simplification). NFVI can be single- or multi-domain (cf. [11]). All VNFs have their EMs (symbolized by red dots) connected to OSS/BSS (red arrows). In case of MEC Apps, their management functions may be embedded in applications, externalized or nonexistent. VNFs and their EMs are also connected to VNFM(s) (single- or multi-VNFM options are possible, cf. [11]), which are responsible for LCM of both MEC Apps and other VNFs (VNFM* in Fig. 2). Even if the ETSI MEC framework assumes *Ve-Vnfm-vnf* variant (light) of MEC App–NFVO reference point, it may be potentially useful in specific cases to implement fully functional *Ve-Vnfm-em* variant, instead.

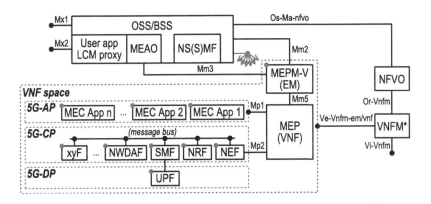

Fig. 2. General slicing architecture of MEC-enabled 5G network (Color figure online)

Orchestration of MEC is located at OSS/BSS together with management of a 5G network and Network Slice (Subnet) Management Function – NS(S)MF. Therefore, all interactions with the ETSI NFV MANO stack are performed via one common OSS–NFVO interface. As MEAO and User app LCM proxy are functional modules of OSS/BSS, some ETSI MEC reference points are internalized. OSS/BSS opens both interfaces *Mx1/Mx2* to the customer domain.

MEP exposes platform's services to MEC Apps (*Mp1*) and in case of 5GS-interacting ones, acts as mediator to 5GC-CP via NEF (*Mp2*, considered as *Naf* at the 5GC-CP bus).

The described generalized architecture is valid both in case of 5G network with its own MEP/MEPM-V (Variant 1) and for MEP/MEPM-V sharing by multiple networks (Variant 2). In case of Variant 1, the "VNF space" in Fig. 2 can be simply renamed to "5G network". As MEP/MEPM-V are dedicated, they can be a part of the template of virtualized 5G network and share its life cycle. In case of Variant 2 (suitable rather for short-lived and simple slices), they will be external to 5G networks (now consisted of AP, CP and DP only). As the shared MEP is interfaced with CPs and APs of separate networks, it has to provide mechanisms for mutual isolation between these networks, i.e. their reciprocal unawareness and prevention of cross-exchange of information or unauthorized access to foreign 5GC-CP. The issue of protection of individual networks privacy is an additional factor for externalization of MEP towards all connected networks in Variant 2. Additionally, inter-App privacy should be ensured in both variants (e.g. awareness of users, their sessions metadata, etc.), but it can be provided by the own 5GC-CP. If network slicing is enabled (the case of multiple-NSI networks, providing services with different characteristics), both MEP/MEPM-V and MEAO have to be NSI-aware, i.e. recognize and distinguish NSIs, as it is required from all 5GC-CP entities (cf. [3]).

3.3   Scalable MEC-enabled Slicing Architecture

In geographically distributed architecturally complex communication networks, moving network functions of high granularity towards the edge has positive consequences for user traffic transport and performance but at the expense of the control and management planes. Centralized management of highly distributed networks is vastly inefficient, especially due to necessity of transporting of huge volumes of data needed for analysis, decision-making and execution of automated management processes. The DASMO architecture faces this problem.

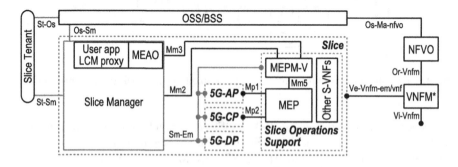

Fig. 3. MEC-enabled DASMO architecture (Color figure online)

The single-domain scalable MEC-enabled slicing architecture (DASMO extended with MEC) is presented in Fig. 3. All VNFs of the slice have their own EEMs, as it is required by the DASMO concept. EEMs are connected to SM, to provide the slice management plane communication. MEP/MEPM-V belong to the SOS area, because their role is in line with the SOS definition, especially the exposure of transparent mechanisms for slice VNFs interconnection. MEAO and User app LCM proxy are located in SM, because it plays a role of slice OSS.

The important task of SM is proper routing of the MEC framework-related exchange. The *Mm1* communication will be forwarded to the global OSS/BSS, which concentrates the exchange with NFV MANO. The *Mx1/Mx2* reference point communication will be exposed through the *St-Sm* interface. Alternatively, it may be forwarded to the global OSS/BSS if the Slice Tenant prefers interactions that way (e.g. utilization of multiple separate NSIs; the consolidated global view is then desired).

It has to be noted that the DASMO architecture also supports the multi-domain sliced networks. The global OSS/BSS contains the Multi-Domain Management and Orchestration Support functions composed of Multi-Domain Slice Configurator (MDSC) and Multi-Domain Orchestrator ("Umbrella NFVO", cf. [11]). MDSC, during the slice run-time, keeps monitoring of the end-to-end slice and coordinates its reconfiguration, taking also care of MEC-related activities. It is responsible for proper configuration of local SOS entities for inter-domain operations.

To enable operations in a multi-domain environment, it is essential to provide means of horizontal end-to-end slice stitching, i.e. concatenation of subslices from different domains. Inter-Domain Operations Support (IDOS), a functional part of SOS, is defined for this purpose. IDOS acts as an inter-slice gateway, implementing information exchange between neighbouring domains, i.e. exposure of domain abstracted view and support for inter-domain communication (relevant protocols, transcoding, mediation, etc.). In the MEC-enabled DASMO architecture, the *Mp3* reference point control information transfer between MEPs shall be carried out via IDOS.

4   5G-MEC Implementation Details

4.1   MEC Service APIs

The MEC framework defines special service APIs exposed by MEP to MEC Apps: Radio Network Information – RNIS [12] (PLMN information, E-RAB information, S1 Bearer information and L2 measurements), Location [13] (zonal presence and terminal location, including information about distance from specific location or between terminals), UE Identity [14] and Bandwidth Management [15] (management of bandwidth on per application session basis). These services shall be provided via the *Mp2* reference point, which will need special enablers within 5GC-CP. It has to be noted that the ETSI MEC framework is currently defined for integration with the 4G network (it is especially reflected in

RNIS data model, which is not radio technology-agnostic). Therefore, specifications of these APIs have to be updated and corresponding 5GS-side enablers have to be available. This mainly applies to mechanisms provided by NEF, NWDAF [16] and LCS [17]. It is particularly important to ensure the availability of RAN-related information. Although the 5G RAN physical layer measurements at UE have been specified [18], the mechanisms similar to 3G/4G radio measurements collection (MDT, cf. [19]) for further processing and use are still undefined, but they are in the scope of Release 17.

Additionally, it is hereby proposed to define the special MEP-facing gateway function located in 5GC-CP to provide a single and standardized interface for MEP and ensure smooth and optimized interaction (especially for avoiding excessive signaling exchange within 5GC-CP). Such initiative needs bilateral cooperation of the 3GPP and ETSI MEC group.

4.2   Application Mobility in Demanding Use Cases

Ksentini *et al.* demonstrated [5] that the total time needed for MEC application deployment can vary from ~60 s (application instantiation only) to ~180 s (onboarding and instantiation) or even ~440 s (full onboarding and instantiation of both MEP and application). In high-mobility use cases (drone, railway or automotive – speeds of several kms per minute) MEC Apps cannot only follow the UE, but they must overtake it. Standard mechanisms of location tracking (even with prediction) will not be sufficient, so integration with drone traffic management system (aware of flight plan), with UE context awareness mechanisms (driven by mechanisms of Artificial Intelligence and Geographic Information Systems to deduce e.g. following a motorway or railway line) or with on-board navigation (aware of the desired route) can be utilized.

4.3   Service Continuity in Roaming

Special concern should be dedicated to roaming cases. Maintaining service continuity requires replication of its architecture at VPLMN and new approach to the re-registration process when changing an operator. This issue is partially discussed in [20]. In case of MEC-enabled service architecture, the entire NSI, along with the MEC App residing in the AP, must be instantiated on VPLMN resources in local breakout mode. To some extent, service architectures (i.e. NSI templates) standardization together with MEC applications porting mechanism can be a solution, but a general mechanism for any NSI portability will be needed.

4.4   Availability of 5G Enablers for MEC

Majority of R&D projects are based on popular 5GS implementations, such as OpenAirInterface, Open5GCore or free5GC. It has to be noted that these solutions implement fundamental functionalities of the 3GPP 5G architecture, but unfortunately NEF, NWDAF or LCS are missing there. Even handover support can be somewhat problematic. Additionally, whenever non UE-based positioning is required, the Network-Assisted Positioning Procedure shall be used, which has to be supported by gNB (positioning based on RAN measurements, cf. [21]). Individual efforts on implementation of these mechanisms or an initiative on public-domain tools are needed. The list, review and status of open source tools for 5G (3GPP Release 15) can be found in [22].

5 Summary and Conclusions

In this paper, a novel concept of scalable MEC integration with slicing-enabled 5G has been presented. It is based on the critical evaluation of the ETSI approach. Several issues of the concept of ETSI, such as separate orchestration of network slices and MEC or improper integration of services offered by the 5GC-CP bus and MEC APIs, have been identified. Moreover, there is a need of filtering of MEC data on per slice basis to provide proper isolation between slices.

It has been proposed to use an ETSI NFV MANO-compliant orchestration based on a single orchestrator, common both for MEC and NFV, and to follow the ISM paradigm for automation of MEC operations and providing slice management scalability. Also, the specifics of use of MEC for network slicing has been outlined – the region of operation is already defined by the slice registration area. Moreover, slice services are generally limited and they rarely change during slice lifetime. The observations have led to the conclusions that it is possible to use many simplifications of MEC and slicing-enabled 5G network integration. The main value of MEC in the context of network slicing is the set of APIs, especially RNIS, Localization and Application Mobility API. Further research and development directions for enabling of commercial implementation and use of the presented concept have been also outlined.

The three defined and described variants of integration of MEC and 5G network may coexist in the network. Their selection is dependent on slice duration, complexity, deployment time requirements or the expected number of slices. The ISM-based integration is recommended as a variant of choice.

References

1. ETSI: ETSI GS MEC 002 Multi-access Edge Computing (MEC); Phase 2: Use Cases and Requirements, V2.1.1. ETSI MEC ISG, October 2018
2. ETSI: ETSI GS MEC 003 Multi-access Edge Computing (MEC); Framework and Reference Architecture, V2.1.1. ETSI MEC ISG, January 2019
3. ETSI: ETSI GR MEC 024 Multi-access Edge Computing (MEC); Support for network slicing, V2.1.1. ETSI MEC ISG, November 2019
4. ETSI: ETSI GR MEC 018 Multi-access Edge Computing (MEC); End to End Mobility Aspects, V1.1.1. ETSI MEC ISG, October 2017
5. Ksentini, A., Frangoudis, P.A.: Towards slicing-enabled multi-access edge computing in 5G. IEEE Netw. **34**(2), 99–105 (2020). https://doi.org/10.1109/MNET.001.1900261

6. Iwai, T., Nakao, A.: Demystifying myths of MEC: rethinking and exploring benefits of multi-access/mobile edge computing. In 2018 IEEE 7th International Conference on Cloud Networking (CloudNet), pp. 1–4. IEEE, Tokyo (2018). https://doi.org/10.1109/CloudNet.2018.8549539

7. Kukliński, S., Tomaszewski, L., et al.: A reference architecture for network slicing. In: 2018 4th IEEE Conference on Network Softwarization and Workshops (NetSoft), pp. 217–221. IEEE, Montreal (2018). https://doi.org/10.1109/NETSOFT.2018.8460057

8. ETSI: ETSI GS NFV 002 Network Functions Virtualisation (NFV); Architectural Framework, V1.2.1. ETSI NFV ISG, December 2014

9. Kukliński, S., Tomaszewski, L.: DASMO: a scalable approach to network slices management and orchestration. In: NOMS 2018–2018 IEEE/IFIP Network Operations and Management Symposium, pp. 1–6. IEEE, Taipei (2018). https://doi.org/10.1109/NOMS.2018.8406279

10. IBM: An architectural blueprint for autonomic computing. Autonomic Computing White Paper, Third Edition, June 2005

11. ETSI: ETSI GS NFV-IFA 009 Network Functions Virtualisation (NFV); Management and Orchestration; Report on Architectural Options, V1.1.1. ETSI NFV ISG, July 2016

12. ETSI: ETSI GS MEC 012 Multi-access Edge Computing (MEC); Radio Network Information API, V2.1.1. ETSI MEC ISG, December 2019

13. ETSI: ETSI GS MEC 013 Multi-access Edge Computing (MEC); Location API, V2.1.1. ETSI MEC ISG, September 2019

14. ETSI: ETSI GS MEC 014 Mobile Edge Computing (MEC); UE Identity API, V1.1.1. ETSI MEC ISG, February 2018

15. ETSI: ETSI GS MEC 015 Mobile Edge Computing (MEC); Bandwidth Management API, V1.1.1. ETSI MEC ISG, October 2017

16. 3GPP: 3GPP TS 23.501 System Architecture for the 5G System, V16.4.0, 3GPP, March 2020. https://portal.3gpp.org/desktopmodules/Specifications/SpecificationDetails.aspx?specificationId=3144

17. 3GPP: 3GPP TS 23.273 5G System (5GS) Location Services (LCS); Stage 2, V16.3.0. 3GPP, March 2020. https://portal.3gpp.org/desktopmodules/Specifications/SpecificationDetails.aspx?specificationId=3577

18. 3GPP: 3GPP TS 38.215 NR; Physical layer measurements, V16.1.0. 3GPP, April 2020. https://portal.3gpp.org/desktopmodules/Specifications/SpecificationDetails.aspx?specificationId=3217

19. 3GPP: 3GPP TS 37.320 Universal Terrestrial Radio Access (UTRA) and Evolved Universal Terrestrial Radio Access (E-UTRA); Radio measurement collection for Minimization of Drive Tests (MDT); Overall description; Stage 2, V16.0.0. 3GPP, April 2020. https://portal.3gpp.org/desktopmodules/Specifications/SpecificationDetails.aspx?specificationId=2602

20. Tomaszewski, L., Kołakowski, R., Korzec, P.: On 5G support of cross-border UAV operations. In: 2020 IEEE International Conference on Communications, Workshop on Integrating UAVs into 5G and Beyond (accepted)

21. 3GPP: 3GPP TS 38.305 NG Radio Access Network (NG-RAN); Stage 2 functional specification of User Equipment (UE) positioning in NG-RAN, V16.0.0. 3GPP, April 2020. https://portal.3gpp.org/desktopmodules/Specifications/SpecificationDetails.aspx?specificationId=3310

22. 5G Americas: The Status of Open Source for 5G. 5G Americas White Paper, February 2019

Business Aspects of the Neutral Host Model: The Immersive Video Services Case

Ioannis Neokosmidis[1(✉)], Vangelis Logothetis[1], Theodoros Rokkas[1],
Luca Vignaroli[2], Davide Desirello[2], Antonino Albanese[3],
Viscardo Costa[3], Mariano Lamarca[4], Maria Rita Spada[5],
Muhammad Shuaib Siddqui[6], Dimitra Simeonidou[7],
and Carlos Colman-Meixner[7]

[1] inCITES Consulting, Strassen, Luxembourg
i.neokosmidis@incites.eu
[2] RAI, Centro Ricerche, Innovazione Tecnologica e Sperimentazione,
Turin, Italy
[3] ITALTEL, Castelletto, Milan, Italy
[4] IMI – Barcelona City Council, Barcelona, Spain
[5] Wind Tre S.p.A, Largo Metropolitana 5, Rho, Milan, Italy
[6] i2CAT Foundation, Barcelona, Spain
[7] High Performance Laboratory, University of Bristol, Bristol, UK

Abstract. The introduction of novel approaches that cause a paradigm shift on a technological level can become the driver of innovative business models that benefit from capabilities that may have emerged. Such is the case for 5G which offers an entirely new way of delivering services that affects consumers and even more fundamentally the providers. The introduction of network slicing and the ability to provide individually configurable parts of the network to providers offer unique opportunities and solutions particularly when it comes to solving the known issue of overlapping infrastructure investments from various stakeholders. In this paper, the scenario of a single wholesale 5G network provider – the Neutral Host – operating in the City of Lucca is examined. Some remarks about the impact of the NH model on Barcelona superblock urbanistic model are also provided.

Keywords: Neutral Host · 5G · Business model · Technoeconomics

1 Introduction

With the emergence of mobile communication networks, a great variety of services have been introduced to consumers along with the relevant revenue streams that emerged for providers of all sorts. With bandwidth demands following a steady increase, the necessity for updating the infrastructure and accommodate the observed trends is emerging. The technology of 5G aims to do just that by providing far greater internet speeds compared to its predecessors. But talking about increased connection speeds is only scratching the surface of what 5G can offer to the telecommunications world since great innovations are adopted into the network's architecture on a foundational level.

© IFIP International Federation for Information Processing 2020
Published by Springer Nature Switzerland AG 2020
I. Maglogiannis et al. (Eds.): AIAI 2020 Workshops, IFIP AICT 585, pp. 25–34, 2020.
https://doi.org/10.1007/978-3-030-49190-1_3

In particular, the ability to create network slices creates unique business opportunities as network sharing could be efficient and very adjustable to different service providers' needs, something that was not the case up until this point. Furthermore, 5G envisions beyond conventional passive networking sharing and encompass active network sharing as well. Based on this major characteristic, the concept of the Neutral Host (NH) becomes more appealing since it provides the foundations that allow the seamless development of a single entity that can build virtual end-to-end slices including various resources (e.g. network storage, computing) that can be leased to mobile network operators that operate these resources per their respective needs.

Thus, the NH model allows for the deployment of a single network capable of hosting various providers reducing infrastructure competition and leading to an overall welfare increase. In the case of urban areas, the deployment of small cells over street furniture will be more intensive while physical coexistence of multiple operators become a Chimera. Even though the NH concept has existed beforehand, the ability that 5G has to parameterize network slices and adhere to providers' needs, is what makes it able to crossover from a theoretical model to an actual implementation that shows promise in overcoming challenges faced by infrastructure providers and vertical actors [1, 2]. Being able to create networks that can be leveraged upon multiple vendors renders the NH model capable to support the fast adoption and exploitation of 5G as there is no longer the need to develop multiple isolated access networks to facilitate services. Apart from the technological aspects that characterize the NH, there also exists the business perspective that surfaces alongside an entity that can potentially be the arbitrator for a whole new array of SLAs that will characterize the network [2–4].

A business model encompassing the characteristics of the described NH is presented followed by a technoeconomic analysis that aims to explore the model's potential gauged in economic terms. Increased flexibility is the main attribute of the modelled wholesaler, not only in terms of services provided, but also when it comes to charging strategies that can be diversified in creative ways. Typical wholesale access pricing is still present but can be shaped in more suitable ways to better suit each hosted entity. Dynamic monthly fees could be the case or even a pay-per-use scheme if periodic access to the infrastructure is needed, as would be the case for some content providers that would only employ the network's capabilities during specific timeframes, for example during Public events. The benefit to this approach is the ability to charge based on actual resources utilized on top of a flat access rate, instead of only the later which is usually encountered in the industry and bound to be pricier if it acts as a universal price for all possible services. This perspective combined with the network slicing will provide additional flexibility as the NH can dynamically adjust to the needs of various interested parties. Additional specialization can be achieved by adopting per-service pricing further increasing possible revenues.

It should be highlighted that Network SLAs stability by compromising coverage and signal to noise ration (SNR), should also be taken into account. 5GCity project's deployments in both Lucca and Barcelona show that it is possible to provide a flat coverage higher than that of the 4G or WIFI model with less transmission power and higher SNR managing adequately distance and height of SCs. That means QoS guarantee independently of phones' position in the coverage area of the SC.

The rest of the paper is organized as follows: Sect. 2 describes the Neutral Host business model. Section 3 discusses the technoeconomic analysis of the NH model. Section 4 discusses and concludes the paper.

2   The Neutral Host Business Model

The telecommunication industry has undoubtedly seen a lot of growth in recent years as connectivity became a staple of everyday life and demand for capacity, both residential and business, steadily increased without showing any signs of slowing down. Regardless of this continued increase in consumption and reliance on ICT and digital services, operators' profits have suffered underlying the need to identify new ways of profiting from infrastructure. Bearing that in mind and understanding the importance of context, a Business Model Canvas methodology is being used to identify the ecosystem that revolves around the NH along the potential opportunities that exist. This methodology looks into external and internal aspects that need to be assessed when developing a business model.

2.1   External Aspects

Initially, the business model examines the external environment of the NH. The proposed idea is for the NH to offer a platform that combines infrastructure and service dashboards. The former allows mobile network operators to deploy network slices in a wholesale manner. Although, operators are interested in 5G, they appear reluctant to invest because 5G antennas size and range ask for much denser deployments that create practical backhauling and powering issues. Additionally, the NH offers, through the service dashboard, access to a service design toolkit (SDK) that allows the further exploitation of 5G's capabilities. Vertical application developers can use it to develop new services and networks functions while service providers can combine available functions and create new services. Such an approach would allow for greater flexibility as a result of the combination of software-based functionalities along with physical access. As such, the reliance on wholesale access is relaxed and the NH can look into entirely new revenue streams and most importantly explore the untapped potential of fluid business models that still benefit from the established ways of exploiting network infrastructure. Moreover, RAN architectures can be innovated with multi-RAT function disaggregation, implemented through SDN-based virtual RAN slicing and RAN function virtualization for LTE and Wi-Fi. Also, the NH can support edge computing capabilities to enable ultra-low latency, high bandwidth and real-time access to radio network information that can be leveraged by applications. All these characteristics render the NH model an enticing option with significant added value.

The NH would be able to reach out to its clients to communicate the mentioned benefits of its business model through direct sales or dealers establishing a clear relationship through the use of online support, call centers and in field assistance.

As the services that can be provided are described, it is crucial to identify the possible revenue streams for the NH's business model. Wholesale access to the infrastructure is the obvious one but with added ability to adopt new pricing schemes such as monthly subscription or even more dynamic choices (e.g. pay-as-you-go, per core etc.) which would substantiate the use of two-part tariffs. Opting for a basic network slice pricing, based on specific KPIs (e.g. maximum throughput, number of users connected or maximum/average latency) which can be adapted based on actual resource usage. This approach would not only incentivize mobile network operators to utilize the Neutral Host's network but also help in keeping up with overall resource usage estimation, opening up the network for better management and exploitation.

Similarly, the platform offering the services development toolkit can be subject to different pricing schemes such as subscription fees or fee per package of N services. Alternatively, a more dynamic scheme could be offered such as charging per service or per number of services and/or per function used for the creation of the new service. This platform, based on the combination of cloud and edge computing and the SDK for service creation, will be able to provide pricing flexibility in order to service providers and OTTs that will need to utilize parts of the network in ways suitable to the products to be delivered.

Another revenue stream that is important to capture is that of private networks that is considered a critical aspect of the potential of 5G networks. A company will be able to utilize infrastructure and service platform to host its own bundle of services for their employees/users and evolution to the "private LTE" networks currently available that is also usable in "mission critical" scenarios. To offer this type of services, the allocation of specific spectrum is needed regardless of where it comes from (the industry itself or a MNO). Finally, the NH can profit from the provision of certifications to developers that intend to certify their services uploaded to the catalogue and from consulting and training services.

2.2   Internal Aspects

Apart from the exterior, an internal analysis is also conducted to understand the aspects that deal with the actions that the NH has to perform as well as the resources that need to be allocated in order to successfully develop and maintain the infrastructure and platform. The key resources used for the proper execution of the business model are the business and technical personnel, the physical assets such as network equipment, and the facilities that need to be made available, e.g. sites for network equipment, lamp-posts, street signs, traffic lights etc. In a City, it is important to have a scalable model for the development of an end to end solution allowing NH to provide same services with same QoS independently of the density of the deployed SCs.

The Neutral Host, apart from building the network is also tasked with its operation and the provisioning of network slices and required services and functions to the hosted entities. Also, an initial collection of available services is a task that may need to be carried out by the NH in order to establish the basic functionalities that can then be enhanced by developers certified by the host himself. Training and consulting should also be considered as entirely new types of functionalities are being proposed.

A crucial component of the project's fruition would be to establish key partnerships with NFV providers and software developers that would provide VNFs, NFI and orchestrators. Partnership with vendors shows a lot of potential as technologies developed by for the NH can be integrated and sold by them in other network implementations.

Apart from business partners, cooperation with the open source and scientific community can also reveal pathways to innovation. Equally important is the ability to come together with facility managers and landlords as without the necessary space that they can offer the infrastructure cannot be realized.

As is true for every network implementation though, the NH needs to allocate significant monetary resources for the deployment and operation of the 5G network. Capital and operational expenditure to build and run the network but also the costs related to the integration of the platform that lies at the heart of the business models. Also, not to be overlooked is the research and development that would need to come before during and after the development of the network to create, integrate and keep in line with technological advancements.

3 Technoeconomic Analysis

To explore the economic side of this model, a technoeconomic (TE) analysis is conducted. The use case under investigation deals with a NH providing wholesale access to MNOs that offer immersive video services (IVS). It should be highlighted that these services are designed to allow end-users to move through parts of the city utilizing VR/AR/MR-like devices and receiving content related to the surrounding environments. This experience is enhanced using additional content in the form of 360° video, further increasing immersion and information delivered to the end user. Another interesting feature examined is the visual search that allows visual content captured by the user (e.g. such as buildings, statues, paintings) to be matched to content present in databases thanks to visual similarities and provide information, for example, looking at the Parthenon could allow the user to examine painted graphical representations of how scientists believe the monument looked like in the past.

Television archives in the form of 2D video, panoramic video and 3D models as well as new UHD/4K content will be available to the users, creating an all-around digital experience. To successfully achieve that, ultra-high bandwidth and very low system latency are required in order to effectively provide the described content to end-users. The services will leverage the NH model that allows the creation of end-to-end segmented slices, which encompass a wide variety of resources. The slices are leased to MNOs, which can then operate their virtual resources by mapping their services with respect to the set of slices that they have been assigned.

The TE analysis, particularly focuses on three main services: (a) on demand immersive tour experience using Oculus [5] headgear in the context of Puccini Museum [6], (b) 360° live content streaming during crowded events, with reference to Piazza Napoleone where music concerts are organized and (c) street immersive augmented walking using HoloLens [7] in the City of Lucca (Sant' Andrea Street).

3.1 Technoeconomic Scenarios

The first service allows a complete immersive experience in an interactive environment. The already deployed services that offer low scale AR features though the use of smartphone screens, can be taken to the next level through the use of VR headgear, something that many museums are exploring as a service. In the frame of this use case, visitors are drawn into the experience by the addition of spatial audio or surround sound. While learning about the history of Puccini life they can also listen to the sound of his concerts and operas and textual infographics.

The 360° live streaming service can be used in several applications allowing people to travel virtually to the location where an event (e.g. concert, interview etc.) is taking place. A technological challenge, in case of crowded events, the economic feasibility of this service is evaluated considering the case of Piazza Napoleone, located in the city centre of Lucca, during a live music concert [8]. The scenario consists of a 360° camera, e.g. an Insta360 Pro device, placed near the stage live streaming the show to remote audience equipped with VR headsets. The concept is to provide an immersive experience for the end user and high engagement by placing the camera directly on the stage. The attendee of the event within the square can also use the service and make himself a part of the show rather than just part of the audience.

Finally, the cultural immersive street walking will allow the user to be involved in a wandering experience in Saint Andrew Street. Using rented AR headsets, the user can walk towards Guinigi Tower [9] can experience the full experience of augmented reality, getting additional content such as video description and the 3D reconstructed model of the tower itself. Other points of interest could be included in the future improving the service content and immersion wise.

3.2 Technoeconomic Methodology

The technoeconomic methodology used to assess telecom network investments and subsequently for the case of 5G has already been adopted in similar studies [10]. The core of a TE model is a database regularly updated with relevant data (e.g. network components) collected from the largest European telecommunication companies and vendors as well as benchmarks from the telecom market [10, 11] used to assess costs incurred to deploy and maintain a network as well as offer services.

The study period is always adapted to the case under investigation. For the deployment of 5G networks and considering the time needed for the technology to reach market maturity and pay back investments, an eight to ten-year period is adopted. A list of provided services and their market penetration over the study period are defined while econometric and price forecast models are used to define their tariffs. Services revenues can be calculated by vombining market penetration and tariff evolution.

To calculate the expenditures, the selected topology and dimensioning rules for radio and IT resources are used. Thus, alternative topologies can be easily incorporated in the TE analysis as long as the right input in terms of assets used is being provided. To calculate the required number of network components, demand forecasting is conducted using existing methodologies and market data. CAPEX is then calculated by combining the required number of components and their price for each year. A price evolution is calculated for all network components by using the extended learning curve model [12]. Maintenance costs consist of two parts: (i) the cost to repair, calculated as a fixed percentage of the total investments in network elements, and; (ii) the cost of repair work, using the mean time between failures (MTBF) and the mean time to repair (MMTR). Operating expenditures (OPEX) are also calculated in the tool, e.g. energy costs are evaluated based on the power consumption of components and the average cost of one kWh [13]. In the scenario investigated, network equipment is only used during the event and switched-off before and after.

By combining of all calculated costs and more general economic inputs (discount rate, cost of capital), the tool calculates the results necessary for Discounted Cash Flow analysis such as cash flows, Net Present Value (NPV), Internal Rate of Return (IRR), payback period and other notable economic figures.

3.3   Demand Forecast

The forecast is a very important part of the TE analysis since it helps quantify present and future costs and revenues. To estimate the 5G population penetration 6 steps were followed: (i) the definition of a 5G mobile subscription, (ii) understanding of regional deployment plans, (iii) understanding of qualitative factors affecting 5G adoption, (iv) observation of 3G and 4G adoption patterns, (v) estimation of 5G population penetration, and (vi) identification of risks that might hinder 5G adoption.

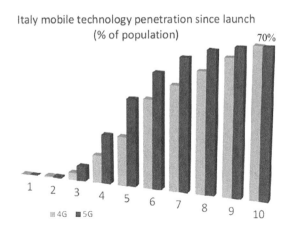

Fig. 1. 5G adoption curve

Following these steps, a global population adoption curve has been defined and shown in Fig. 1. Keep noted that machine-to-machine connections are not being considered for the purpose of this exercise.

4   Results

4.1   Financial Results

The financial results are what is to be studied and analyzed after the completion of TE model. During the study period, the NH invests in the necessary equipment in order to deploy the network including switches, servers, small cells etc. The length of fiber cables needed is also included using a geometric model. All individual cash flows as well as a cumulative cash flow line are presented in Fig. 2 for the underlying analysed network. The cumulative discounted cash flow, widely known as the cash balance, summarizes the total profit/loss at the end of each year of the business case.

From Fig. 2, it can be deduced that the balance is initially negative. This is somehow expected due to the high initial investments needed to deploy the network together and the relatively low demand for 5G services. As service demand increases, revenues grow at a faster pace than outflows, making the investment profitable within the study period. Specifically, our calculations show that the payback period for the investment is approximately 7 years with an IRR of 13% and a NPV of approximately 93 k€. Although initially CAPEX accounts for the bulk of the outflows, OPEX costs become more dominant towards the end of the study period.

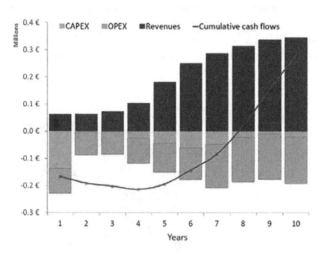

Fig. 2. Cash flows by year

4.2 Sensitivity and Risk Analysis

Having conducted the TE analysis, key outputs are the revenues, investments, lifecycle cost, cash balance, NPV and IRR, all important outputs that allow the evaluation of the investment analyzed leading to the next stage of understanding the most impactful parameters that surface within the TE model. To achieve this, sensitivity and risk analysis are being conducted allowing to take into consideration uncertainties involved. In the examined case, the parameters chosen for the sensitivity analysis were service tariffs, Napoleone piazza's capacity, CAPEX and the maximum number of HoloLens/Oculus devices at the end of the study period. Changed by ±60% of their initial assumed values, the impact that each parameter has on the NVP is evaluated. As seen in Fig. 3, service tariffs have the biggest impact on NPV both positive and negative following their increase or decrease. Max number of headgear and CAPEX have similar impact on absolute terms while piazza capacity is not very impactful. It is worth noting that NPV's sensitivity to CAPEX will be diminished in the future along with advances in performance and capabilities of network components.

A risk analysis follows to further analyze risky parameters that could influence the results of the use case. The tariffs of basic, 360, oculus and HoloLens services, 5G demand, CAPEX, piazza capacity and the maximum number of Oculus and HoloLens at the end of the study period were identified as the most impactful to the project. Modelling said variables using a probability density function that follows uncertainty assumptions that produce upper and lower limits, optimistic and pessimistic results all used as input into a ten thousand samples Monte Carlo simulation to output differentiated NPV results, useful in evaluating the project. The parameters showing the greatest influence on variance is the demand followed by tariff Oculus and Basic.

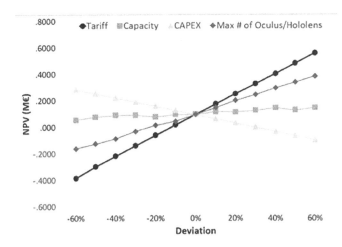

Fig. 3. Sensitivity analysis on the Net Present Value

5   Conclusions

In this paper, the business model of the Neutral Host was described, an entity providing wholesale 5G access in the form of end-to-end virtualized network slices along with a platform of functions and services able to support the individual providers. Due to the fact that 5G networks need much denser cell deployments, the 5GCity NH model, tested in Lucca and Sant Marti Superblock of Barcelona, seems as an enticing way to accelerate 5G networks' deployment. Additionally, the access to a service design toolkit opens up pathways for new revenue streams.

The model proposed is further examined through the technoeconomic analysis of a particular use case where MNOs in the City of Lucca is offering immersive video services using the NH network. The investment is breaking even in year seven of the study, due to an increase in revenues as the adoption of 5G brings along more end-users from year six and onwards, enough to counter increases in operational costs. As seen in the sensitivity analysis, demand will be a main contributing factor for the investment's viability as well as the ability to cut down on some of the costs that come along with improvements in small cell's technological capabilities.

Acknowledgment. The research leading to these results has been supported by the EU funded H2020 5G-PPP project 5GCity (grant agreement No. 761508).

References

1. 1ITU-R Rec. M.2083-0: 2015IMT Vision – Framework and overall objectives of the future development of IMT for 2020 and beyond, September 2015
2. Colman-Meixner, C., et al.: Deploying a novel 5G-enabled architecture on city infrastructure for ultra-high definition and immersive media production and broadcasting. IEEE Trans. Broadcast. **65**(2), 392–403 (2019). https://doi.org/10.1109/TBC.2019.2901387
3. Neokosmidis, I., Rokkas, T., Parker, M.C., Koczian, G., Walker, S.D., Escalona, E.: Assessment of socio-techno-economic factors affecting the market adoption and evolution of 5G networks: evidence from the 5G-PPP CHARISMA project. Telematics Inform. **34**(5), 572 (2017)
4. Ksentini, A., Iqbal, M., Flinck, H.: Mobile edge computing potential in making cities smarter. IEEE Commun. Mag. **55**(3), 38–43 (2017)
5. https://www.magicleap.com/
6. http://www.puccinimuseum.org/en/
7. https://www.microsoft.com/en-gb/HoloLens?icid=SSM_AS_Promo_Devices_HoloLens2
8. https://www.summer-festival.com/
9. http://www.turismo.lucca.it/en/luoghi-di-interesse/guinigi-tower
10. Monath, T., Kristian, N., Cadro, P., Katsianis, D., Varoutas, D.: Economics of fixed broadband access network strategies. IEEE Commun. Mag. **41**(9), 132–139 (2003)
11. Katsianis, D., et al.: The financial perspective of the mobile networks in Europe. IEEE Pers. Commun. **8**(6), 58–64 (2001)
12. Ims, L.A.: Broadband Access Networks. Springer, Boston (1998). https://doi.org/10.1007/978-1-4615-5795-1
13. Energy price statistics (2017). http://ec.europa.eu/eurostat/statistics-explained/index.php/Energy_price_statistics

Combined 5G-*Based* Video Production and Distribution in a Crowded Stadium Event

Ioannis P. Chochliouros[1](✉) 📷, Anastasia S. Spiliopoulou[1],
Pavlos Lazaridis[2], Michail-Alexandros Kourtis[3],
Zaharias Zaharis[4], and Alexandros Kostopoulos[1]

[1] Hellenic Telecommunications Organization (OTE) S.A., 99 Kifissias Avenue,
15124 Maroussi-Athens, Greece
{ichochliouros,alexkosto}@oteresearch.gr,
aspiliopoul@ote.gr
[2] The University of Huddersfield, Queensgate, Huddersfield HD13DH, UK
P.Lazaridis@hud.ac.uk
[3] National Centre for Scientific Research "Demokritos",
15310 Aghia Paraskevi-Athens, Greece
akis.kourtis@iit.demokritos.gr
[4] Aristotle University of Thessaloniki, 54124 Thessaloniki, Greece
zaharis@auth.gr

Abstract. Based upon the scope of the original 5G ESSENCE research effort and by considering the related fundamental architecture, we develop a dedicated scenario for the implementation and demonstration of a setup for a 5G edge network acceleration in the context of a sport event, taking place in a stadium. Specifically, we demonstrate a combined 5G-*based* video production and video distribution scenario towards delivering benefits to both media producers/content providers and mobile operators, with those being able to offer enriched event experience to their subscribers. The production/distribution of locally generated content through the respective platform, coupled with value-added services and rich user context, enables secure, high-quality and resilient transmission in real-time, thus ensuring minimal latency. In the selected scenario, massive data traffic does not affect nor overload the backhaul connection as it is produced, processed and consumed just locally, aligned to the 5G 3GPP specifications. We also discuss details about the proposed services and functionalities of the use case, together with an approach for a potential projection to the market.

Keywords: 5G · Cloud-Enabled Small Cell (CESC) · evolved Multimedia Broadcast Multicast Services (eMBMS) · Multi-access Edge Computing (MEC) · Network Functions Virtualisation (NFV) · Small Cell (SC) · Virtual Network Function (VNF)

1 Introduction

The introduction of 5G technologies in economic and societal procedures of everyday life is a "key" asset that supports transformation of the vertical industries and focuses upon the development of cloud infrastructure and the concomitant development of

I. Maglogiannis et al. (Eds.): AIAI 2020 Workshops, IFIP AICT 585, pp. 35–46, 2020.
https://doi.org/10.1007/978-3-030-49190-1_4

mobile broadband digital access networks [1, 2]. The advent of the Internet of Things (IoT) and the predictive and real-time intelligence on network devices act as a "catalyst" to the growing adoption of edge cloud solutions and services. To respond, the next generation of communication and services includes virtualised applications that "run" much closer to mobile users ensuring network flexibility, economy and scalability [3]. The delivery of services from an edge cloud represents a new synergistic business model between network service providers or edge cloud providers and enterprises [4]. For the edge cloud provider, it represents an opportunity to nearly double the revenues associated with the new services, while for an Information Communication Technology (ICT) services enterprise it shows a potential opportunity to "add" a new revenue stream to its portfolio by using and delivering over the top (OTT) services [5].

The 5G ESSENCE project [6] addresses the paradigms of Multi-access Edge Computing (MEC) and Small Cell as-a-Service (SCaaS) [7] by fueling the drivers and removing the barriers in the Small Cell (SC) market, forecasted to grow at an impressive pace up to 2020 and beyond and to play a "key" role in the 5G ecosystem. The proposed approach provides a highly flexible and scalable platform, which is able to support new business models and revenue streams by creating a neutral host market and reducing operational costs by providing new opportunities for ownership, deployment, operation and amortisation [8].

Among other potential applications and within all proposed use cases, this scope delivers benefits to media producers and mobile operators, enabling them to offer a highly interactive fan experience and to optimise operations by deploying key functionalities at the edge (i.e., evolved Multimedia Broadcast Multicast Services (eMBMS) together with multitenancy support from small cells). By leveraging the benefits of small cell virtualisation and radio resource abstraction, as well as by optimising network embedded cloud, it becomes possible to "ease" the coverage and capacity pressure on the multimedia infrastructure, and also to increase security since content will remain locally. Furthermore, additional benefits for the operators and the venue owners arise such as: (i) Lower latency, due to shortening the data transmission path, *and*; (ii) increased backhaul capacity, due to playing out the live feeds and replays locally, that practically "puts" no additional strain on the backhaul network and upstream core network components. Among the fundamental 5G ESSENCE use cases [9] is the one about supporting 5G edge network acceleration in a crowded event, that is discussed and further assessed in the continuity of the present work.

2   Basic Architecture and Use Case Description

The 5G ESSENCE project realises a two-tier cloud architecture that enables the provision of dynamically repurposed virtual network infrastructures with tailored computing and flexible networking capabilities. Following the related approach, the Small Cell concept is evolved as not only to provide multi-operator radio access, but also to achieve an increase in the capacity and the performance of current RAN (Radio Access Network) infrastructures, and to extend the range of the provided services while maintaining its agility [10]. To achieve these ambitious goals, our scope provides an enhanced, edge-*based*, virtualised execution environment attached to the small cell, taking advantage and reinforcing the concepts of MEC [11] and network slicing [12, 13]. The existing 5G architecture is a solid reference point for our original approach, which combines the current 3GPP framework to network management in RAN sharing scenarios [14] and the ETSI NFV framework for managing virtualised network functions [15].

The CESC (Cloud-Enabled Small Cell) provides the computing, storage and radio resources at the edge, while the CESC cluster is the cloud platform. This cloud platform can also be "sliced" to enable multi-tenancy, and it is used to support Virtualised Network Function (VNFs) implementing the different features of the SCs as well as to support the mobile edge applications delivered to the end-users.

The technical approach is presented in Fig. 1, where the working architecture is illustrated with specific emphasis upon the functional elements and interfaces. The corresponding system is equipped with a two-tier virtualised execution environment, materialised in the form of the Edge DC (Data Centre), which allows also the provision of MEC capabilities to the mobile operators for enhancing the user experience and the agility in the service delivery [16–18].

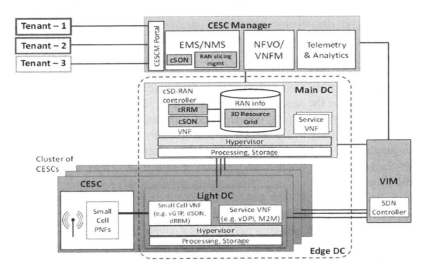

Fig. 1. 5G ESSENCE system architecture.

Both tiers are briefly discussed as follows:

- *The first tier*, that is the *Light DC* hosted inside the CESCs, is used to support the execution of VNFs for carrying out the virtualisation of the Small Cell access. In this regard, network functions supporting traffic interception, GTP encapsulation/decapsulation and some distributed RRM (Radio Resources Management)/SON (Self-Organising Networks) functionalities are expected to be executed therein. VNFs that require low processing power such as, *for example*, a Deep Packet

Inspection (DPI), a Machine-to-Machine (M2M) Gateway and so on, could also be hosted here.

- *The second cloud tier*, that is the *Main DC*, hosts more computation intensive tasks and processes that need to be centralised in order to have a global view of the underlying infrastructure. This encompasses the cSD-RAN (centralised Software-Defined RAN) controller which will be delivered as a VNF running in the Main DC and makes control plane decisions for all the radio elements in the geographical area of the CESC cluster, including the centralised Radio Resource Management (cRRM) over the entire CESC cluster.

Our intended approach demonstrates a combined 5G-*based* video production and video distribution towards delivering benefits to both media producers and mobile operators, who will be able to offer enriched event experience to their subscribers. The production/distribution of locally generated content through the respective platform, coupled with value-added services and rich user context, can enable secure, high-quality and resilient transmission, in real-time and with minimal latency [19].

In the context of the 5G ESSENCE infrastructure sharing support, each network operator will be in position to optimise his network usage, resulting in lower operating expenses (OPEX). Additionally, network operators will be able to rapidly deploy new services, to deliver directly to users higher quality of experience (QoE) and offer "Content as-a-Service", increased bandwidth and storage solutions to content providers and venue owners [9].

The content providers will also benefit from reduced latency and improved user QoE by positioning content on mobile edge and, *in addition*, they can offer augmented services by leveraging the network information. Finally, the stadium owner will obtain additional benefits by leveraging the deployed dedicated infrastructure and its functionalities, by capitalising live content to spectators from many cameras, statistics, etc.

The developed scenario provides the logic for distributing the live video feeds received from the local production room to local spectators in a highly efficient manner. The Municipal Football Stadium "Stavros Mavrothalassitis" in the city of Egaleo-Athens in Greece is covered with a cluster of multitenant, eMBMS-*enabled* as CESCs and, together with the CESCM (CESC Manager) and the Main DC, they can all potentially be connected to the core networks of multiple telecom operators [20]. The video content from cameras is sent for processing locally at the Edge DC (similar to the proposed use case by ETSI MEC [21]). MEC offers application developers and content providers cloud-computing capabilities and an IT service environment at the edge of the network [22]. This environment is characterized by ultra-low latency and high bandwidth as well as real-time access to radio network information that can be leveraged by applications. MEC provides a new ecosystem and value chain. Operators can open their RAN edge to authorized third-parties, allowing them to flexibly and rapidly deploy innovative applications and services towards mobile subscribers, enterprises and vertical segments. Then the video streams are broadcasted locally using the CESCs and spectators are able to dynamically select between different streams offered. In this and in similar massive event scenarios, the data traffic does not impact the backhaul connection since it is produced, processed and consumed locally (Fig. 2).

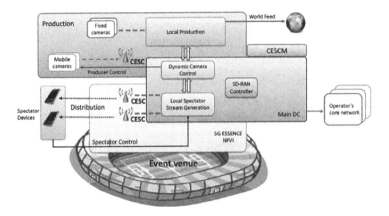

Fig. 2. 5G edge network acceleration in a stadium.

To provide a comprehensive overview of the use case, it is worth highlighting the business roles that can be envisaged. Actors involved in this scenario are listed below:

- *Small Cell Network Operator (SCNO):* Owner of the infrastructure deployed in the stadium.
- *Virtual Small Cell Network Operator (VSCNO):* Users of the infrastructure available in the stadium to provide services to the end-users.
- *End-Users:* Users of the networking services.
- *Mobile Operators (MOs):* Network operators responsible for bringing the network and communication services to the stadium.
- *Service Providers (SPs):* Companies providing some of the VNFs to the SCNO. Examples of key service providers for this use case are as follows: (i) Football/sport society; (ii) live event organizer; (iii) municipality, and; (iv) video/content provider.
- *Spectrum Owner:* In the licensed spectrum case, it is the stadium which leases the spectrum from an operator or a mobile operator that offers a service.

3   Technical Enablers and Functionalities

This section intends to present the mapping between the testbed architecture for assessing the respective stadium use case, based on the testbed components presented in previous sub-sections and the corresponding general 5G ESSENCE architecture (as shown in Fig. 1). This architecture serving our stadium use case is illustrated in Fig. 3, and consists of several main elements that are briefly discussed as follows:

- The CESC is composed by a small cell physical network function attached to an execution platform (i.e. micro-server) able to run VNFs corresponding to either small cell functionality or specific service-level functions [23].

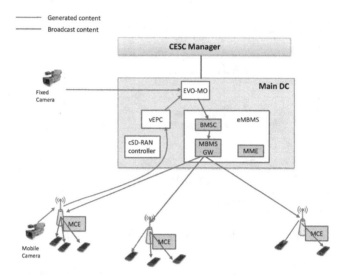

Fig. 3. Stadium demonstration architecture.

- The Edge DC is a two-tier virtualised execution environment composed by the Light DC (resulting from the aggregation of the micro-servers of each CESC) and the Main DC (it is centralised and can host more computation intensive tasks).
- The CESCM includes the components of the ETSI NFV MANO (Management and Orchestration) framework [15], that is the NFVO (NFV Orchestrator) and VNF Manager (VNFM) for carrying out the lifecycle management of network services and VNFs, the Element Management System (EMS)/Network Management System (NMS) for carrying out the management of the deployed CESCs in terms of Fault, Configuration, Accounting, Performance, Security (FCAPS) operations, and a telemetry and analytics module that collects and analyses relevant indicators of the network operation [24].
- The Virtualised Infrastructure Manager (VIM) manages, monitors and optimises the operation of the NFVI (NFV Infrastructure) resources.

The support of eMBMS in this relies upon several functionalities hosted at different components of the original architecture. At the CESC side, the small cells should incorporate the functionality associated to the Multi-Cell/Multicast Coordination Entity (MCE) that manages the allocation of resources for eMBMS transmissions [25]. In turn, the Main DC hosts the rest of components of the eMBMS architecture in the form of a VNF that includes the BMSC (Broadcast Multicast Service Center), the MBMS (Multimedia Broadcast/Multicast Service) GW (Gateway) [26, 27] and the MME (Mobility Management Entity). The video content to be delivered to the eMBMS-*capable* UEs will be produced by the Edge Video Orchestrator - Master Orchestrator (EVO-MO) that will also run as a VNF in the Main DC [28]. In the selected stadium use case, the EVO-MO does not perform CPU (Central Processing Unit) intensive tasks (such as transcoding for external video sinks) and, thus, a simple DC will have enough capacity.

At the same time, this choice ensures that the video content is confined within the area covered by the small cell. The Main DC also incorporates a virtual EPC (Evolved Packet Core) function (the EPC is the latest evolution of the 3GPP core network architecture) that allows the video upstreaming and offloading the traffic locally in the stadium, where the CESCs have been deployed without the need to have access to the backbone of the operator [29].

At the CESCM side, Fig. 1 illustrates the EMS/NMS, which is in charge of configuring the parameters of the small cells, and the NFVO/VNFM components, in charge of, *for example*, instantiating and terminating the abovementioned VNFs. In Fig. 3 we illustrate the interrelationships between the different components of the architecture for demonstrating the delivery of eMBMS data to the User Equipments (UEs). The demonstration assumes that the eMBMS content can be originated either from fixed cameras or from mobile cameras hosted at different UEs. In both cases the images captured by the cameras are delivered to the EVO-MO in upstream via the virtual EPC (vEPC) for processing it. For that purpose, mobile cameras will have access to the CESCs as other UEs and will transmit information through the radio interface by means of a data radio bearer. At the main DC, this data will be received by the local vEPC who will deliver it to the EVO-MO. Based on the data received from the cameras, the EVO-MO will produce the content to be distributed to the UEs [30]. As seen in Fig. 3, this content is injected to the BMSC inside the eMBMS VNF and then it is passed to the MBMS GW who delivers it to the involved small cells.

4 Pilot Description

The selected facility is covered with a cluster of multitenant, eMBMS-*enabled* CESCs and, together with the CESCM and the Main DC, can be connected to the core networks of several participating telecom operators. The video content from cameras is sent for processing locally at the Edge DC. The video streams are broadcasted locally by using the CESCs. Spectators are able to dynamically select between different offered broadcast streams. The main infrastructure needed for this demo is depicted as in Fig. 4, below:

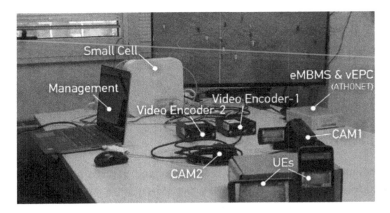

Fig. 4. Main infrastructure of the realization of the use case.

Following to the successful integration and testing of this use case infrastructure, the following network services have been deployed:

- *Multicast Video Delivery in Multi/Single View:* Here the intended objectives have been to assure that: (i) the multicast video is delivered to the small cell and UEs, by receiving related multicast streams; (ii) multicast video is delivered to UEs and can be watched in Multi/Single View (in this case the aim has been to confirm that users can watch videos delivered by multicast in single view and multi-view with the quality known from unicast transmission); (iii) the small cell provides sufficient capacity to all available multicast videos; (iv) stable delivery of multicast to UEs is feasible; in particular, no significant performance degradation observed during evaluation period; (v) the multicast delivery effectively covers all areas of interest in the stadium, and; (vi) audio/video synchronization is achieved for multicast delivery.
- *UE View Switching during the Video Delivery:* In this service the intended objective has been to assure that quality of experience is preserved when switching from multi-view to single view and *vice versa;* in fact, relevant switching times have been small and do not affect user experience significantly.
- *Video Delivery with Handover:* In the context of this service the intended objectives have been to assure that: (i) seamless handover for multicast video transmission takes place; in fact, no video degradation observed when moving from one cell to another, and; (ii) seamless multicast video transmission for mobile encoder is feasible; in particular, no difference in unicast and multicast delivery observed when the video source moves from cell to cell.
- *Unicast vs. Multicast Video Delivery:* In this service case, the intended objectives have been to: (i) demonstrate the reduction in resource usage when using multicast delivery; in fact, significant reductions in resource usage (radio, backhaul) have been performed when using multicast instead of unicast, and; (ii) compare transmission delay in unicast and multicast video delivery; here results have demonstrated that the transmission delay for multicast delivery is very slightly higher compared to unicast transmission (due to the longer chain of entities crossed) but not affecting the user experience.

Two successful demos already took place in the stadium. The first demo took place in July 2019, during Egaleo team's training. The second one took place in October 2019, where two football teams had a typical 90-min match. The event was broadcasted via the 360° camera to the eMBMS-*enabled* end-devices of the viewers. Apart from the 5G ESSENCE partners, many external viewers also attended this event, including two members of the Greek Parliament, the Mayor of Egaleo with two his predecessors, as well as the Deputy Minister of Digital Governance.

5 Market Projection

5G will undoubtedly change our everyday lives and the world *as a whole*. It will have many political, social and economic consequences. New applications and use cases will emerge, which will allow not only for the operators to expand their businesses, but also for new players to enter the market [31]. In the 5G era, different industry verticals are looking for leveraging the influence of modern technologies to boost productivity across paths of the economy [32]. The main idea of the present use case has been to overcome the "hiccups" while at a stadium, including missing parts of the actual game due to different factors, as well as not receiving a good signal while attending an event in a limited space with over several thousands other people. This use case has become able to demonstrate the broadcast capabilities of LTE/5G networks for video processing at the edge by reducing the backhaul traffic to the macro network by leveraging SCs which are connected to a local EPC. The use of the EPC expands the coverage and capacity and paves the way to multimedia transmission to tackle viewing problems audiences' in a stadium face [33]. This is done by multi-angled streaming which will be offered to the audience as a service to improve the QoE.

Considering that the majority of attendees at live events check regularly their phones during the event, there is enough space for introduction of this product. The estimated price that will be charged for the service is 65.00 Euros per year per user, which can be considered a fairly low-price which will leave the business owners a good margin for profit. We take an assumption that the stadium where the respective service will be installed has average match attendance of 48,000 people (which is around the average spectator number in Bundesliga in Germany), out of whom 10% will be using our service on year 1.

That 10% is a very conservative estimation considering the following facts [34]: (i) 18% of overall fans check their phones at matches; (ii) 31% of millennials check their phones during a live event; (iii) 80% of all age groups use a second screen to check scores in other matches, to get expert analysis or to engage with others online over the match; (iv) 50% of the attendees believe that virtual view would improve experience, and; (v) 63% of the attendees believe that video replay would generate excitable experience.

Then we assess that an additional 3% increase of users per year will occur, and each small cell can support up to 400 simultaneous active subscribers; thus for 4,800 users we will be requiring 14 small cells but with a 3% increase per year in a 10 years period we will be needing a total of 16 small cells for 6,263 users. Further parameters in our calculation have been:

- 25 events per year per stadium (i.e.: in Bundesliga 17 matches per year + 7 for cup + 8 for European events).
- Energy consumption is estimated as 1,000.00 Euros per year since the infrastructure will be active only 3 h per event (pre-match and after match along with actual game time reaching a total of $25 \times 3 = 75$ h of use per year) including small cells, cameras, backhaul, router and server energy consumption.
- Tax rate = 29.8% [35].
- WACC (Weighted Average Cost of Capital) = 7.45% considering that the project on this scenario will be co-financed on a 50-50 basis by the involved 5G ESSENCE network operators (i.e.: OTE S.A. (Greece) and Wind TRE SpA (Italy)).

Taking into consideration the sales forecast and the cost estimation, and assessing the NPV (net present value) as 300,190.00 Euros, the payback period as is in year 4 and the IRR (internal rate of return) as 14.33%, we can conclude that the initial investment required is 516,340.00 Euros including 469,400.00 Euros for the CAPEX and 46,940.00 Euros for OPEX costs.

6   Conclusion

The 5G ESSENCE project demonstrates a combined 5G-*based* video production and video distribution towards delivering benefits to both media producers and mobile operators, who will be able to offer enriched event experience to their subscribers. The production/distribution of locally generated content through the related platform, coupled with value-added services and rich user context, enables secure, high-quality and resilient transmission in real-time, thus ensuring minimal latency. This delivers benefits to media producers and mobile operators as it allows them offering a highly interactive fan experience and optimises operations by deploying key functionalities at the edge (i.e., eMBMS or local network services like real-time analytics together with multitenancy support by small cells).

A large-scale facility in a municipality stadium was used for the validation of the respective use case. The coverage in this facility was provided by a cluster of multi-tenant, eMBMS-*enabled* SCs and a main DC able to be connected to the core networks of multiple telecom operators. The Edge DC is processing video content from cameras deployed on-site, which is broadcasted locally without affecting the backhaul. In order to "address" the needs and requirements of a robust and agile network management, and building upon the pillars of network functions virtualisation, mobile-edge computing and cognitive management, our attempt aimed to deliver new business models and revenue streams in the real-life use cases associated to the vertical industry of entertainment, which is purely the case of edge network acceleration in a crowded event. This "opens the door" to venue owners (e.g., municipalities, stadiums, site owners and virtually anyone who manages a property and can install and run a local Small Cell network) to deploy a low cost infrastructure and to act as neutral host network and service provider. Although probably none of such entities would offer static network coverage, many of them could foresee adequate chances for profits generated by exploiting the 5G ESSENCE concepts of multitenant small cells, able to provide wireless network coverage coupled with added value services in close proximity to customers and visitors that belong to multiple network operators and vertical industries.

Acknowledgments. This work has been performed in the joint scope of the *5G ESSENCE* and the *MOTOR5G* European Research Projects and has been supported by the Commission of the European Communities/*H2020* under *Grant Agreements No. 761592 and No. 861219, respectively*.

References

1. Andrews, J.G., Buzzi, S., Choi, W., Hanly, S.V., et al.: What will 5G be. IEEE JSAC. **32**(6), 1065–1082 (2014). Special Issue on 5G Wireless Communications Systems

2. Chochliouros, I.P., et al.: Challenges for defining opportunities for growth in the 5G era: the SESAME conceptual model. In: Proceedings of the 25th European Conference on Networks and Communications (EuCNC), pp. 1–5 (2016)

3. Chochliouros, I.P., et al.: Putting intelligence in the network edge through NFV and cloud computing: the SESAME approach. In: Boracchi, G., Iliadis, L., Jayne, C., Likas, A. (eds.) EANN 2017. CCIS, vol. 744, pp. 704–715. Springer, Cham (2017). https://doi.org/10.1007/978-3-319-65172-9_59

4. Weldon, M.K.: The Future X Network: A Bell Labs Perspective. CRC Press, Boca Raton (2016)

5. Chochliouros, I.P., et al.: Business and market perspectives in 5G Networks. In: Proceedings of the Joint 13th CTTE and 10th CMI Conference 2017, pp. 1–6. IEEE (2017)

6. 5G ESSENCE H2020/5G-PPP Project (GA No. 761592). http://www.5g-essenceh2020.eu

7. Chochliouros, I.P., et al.: A model for an innovative 5G-*oriented* architecture, based on small cells coordination for multi-tenancy and edge services. In: Iliadis, L., Maglogiannis, I. (eds.) AIAI 2016. IFIP AICT, vol. 475, pp. 666–675. Springer, Cham (2016). https://doi.org/10.1007/978-3-319-44944-9_59

8. Goratti, L., et al.: Network architecture and essential features for 5G: the SESAME project approach. In: Iliadis, L., Maglogiannis, I. (eds.) AIAI 2016. IFIP AICT, vol. 475, pp. 676–685. Springer, Cham (2016). https://doi.org/10.1007/978-3-319-44944-9_60

9. Kostopoulos, A., et al.: Use cases for 5G networks using small cells. In: Iliadis, L., Maglogiannis, I., Plagianakos, V. (eds.) AIAI 2018. IFIP AICT, vol. 520, pp. 39–49. Springer, Cham (2018). https://doi.org/10.1007/978-3-319-92016-0_4

10. Costa-Perez, X., Swetina, J., Guo, T., Mahindra, R., Rangarajan, S.: Radio access network virtualization for future mobile carrier networks. IEEE Commun. Mag. **51**(7), 27–35 (2013)

11. Fajardo, J.O., et al.: Introducing mobile edge computing capabilities through distributed 5G Cloud enabled small cells. Mobile Netw. Appl. **21**(4), 564–574 (2016). https://doi.org/10.1007/s11036-016-0752-2

12. Afolabi, I., Taleb, T., Samdanis, K., Ksentini, A., Flinck, H.: Network slicing and softwarization: a survey on principles, enabling technologies, and solutions. IEEE Commun. Surv. Tutor. **20**(3), 2429–2453 (2018)

13. Sallent, O., Pérez-Romero, J., Ferrús, R., Augusti, R.: On radio access network slicing from a radio resource management perspective. IEEE Wirel. Commun. J. **24**(5), 166–174 (2017)

14. The 3rd Generation Partnership Project (3GPP): 3GPP TR 32.851 V12.2.0: Telecommunications management; Study on operations, administration and management (OAM) aspects on network sharing (Release 12) (2014)

15. European Telecommunications Standards Institute (ETSI): NFV Management and Orchestration - An Overview, GS NFV-MAN 001 v1.1.1. ETSI (2014)

16. Chochliouros, I.P., et al.: Enhancing network management via NFV, MEC, cloud computing and cognitive features: the "5G ESSENCE" modern architectural approach. In: Iliadis, L., Maglogiannis, I., Plagianakos, V. (eds.) AIAI 2018. IFIP AICT, vol. 520, pp. 50–61. Springer, Cham (2018). https://doi.org/10.1007/978-3-319-92016-0_5

17. Chochliouros, I.P., Kostopoulos, A., Spiliopoulou, A.S., Kourtis, A., et al.: Small cells, NFV, and cloud computing as enablers for offering innovative 5G services: from the SESAME to the 5G ESSENCE architectural framework. In: Proceedings of the 27th European Conference on Networks and Communications (EuCNC), pp. 570–574. IEEE (2018)

18. Chochliouros, I.P., Giannoulakis, I., Spiliopoulou. A.S., et al.: A novel architectural concept for enhanced 5G network facilities. In: MATEC Web of Conferences, CSCC-2017, vol. 125, no. 03012, pp. 1–7 (2017)

19. Fajardo, J.O., Taboada, Y., Liberal, F.: Improving content delivery efficiency through multi-layer mobile edge adaptation. IEEE Netw. Manag. **29**(6), 40–46 (2015)
20. Giannoulakis, I., Kafetzakis, E., Trajkovska, I., et al.: The emergence of operator-neutral small cells as a strong case for cloud-like computing at the mobile edge. Trans. Emerg. Telecommun. Technol. **27**(9), 1152–1159 (2016)
21. European Telecommunication Standards Institute (ETSI): Multi-Access Edge Computing. http://www.etsi.org/technologies-clusters/technologies/multi-access-edge-computing
22. Kostopoulos, A., Chochliouros, I.P., Giannoulakis, I., Kourtis, A., Kafetzakis, E.: Small cells-as-a-service in 5G networks. In: Proceedings of the IEEE 2018 International Symposium on Broadband Multimedia Systems and Broadcasting (BMSB), pp. 1–4. IEEE (2018)
23. Kostopoulos, A., Chochliouros, I.P., et al.: Network functions for supporting 5G services. In: Proceedings of the 28th European Conference on Networks and Communications (EuCNC), pp. 1–4. IEEE (2019)
24. Chochliouros, I.P., et al.: Using small cells for enhancing 5G networks. In: Proceedings of the IEEE 2017 Conference on Network Function Virtualization and Software Defined Networks (NFV-SDN), pp. 1–6. IEEE (2017)
25. The 3rd Generation Partnership Project (3GPP): TS 23.246 v13.3.0: Multimedia Broadcast/Multicast Service (MBMS); Architecture and functional description (2015)
26. The 3rd Generation Partnership Project (3GPP): TS 22.146 V15.0.0: Technical Specification Group Services and System Aspects; Multimedia Broadcast/Multicast Service (MBMS); Stage 1 (Release 15) (2019)
27. The 3rd Generation Partnership Project (3GPP): TS 22.246 V15.0.0: Technical Specification Group Services and System Aspects; Multimedia Broadcast/Multicast Service (MBMS) user services; Stage 1 (Release 15) (2018)
28. Smart Mobile Labs AG: Edge Video Orchestration EVO - Product description, Release 2.1 (2018)
29. Kostopoulos, A., Chochliouros, I.P., Sfakianakis, E., Munaretto, D., Keuker, C.: Deploying a 5G architecture for crowd events. In: Proceedings of the 2019 IEEE International Conference on Communications (ICC) Workshops, pp. 1–6. IEEE (2019)
30. Kostopoulos, A., Chochliouros, I.P., Sfakianakis, E., Munaretto, D., Keuker, C.: A cloud-based architecture for video services in crowd events. In: MacIntyre, J., Maglogiannis, I., Iliadis, L., Pimenidis, E. (eds.) AIAI 2019. IFIP AICT, vol. 560, pp. 7–18. Springer, Cham (2019). https://doi.org/10.1007/978-3-030-19909-8_1
31. Mordor Intelligence: 5G Infrastructure Market - Growth, Trends and Forecast (2020–2025). Mordor Intelligence (2020)
32. Kostopoulos, A., Chochliouros, I.P., Spada, M.R.: Business challenges for service provisioning in 5G networks. In: Abramowicz, W., Corchuelo, R. (eds.) BIS 2019. LNBIP, vol. 353, pp. 423–434. Springer, Cham (2019). https://doi.org/10.1007/978-3-030-20485-3_33
33. Kostopoulos, A., Chochliouros, I.P., Sfakianakis, E., Munaretto, D., Keuker, C., Giannoulakis, I.: 5G edge network acceleration for crowd events. In: Proceedings of the 19th International Conference WWW/Internet, ICWI 2019, pp. 117–124. IADIS (2019)
34. McIntyre, H.: Millennials, Live Events, and Smartphones: A Look Into Their Behavior. Hollywood & Entertainment (2015). https://www.forbes.com/sites/hughmcintyre/2015/05/07/millennials-live-events-and-smartphones-a-look-into-their-behavior/#2b7ea5623e79
35. Asen, E.: Corporate Income Tax Rates in Europe. Tax Foundation (2019). https://taxfoundation.org/corporate-tax-rates-europe-2019/

Dynamic Network Slicing: Challenges and Opportunities

Ioannis P. Chochliouros[1(✉)] ⓘ, Anastasia S. Spiliopoulou[1],
Pavlos Lazaridis[2], Athanassios Dardamanis[3], Zaharias Zaharis[4],
and Alexandros Kostopoulos[1]

[1] Hellenic Telecommunications Organization (OTE) S.A., 99 Kifissias Avenue,
15124 Maroussi-Athens, Greece
{ichochliouros,alexkosto}@oteresearch.gr,
aspiliopoul@ote.gr
[2] The University of Huddersfield, Queensgate, Huddersfield HD13DH, UK
P.Lazaridis@hud.ac.uk
[3] SmartNet S.A., 2 Lakonias Street, 17342 Ilioupolis-Athens, Greece
adardamanis@smartnet.gr
[4] Aristotle University of Thessaloniki, 54124 Thessaloniki, Greece
zaharis@auth.gr

Abstract. Network Slicing (NS) is an evolving area of research, performing a logical arrangement of resources to operate as individual networks, hence allowing for massively customizable service and tenant requirements. NS, via the respective network architecture can enable an effective deployment of 5G networks and support a great variety of emerging use cases and/or related services. In this scope and with the aim of extending all potential network and service benefits, the concept of dynamic NS becomes a prominent feature of 5G allowing for connectivity and data processing tailored to specific customers' requirements. We discuss several essential features and fundamental designing principles that can affect the realization of a reliable dynamic NS, capable of serving an immense multiplicity of 5G-based innovations, towards structuring a fully mobile and inclusive society. Furthermore, due to its context, dynamic NS can support digital transformation and mobilization of industry vertical customers, implicating for significant commercial potential. To this aim, we also discuss related perspectives for market growth coming from proposed business models, together with regulatory concerns that could affect future growth of dynamic NS.

Keywords: 5G · Dynamic network slicing · Network functions virtualisation (NFV) · Network slicing (NS) · Orchestration · Programmability · Software-Defined Networking (SDN) · Virtual network function (VNF)

1 Introduction

Network Slicing (NS) refers to partitioning of one physical network into multiple virtual networks, each architected and optimized for a specific application/service [1, 2]. Specifically speaking, a network slice is a virtual network that is created on top of a

© IFIP International Federation for Information Processing 2020
Published by Springer Nature Switzerland AG 2020
I. Maglogiannis et al. (Eds.): AIAI 2020 Workshops, IFIP AICT 585, pp. 47–60, 2020.
https://doi.org/10.1007/978-3-030-49190-1_5

physical network in such a way that it gives the illusion to the slice tenant of operating its own dedicated physical network. Consequently, a network slice can be assessed as a self-contained network with its own virtual resources, topology, traffic flow and provisioning rules [3]. Each slice may have its own network architecture and protocols. The related customizable network capabilities can include data speed, quality, latency, reliability, security and services. These capabilities are always provided based on a relevant Service Level Agreement (SLA) between the involved network operator and the business customer.

In its simplest description, NS is the capability to modify a set of functions to improve use of the network for each involved device. All of the functionality needed is accumulated so that to optimize a devices' ability to find the correct underlying network and access it in an efficient and secure manner and then to be attached to the respective core network with the appropriate set of functionality, as needed by that specific device. From a business perspective, a slice can include a combination of all the relevant network resources, functions and other assets required to fulfil a specific business case or a dedicated service, including OSS (Operations Support Systems), BSS (Business Support Systems) and DevOps processes. There may be various network slices to "meet" the detailed communication needs of diverse users in future network systems: for example, a massive industrial IoT slice may need a light 5G core network, no handover but a large number of connections; on the other hand, a mobile broadband slice may need a high capacity core, full feature of mobility and low latency. Slices are logically isolated, but involved resources can be shared among them [4]. NS allows core networks to be logically separated, with each slice providing customized connectivity and all slices running on the same, shared infrastructure or on separate infrastructures as the operator desires, following to related market needs. This is a much more flexible solution than a single physical network providing a maximum level of connectivity.

In any case, a network slice comprises of dedicated and/or shared resources (e.g. in terms of processing power, storage, and bandwidth) and has isolation from the other network slices. In this context, NS is an innovative technology permitting multiple logical networks to be created on the top of a common shared physical infrastructure. The "key" benefits [5] can include, *among others*: (i) Greater elasticity, robustness, secure and stable operations and functionalities through the compartmentalization of the network, applied end-to-end (E2E); (ii) uncompromising and customizable slices, each optimized for the needs of the services -or segment- cluster they are defined to serve, and; (iii) built-in flexibility and efficiency with Artificial Intelligence-powered automated service orchestration, from test to launch to the maintenance of new services.

In the scope of the efforts towards achieving the much promising 5G potential [6], NS explicitly responds to any request about how to perform both increased efficiencies and revenues, through differentiation and faster time-to-market [7]. 5G NS includes slicing 5G radio access network (RAN), 5G core network and even end-user devices. Based on recent technological trends coming from the 5G growth [8], it appears that networks will need to be deployed using different hardware technologies, with different feature sets placed at different physical locations in the network, depending on the use case [9]. To support a specific set of services efficiently, a network slice should have access to different types of resources, such as infrastructure -including virtual private networks (VPNs), cloud services and access- as well as resources for the core network in the form of virtual network functions (VNFs). The flexibility of 5G core networks will improve significantly by supporting a full separation of control plane and user plane, and through adopting selected SDN (Software-Defined Networking) principles and technologies.

NS will allow 5G networks to be sliced logically into multiple virtual networks [10]. Each slice can be optimized to serve a specific vertical application to efficiently support network services, thus providing high degree of flexibility in enabling several use cases to be active concurrently. This is already a well understood methodology in the wireless industry in some limited environments, such as software-defined core networks [11]. In this scope, NS is a fundamental feature of 5G networks and can offer significant advantages when compared to the traditional networks, such as: (i) It can provide logical networks with better and more enhanced performance; (ii) a network slice can scale up or down, depending on the service requirements and the number of involved users, as both they may vary in time; (iii) network slices can separate the network resources of one specific service from the others; in this scope the configurations between various slices do not affect each other, implicating that both reliability and security of each separate slice can be improved, and; (iv) a slice is tailored to dedicated service requirements, which can optimize the allocation and the respective use of involved physical network resources. The NGMN alliance proposed a three layer model [12]; 3GPP defined the required network functions for NS selection and management and so proposed three network slice types [13, 28].

The NS concept is currently a topic of numerous research projects, mostly linked with 5G. The projects have provided some progress, but there is no integrated NS approach that combines the research efforts into a single, coherent concept. Moreover, many details of the proposed approaches still have to be developed. So far, there is no standardized approach to NS that addresses the typical carrier-grade requirements as interoperability, scalability, controllable performance, security, accounting and more. The above implicate for the challenging character of introducing dynamic network slicing, within a fully competitive and fast growing environment.

2 Trends Towards Defining Dynamic Network Slicing

As noted by the NGMN 5G White Paper [14], the success of the forthcoming 5G technology will depend on the ability of the involved operators/market actors to provide multiple solutions for all implied requirements and the ability to provide all participating stakeholders with a unique (set of) solution(s) tailored to everyone's specific needs, under a dynamic consideration. Nevertheless, existing network architectures are not entirely up to this challenge. The current approach, usually assessed as the "one-size-fits-all", cannot be effective to wireless networks for all potential use cases and/or services related to any sort of device/equipment everywhere. Especially, this does not offer the level of adaptability needed to "meet" the performance expectations for new and legacy use cases, services, business models, infrastructure usage approaches and radio access needs that will emerge with 5G growth and penetration. Driven by the new business paradigms such as 5G verticals, the future 5G network should support very heterogeneous services on the same infrastructure.

Furthermore, among the core challenges for 5G network operators is about allocating existing network resources in a way to maximize their advantages. NS provides a network as-a-Service (NaaS) model, which can be very flexible to allocate and reallocate resources according to the dynamic demands such that it can customize network slices for diverse and complex 5G communication scenarios. Within this framework, the life-cycle management of the network slices becomes a critical problem to be taken into account and solved, accordingly. Aiming to support the maximum possible number of diversified service requests, 5G network operators have to deploy VNFs [15] and allocate network resources quickly so that to be able to "structure" related network slices [16]. Moreover, they need to scale slices dynamically [17], according to the varying service load of the underlying infrastructure(s). In contrast, although a network operator has the maximum control over his own network slices, it is essential that one slice may still need to perform some sort of control over itself, so that to improve the corresponding service quality. Therefore, the intended dynamic NS technique has to consider how to "open" partial permissions to each slice to configure and manage it, without rising unnecessary -or complex- security issues [18]. In addition, management of network slice has to take place automatically, to avoid manual efforts and respective errors. To this aim, it can be expected that dynamic NS deployment will benefit from network automation. The automation in rolling network slices will be subject to normal learning curve that new technologies are commonly experiencing, thus it can be expected that the degree of automation of deployment of a network slice will further evolve.

On the other hand, the perspective of 5G dynamic network slicing can be assessed as a suitable "means" to guarantee that intended E2E performance fulfils specific customer prospects together with requirements implied by the services that are to be offered (within several platforms and/or infrastructures and also involving a diversity of related equipment/devices and tools, in a fully converged context). With the aim of properly maximising the efficiency of NS, all individual network segments (such as core, transport, metro, radio access, edge cloud and central cloud) have to be examined "overall", although these are usually treated separately. Simultaneously, performance optimization has to be coordinated and assessed through the entire network; thus, the intended slicing actions can be relevant to a multiplicity of industrial use cases with several instances on one physical network and this offers both reliability and viability in market terms.

Any consistent effort for the realization of an efficient 5G dynamic network slicing process has either to incorporate or to consider several essential features, such as those listed as follows [19]. These could implicate, *inter-alia*, for: (i) Coverage of requests as these are implied by actual business models, tailored to satisfy industrial needs and, preferably, within a broader context for multi-tenancy support [20]; network multi-tenancy aims to reduce capital and operational costs by allowing infrastructure providers to make the best use of available resources, including spectrum and infrastructure; hence, multiple tenants may share resources within the mobile network while offering diverse services; (ii) substantial reduction of new service creation and activation times, so that to enhance network efficiency; (iii) inclusion of an adequate level of network agility, so that to fulfil various service-specific needs; (iv) provision of a (substantial) elasticity to the underlying network infrastructure, thus making it capable to respond to traffic demands that may vary dynamically; (v) consideration of a framework to adapt services and networks in a predictive way and in real time; (vi) structuring of a reliable operating environment for the promotion of open and innovative services with the participation of several market actors from various sectors, to satisfy specific user or industry demands; (vii) care for extension of the intended network and service activities to enterprises and industry verticals as well as to application and content providers; (viii) inclusion of programmability features [21], so that to support easy and fast integration of new network capabilities, extension of existing ones and creation of new services and/or business models; (ix) incorporation of management and orchestration techniques and of related capabilities allowing for dynamic network (re-)configuration to support E2E performance purposes, and; (x) support a high level of automation, powered by advances in analytics and machine learning [22].

The fundamental aim proposed by the innovative context of the dynamic network slicing is to "extend", *further*, the capabilities of 5G networks so that for the latter to become able to effectively "address" a variety of related use cases and possible applications [23] covering actual 5G trends. This permits market telecom operators to design, deploy, customize and optimize the various network slices that are running on the commonly assessed network infrastructure. In addition, beyond its conceptual dependence upon the well-known SDN and NFV features [24–26], the dynamic network slicing also depends on E2E orchestration and analytics. However, although the 5G NS process brings flexibility, it also "increases" the complexity of network management [27]. Thus, there is a need to design automated management schemes, implicating that a proper lifecycle network management is responsible for slice creation, reconfiguration, deletion, etc., but it also involves orchestrating and allocating of infrastructure resources. Vendors usually take into account the term of dynamic network slicing because operators will be able to deliver these network slices quickly and on demand, to any applicant; as a consequence, operators can rapidly start deployments, architecture types and performance thresholds for distinct use cases or service groups, responding to market needs. The dynamic network slicing concept practically extends the slicing vision (as proposed in [28]) and satisfactorily covers diverse requirements, as identified above. The "outcome" is that dynamic network slicing partitions a common network infrastructure into multiple, logical, E2E, virtual network instances -or slices- with several key characteristics summarized as follows:

- *The related slices support a group of services, use-cases and business models with associated requirements:* For example, an operator can "run" enhanced broadband slices to offer a variety of broadband services to its customers, which may include web browsing, audio and video streaming and chat.
- *The slices are built with only relevant network capabilities that do "match" the needs of the corresponding supported service, use case or business case*: For example, an ultra-low latency capability can be created for a slice supporting ultra-low latency use cases. The capabilities in the slice are not restricted to the user plane. The slices can also control and manage plane-relevant capabilities, such as a dynamic video stream controller or a specific type of billing application relevant to the business case.

- *The slices are dynamic in runtime*: They comprise an automation framework that uses real-time analytics and monitoring for efficient use of network, cloud resources and optimization for the dynamic needs of services or traffic demands.

3 Dynamic E2E Network Slicing as Enabler for 5G Promotion

5G is an E2E ecosystem allowing the structuring of a fully mobile and connected society. It empowers value creation towards customers and partners, via current and emergent use cases, delivered with reliable experience and enabled by sustainable business models. The 5G networks need to incorporate various services with dissimilar performance requirements (such as high throughput, low latency, high reliability, high mobility and high security) into a single physical network infrastructure and also to provide each service with a customized logical network (via NS). One among the fundamental concerns for future 5G network operators is about how to allocate network resource in a way to maximize their benefits and, *in this perspective*, the life-cycle management of the network slices becomes a critical issue to deal with. In order to accommodate the maximum number of diversified service requests, 5G network operators need to deploy suitable VNFs and allocate network resources rapidly so that to build *ad-hoc* network slices [26]. Moreover, they need to scale slices dynamically, according to the varying service load, *per case*. On the other hand, although a network operator has the maximum control over his network slices, one slice may still need to exercise some "control" over itself for improving the service quality; therefore, the NS technique should consider how to "open" partial permissions to each slice to configure and manage it, without raising any security issues. In all such actions, the intended management of network slice need to be implemented in an automated fashion for the avoidance of manual efforts and errors.

The response to this challenge can be a dynamic E2E network slicing, thus providing an optimal approach to NS in 5G networks [29]. This allows operators to support the miscellaneous and occasionally demanding requirements for latency, throughput and availability that are essential for the delivery of 5G services to a wide variety of "recipients" such as users, machines, industries and other entities [30, 31]. The dynamic network slicing concept will be beneficial in the 5G framework, especially by allowing dynamic E2E network partitioning at all network levels (i.e.: from the Radio Access Network (RAN) to the transport network and to the core network). This offers to the 5G operators the possibility to promote appropriate deployments and architectures for each separate business model, thus enabling the appearance of new use cases, and occasionally for dedicated service group(s). Furthermore, the operators can "run" and deploy existing network implementations in parallel and simultaneously upon a common network infrastructure, which promotes new communications possibilities. Monetizing the quality of experience (QoE) is another area where operators can benefit from dynamic network slicing [32]. In 5G it is possible to define a QoS based on each application's unique requirements, as an involved network operator may create different slices for different participating Mobile (Virtual) Network Operators (MNOs/MVNOs) and each respective slice may have different QoE values [33].

Following to the above and in order to "address" a variety of miscellaneous requirements, modern 5G network architectures have to "shift" from the current network of entities to a sort of network of capabilities, implicating a way of "transition" from a network for connectivity to a network for services model [34]. Dynamic network slicing offers an effective way to enable this "shifting" and the partition of a single common 5G infrastructure into multiple logical E2E networks. This provides the service agility needed to deal with a diversity of factors including, *inter-alia*: (i) "Users" (i.e.: both people and machines or other type(s) of equipment); (ii) corresponding use cases that support new services and devices, connect new industries and empower new user experiences [35], and; (iii) related requirements for latency throughput and availability. The dynamic network slicing allows network operators to: perform various deployments; implement specific architectural features and; achieve a considerable variety of performance for different use cases of practical interest [36]. This approach permits for simultaneous network implementations that can take place in parallel and it is strongly affected by several "key principles" [5], implicating for the consideration of:

A distributed cloud infrastructure including virtualization features: Virtualization allows for (mobile) networks to be less "tied" to physical resources and, *therefore*, to be more customizable in their design and users. Thus, *whenever possible*, there is a trends for the 5G network functions and/or capabilities to be developed upon distributed cloud and virtualization infrastructures. Furthermore, dedicated and purpose-built network entities are only used when necessary [37].

A network of capabilities instead of network of entities: In this scope, the 5G network slices are made of modular network capabilities. Related Network Capability Units (NCUs) are the "abstractions" of these network capabilities and can have varying degrees of granularity, although usually expected to be modular for easy "plug-and-play" deployment and operation.

A network for services in place of a network for connectivity: The 5G network slices are designed with the aim of offering and supporting diverse classes of services. Consequently, the 5G network slices can have unique capabilities required for supporting dedicated group(s) of services but also for individual services.

Easy and effective design and dynamic creation of E2E slices: Dynamic 5G network slices need to be easily designed by packaging the related and necessary NCUs. Network slices need to be created dynamically by using proven orchestration and management technologies [28]. Moreover, customization through a virtual network allows for the exact definition of the network slice to no longer be pre-defined. This means that anything could actually be provided "as-a-service", since the combination of resources is not restricted. This further "opens up" the market to a broader range of usage cases [38].

Inclusion of dynamic programmability and control: The 5G network slices have to support dynamic programmability and control by leveraging SDN principles [39], thus allowing for the inclusion of a multiplicity of benefits for their operation.

Automation of the network operation and optimization: Although beneficial, the creation of network slices practically increases both the complexity of network operations and also of the ongoing optimization efforts. To overpass this "obstacle", dynamic network slices have to enable automation of operations and optimizations via several means such as analytics, machine learning, big-data, etc. [22].

End-to-end perspective and approach: The 5G network slices are composed of capabilities from multiple network segments that span the network from access to core, as well as network applications. This E2E perspective is needed to satisfactorily meet the needs of diverse services, use cases, and business models.

4   Market and Regulatory Challenges

In the 5G era, different industry verticals are looking for leveraging the influence of modern technologies to boost productivity across paths of the economy [7]. NS builds upon this expectation and, *together with the promise of Massive IoT and ultra-reliable/low latency services*, it can support digital transformation and mobilization of industry vertical customers. Providing "tailored" services to business customers has significant commercial potential; thus, NS does "drive" the business models behind 5G ecosystem [18] by providing an effective way to delivery heterogeneous services of interest for different verticals [40]. In the literature there are three different of business models for NS, that is: B2B, B2C and B2B2C [41, 42]. In the B2B model, operators sell customized network resources to enterprises and release full control of end-consumers to enterprises. In the B2C model, customers purchase customized network resource based on their requirements without considering which operator provides the requested resources. In the B2B2C model, operators just provide customized network resources to a broker, and the broker gets more control of the network and engages with the end-consumer directly. All previously mentioned business models deal with the allocation of network resources and, *consequently*, the effective revenue as well as the network performance directly depend on the way the operator manages such resources [43]. Following to the above, it is expected that dynamic network slicing will further support market growth and related investments [44]. A probable "go-to-market" strategy may implicate for three distinct stages, able to deliver value across the value chain [45]. These stages may happen in parallel, depending on local market conditions. These are briefly summarised as follows:

- *Deployment of NS for internal use*: This will prove the NS validity by using the solution to serve internal customers within an operator. This option offers a low risk opportunity to experiment and to validate the proposition, in order to refine it ahead of rollout to commercial customers.
- *Upsell NS capabilities to existing enterprise customers*: This will prove value to existing enterprise customers and based on the typical buying behaviour of such

customers, upselling network slicing capabilities needs to be an easier opportunity than targeting new customers. These customers can then become proof points and advocates for the new capabilities.

- *Sell to new enterprise customers*: When commercially ready, slicing will be made more broadly available to enterprise customers who often require a proven solution and seek market validation, before they buy.

NS will be an essential attribute of 5G, based upon SDN and NFV [41]. Assessing the importance of NS for future 5G networks implicates that regulation shall be around several fundamental domains/areas as briefly discussed in the following sections. It is important to mention that regulators need to assess practically whether -or not- NS is able to affect customers regarding their common actions and/or their market-related behaviour(s). In the scope of the present work, we only identify several regulatory issues that could be affected to a certain extent by dynamic NS growth and, by turn, they could able to influence further development. These are described as follows.

Security and privacy policy requirements: The notion of sharing resources among slices may create security problems in 5G NS [18]. This is so because network slices that serve different types of services -for different verticals- may have different levels of security and privacy policy requirements [46]. This calls for the new development of 5G (dynamic) NS security and privacy protocols that consider the impact on other slices and the entire network systems, while allocating resources to a particular slice(s). Also, security issues become even more complicated when 5G NS is implemented in multi-domain infrastructures. To address this issue, security policy and efficient coordination mechanisms among different administrative domains infrastructure in 5G systems need to be designed and developed [47].

Net neutrality: While there is no single definition of "net neutrality", the term is frequently used to denote issues related to the optimization of traffic over underlying networks. In particular, due to current market needs, involved network operators have to act so that to offer fast and reliable Internet access to their customers, by taking into account any actual shared use of network resources as well as the limited availability of spectrum. Dynamic NS can be a "tool" to deliver suitable choices and to satisfy customers' needs via managing corresponding traffic patterns and by offering flexibility for differentiation between them. The core objective is to guarantee that consumers shall have the possibility to choose the best offered solution to meet their own needs. Here, the large concern is the way that prioritization and differentiation of network slices might account to discrimination under the net neutrality laws, causing a fear that the development of the technology might be hindered by the lack of regulatory clarity [48]. The intent of the laws are both clear and desirable.

Quality of Service (QoS): The quality of a mobile data services is delineated by several parameters, including but not limited to speed, packet loss, delay and jitter [49]. QoS is also affected by signal strength, network load and user device and application design; however OoS is also influenced by several extra factors that can be beyond the control of operators (such as the type of the devices, the application and propagation environment). In the 5G scope, continually changing traffic patterns and congestions may have a critical result upon the whole performance. The QoS differentiation that is at the heart of the dynamic NS value proposition, what the EU regulation [50] calls as "traffic management". This respective regulation allows for differentiation to take place on the Internet, in a limited capacity. Applied to NS, we can mention that different use cases like virtual reality (VR) video content, smart grid solutions and automated cars fit into having "objectively different" QoS demands, and thus discrimination between them would be within the framework of the regulation.

Cross-border data transfers: The worldwide digital economy is also influenced by the cross-border data transfers aiming to provide important (form both social and economic point of view) benefits to all potential categories of end-users (individuals, businesses and governments). When data is allowed to flow freely across national borders, this permits the involved legal entities operate, innovate, access solutions and offer global support. Policies constraining free flow of data through unjustified restrictions or local data storage requirements can have an adverse impact on all involved market players and the economy. Cross-border transfers of personal data are now regulated by a number of international, regional and national instruments and laws intended to protect individuals' privacy, the local economy or national security. It is foreseen that network slices may be utilised to offer services outside of the home jurisdiction, potentially in a similar manner to international roaming. If so, any transfer of data across borders may need to consider regulatory requirements.

Illegal content: In our current market framework, mobile networks not only offer traditional services but can also deliver virtual access to all forms of digital content via the Internet. Thus, mobile network operators can be assessed as the "equivalent" of other Internet Service Providers (ISPs). However, this also implicates that the involved mobile networks can also be occasionally used to access various forms of illegal content. The respective legal framework affecting this domain demonstrates a significant degree of variation at the global level. Mobile network operators are warned for transfer of or access to illegal content by the national hotline organisations or law-enforcement agencies. When content is reported, the operators follow procedures according to the relevant data protection, privacy and disclosure legislation. The related issues and/or and commitments have to be addressed with the introduction of NS and can vary depending on the implementation of slices.

5   Conclusion

Network slicing is an emerging area of research, featuring a logical arrangement of resources to operate as individual networks, thus allowing for massively customizable services and tenant requirements. NS offers an effective way to support different use cases with diverse requirements and exploits the benefits of a common network infrastructure. It enables operators to establish different deployments, architectural flavors and performance levels for each use case -or service group- and it can "run" all network implementations, occasionally in parallel. Due to its innovative features and to the multiplicity of the beneficial impacts, the NS has been identified as among the fundamental "building blocks" of 5G towards the successful adoption of respective modern infrastructures and for the offering of related services/facilities.

However, as the success of the upcoming 5G technology and its market inclusion is strongly dependent on the capability of the involved market actors/players to provide "suitable" sets of solutions tailored to specific end-users' (i.e.: residential, corporate, governmental and all potential ones) needs/requests, under a continuously evolved context (so that to ensure "alignment" and conformance to any sort of performed technological, business, financial, regulatory or other evolution), a dynamic NS concept has to be taken into account. This allows for a more flexible and more reliable design, establishment, assessment and exploitation of the intended 5G realization and becomes a practical 5G enabler. Towards an effective market-oriented approach, the dynamic NS leverages "key technology" advancements in a variety of sectors, including but not limited to: (i) Distributed cloud infrastructure and cloud native applications; (ii) NFV; (iii) E2E orchestration; (iv) SDN and programmable networking; (v) network big data, analytics and machine learning; (vi) services oriented architectures, and; (vii) intent based network programming. These implicate for innovative attributes to become indispensable parts of the networks of the future and support a variety of services.

In the development of the 5G world, there are also challenges for the market sector and especially for the participating industry verticals, who desire increasing their productivity. To this aim (dynamic) NS enables operators to create pre-defined, differing levels of services to different enterprise verticals, allowing them to customize their own operations. There are several market models for adopting NS and for the support of related "go to market" strategies. However, in order to realize an effective market penetration, dynamic NS also depends on several regulatory perspectives that have to be examined in every attempt for future growth, to avoid potential uncertainties that could harm market growth. In our approach we have also identified several such factors and have realised a first assessment. Due to its nature, the dynamic NS can offer a substantial support for the 5G success.

Acknowledgments. This work has been performed in the scope of the *5G-DRIVE* European Research Project and has been supported by the Commission of the European Communities/ *H2020, Grant Agreement No. 814956.*

References

1. Global System for Mobile Communications Alliance (GSMA): An introduction to 5G network slicing. GSMA, November 2017. https://www.gsma.com/futurenetworks/wp-content/uploads/2017/11/GSMA-An-Introduction-to-Network-Slicing.pdf
2. Sharma, S., Miller, R., Francini, A.: A cloud-native approach to 5G network slicing. IEEE Commun. Mag. **55**(8), 120–127 (2017)
3. Rost, P., Banchs, A., Berberana, I., Reitbach, M., Doll, M., et al.: Mobile network architecture evolution toward 5G. IEEE Commun. Mag. **54**(5), 84–91 (2016)
4. Einsiedler, H.-J., Gavras, A., Sellstedt, P., et al.: System design for 5G converged networks. In: Proceedings of the 24th European Conference on Networks and Communications (EuCNC), pp. 391–396. IEEE (2015)
5. Elliott, J., Sharma, S.: Dynamic end-to-end network slicing unlocks 5G possibilities. Nokia (2016). https://www.nokia.com/blog/dynamic-end-end-network-slicing-unlocks-5g-possibilities/

6. Chochliouros, I.P., et al.: Putting intelligence in the network edge through NFV and cloud computing: the SESAME approach. In: Boracchi, G., Iliadis, L., Jayne, C., Likas, A. (eds.) EANN 2017. CCIS, vol. 744, pp. 704–715. Springer, Cham (2017). https://doi.org/10.1007/978-3-319-65172-9_59

7. Chochliouros, I.P. et al.: Business and market perspectives in 5G networks. In: Proceedings of the Joint 13th CTTE and 10th CMI Conference 2017, pp. 1–6. IEEE (2017)

8. Andrews, J.G., Buzzi, S., Choi, W., Hanly, S.V., et al.: What will 5G be. IEEE JSAC, Spec. Issue 5G Wireless Commun. Syst. **32**(6), 1065–1082 (2014)

9. Makhijani, K., et al.: Network slicing use cases: network customization and differentiated services. Internet Engineering Task Force (IETF) (2017). https://datatracker.ietf.org/doc/draft-netslices-usecases/

10. Sama, M.L., An, X., Wie, Q., Beker, S.: Reshaping the mobile core network via function decomposition and network slicing for the 5G era. In: Proceedings of the 2016 IEEE Wireless Communications and Networking Conference, pp. 1–7. IEEE (2016)

11. Afolabi, I., Taleb, T., Samdanis, K., Ksentini, A., Flinck, H.: Network slicing and softwarization: a survey on principles, enabling technologies, and solutions. IEEE Commun. Surv. Tutor. **20**(3), 2429–2453 (2018)

12. Hedman, P.: Description of Network Slicing Concept. Next Gener. Mob. Netw. Alliance (2016). https://www.ngmn.org/publications/description-of-network-slicing-concept.html

13. The 3rd Generation Partnership Project (3GPP): 3GPP TR 28.801 V15.0.0 (2018-01): Telecommunications management; Study on management and orchestration of network slicing for next generation network (Release 15)

14. Next Generation Mobile Networks Alliance: 5G White Paper. NGMN e.V. (2015). https://www.ngmn.org/fileadmin/ngmn/content/images/news/ngmn_news/NGMN_5G_White_Paper_V1_0.pdf

15. Chochliouros, I.P., et al.: Enhancing network management via NFV, MEC, cloud computing and cognitive features: the "5G ESSENCE" modern architectural approach. In: Iliadis, L., Maglogiannis, I., Plagianakos, V. (eds.) AIAI 2018. IAICT, vol. 520, pp. 50–61. Springer, Cham (2018). https://doi.org/10.1007/978-3-319-92016-0_5

16. Galis, A., Lin, C.: Towards 5G network slicing - motivations and challenges. IEEE 5G Technol. Focus **1**(1), 1–6 (2017). http://5g.ieee.org/tech-focus/march-2017#networkslicing

17. International Telecommunication Union - Telecommunications Standardization Sector (ITU-T): Recommendation Y.3112 (12/2008): Framework for the Support of Multiple Network Slicing. https://www.itu.int/rec/T-REC-Y.3112-201812-I/en

18. Next Generation Mobile Networks Alliance: 5G Security Recommendations Package#2: Network Slicing. NGMN e.V., April 2016. https://www.ngmn.org/fileadmin/user_upload/160429_NGMN_5G_Security_Network_Slicing_v1_0.pdf

19. Nokia Oyz: Dynamic End-To-End Network Slicing for 5G - White Paper, Nokia (2016). http://www.hit.bme.hu/~jakab/edu/litr/5G/NOKIA_dynamic_network_slicing_WP.pdf

20. Samdanis, K., Costa-Perez, X., et al.: From network sharing to multi-tenancy: the 5G network slice broker. IEEE Commun. Mag. **54**(7), 32–39 (2016)

21. Raza, M.R., Fiorani, M., Rostami, A., Öhlen, P., et al.: Benefits of programmability in 5G transport networks. In: Proceedings of OFC-2017, pp. 1–3. IEEE (2017)

22. Chochliouros, I.P., et al.: Inclusion of telemetry and data analytics in the context of the 5G ESSENCE architectural approach. In: MacIntyre, J., Maglogiannis, I., Iliadis, L., Pimenidis, E. (eds.) AIAI 2019. IAICT, vol. 560, pp. 46–59. Springer, Cham (2019). https://doi.org/10.1007/978-3-030-19909-8_4

23. Chochliouros, I.P., Sallent, O., Pérez-Romero, J., Spiliopoulou, A.S., Dardamanis, A.: Implications of multi-tenancy upon RRM/Self-x functions supporting mobility control. In:

Boracchi, G., Iliadis, L., Jayne, C., Likas, A. (eds.) EANN 2017. CCIS, vol. 744, pp. 657–668. Springer, Cham (2017). https://doi.org/10.1007/978-3-319-65172-9_55

24. Odini, M.-P.: SDN and NFV evolution towards 5G. IEEE Softwarization Magazine, September 2017. https://sdn.ieee.org/newsletter/september-2017/sdn-and-nfv-evolution-towards-5g

25. Barakabitze, A.A., et al.: 5G network slicing using SDN and NFV: a survey of taxonomy, architectures and future challenges. Comput. Netw. **167**(11), 1–40 (2020)

26. Mijumbi, R., Serrat, J., et al.: Network function virtualization: State-of-the-art and research challenges. IEEE Commun. Surv. Tutor. **18**(1), 236–262 (2016)

27. European Telecommunications Standards Institute: ETSI GR NGP 011 v1.1.1: E2E Network Slicing Reference Framework and Information Model. ETSI (2018)

28. The 3rd Generation Partnership Project (3GPP): 3GPP TS 28.531 V15.0.0: Provisioning of network slicing for 5G networks and services: Detailed specification of network slice provisioning/Network slice management (2018)

29. Costanzo, S., Fajjari, I., Aitsaadi, N., Langar, R.: Dynamic network slicing for 5G IoT and eMBB services: a new design with prototype and implementation results. In: Proceedings of CIoT 2018, pp. 1–7. IEEE (2018)

30. Katsalis, K., Nikaein, N., et al.: Network slices toward 5G communications: slicing the LTE network. IEEE Commun. Mag. **55**(8), 146–154 (2017)

31. Rost, P., Mannweiler, C., et al.: Network slicing to enable scalability and flexibility in 5G mobile networks. IEEE Commun. Mag. **55**(5), 72–79 (2017)

32. Yousaf, F.Z., Gramaglia, M., et al.: Network slicing with flexible mobility and QoS/QoE support for 5G Networks. In: Proceedings of ICC Workshops 2017, pp. 1–7. IEEE (2017)

33. Le Callet, P., et al.: Definitions of Quality of Experience (COST IC1003), Qualinet (2013). http://www.qualinet.eu/index.php?option=com_content&view=article&id=45&Itemid=52

34. Xin, L., Mohammed, S., Anthony, C.H., Bhamare, D., Guopta, L., et al.: Network slicing for 5G: challenges and opportunities. IEEE Internet Comput. **21**(5), 20–27 (2017)

35. Afolabi, I., Ksentini, A., et al.: Towards 5G network slicing over multiple-domains. IEICE Trans. Commun. **E100B**(11), 1992–2006 (2017)

36. Raza, M.R., et al.: Dynamic slicing approach for multitenant 5G transport networks. J. Opt. Commun. Netw. **10**(1), A77–A90 (2018)

37. Abdelwahab, S., Hamdaoui, B., Guizani, M., Znati, T.: Network function virtualization in 5G. IEEE Commun. Mag. **54**(4), 84–91 (2016)

38. Taleb, T., Ksentini, A., Jäntti, R.: "Anything as a service" for 5G mobile systems. IEEE Netw. **30**(6), 84–91 (2016)

39. Galis, A.: Programmability, Softwarization and Management in 5G Smart Networking. AICT (2017). https://www.ee.ucl.ac.uk/~agalis/

40. Gomes, J.F., Ahokangas, P., Moqaddamerad, S.: Business modeling options for distributed network functions virtualization: operator perspective. In: Proceedings of the 22th European Wireless Conference, pp. 1–6 (2016)

41. Zhou, Z., Li, R., et al.: Network slicing as a service: enabling enterprises' own software-defined cellular networks. IEEE Commun. Mag. **54**(7), 146–153 (2016)

42. Jiang, M., Condoluci, M., Mahmoodi, T., Guijarro, L.: Economics of 5G network slicing: optimal and revenue-based allocation of radio and core resources in 5G. https://nms.kcl.ac.uk/toktam.mahmoodi/files/TWC-16.pdf

43. Bega, M., Gramaglia, M., et al.: Optimising 5G infrastructure markets: the business of network slicing. In: Proceedings of INFOCOM 2017, pp. 1–9. IEEE, May 2017

44. Global System for Mobile Communications Alliance: Smart 5G Networks: Enabled by Network Slicing and Tailored to Customers' Needs. GSMA, September 2017

45. Han, B., Tayade, S., Schotten, H.D.: Modeling profit of sliced 5G networks for advanced network resource management and slice implementation. In: Proceedings of the ISCC-2017, pp. 1–7. IEEE, July 2017
46. Cunha, V.A., da Silva, E., de Carvalho, M.B., Corujo, D., et al.: Network slicing security: Challenges and directions. Internet Technol. Lett. 2(5), e125–e130 (2019)
47. Fang, D., Qian, Y., Hu, R.Q.: Security for 5G mobile wireless networks. IEEE Access 6, 4850–4874 (2017)
48. Morris, I.: Net Neutrality Threatens 5G. Ericsson (2019). https://www.lightreading.com/net-neutrality/ericsson-ceo-net-neutrality-threatens-5g/d/d-id/740854
49. Varela, M., Zwickl, P., Reichl, P., Xie, M., Schulzrinne, H.: From Service Level Agreements (SLA) to Experience level Agreements (ELA): the challenges of selling QoE to the user. In: Proceedings of IEEE ICC QoE-FI, pp. 1741–1746. IEEE (2015)
50. European Parliament and Council (2015): Regulation (EU) 2015/2120 of 25 November 2015. European Union, Official Journal L310-L318 (2015)

Dynamic Resource Allocation and Computation Offloading for Edge Computing System

Zheng Chang[1(✉)], Liqing Liu[2], Xijuan Guo[2], Tao Chen[3],
and Tapani Ristaniemi[1]

[1] Faculty of Information Technology, University of Jyvaskyla,
P. O. Box 35, 40014 Jyvaskyla, Finland
zheng.chang@jyu.fi
[2] College of Information Science and Engineering,
Yanshan University, Qinhuangdao 066004, China
[3] VTT Technical Research Centre of Finland, Espoo, Finland

Abstract. In this work, we propose a dynamic optimization scheme for an edge computing system with multiple users, where the radio and computational resources, and offloading decisions, can be dynamically allocated with the variation of computation demands, radio channels and the computation resources. Specifically, with the objective to minimize the energy consumption of the considered system, we propose a joint computation offloading, radio and computational resource allocation algorithm based on Lyapunov optimization. Through minimizing the derived upper bound of the Lyapunov drift-plus-penalty function, the main problem is divided into several sub-problems at each time slot and are addressed separately. The simulation results demonstrate the effectiveness of the proposed scheme.

Keywords: Edge computing · Dynamic computation offloading ·
Lyapunov optimization · Resource allocation

1 Introduction

In mobile cloud computing (MCC), by offloading the computational tasks to the distant cloud for execution, the system performance, e.g., energy consumption and latency, is able to be improved [1]. Among all different types of MCC technologies, fog/edge computing system, emerges as a proximity solution to provide pervasive and distributed computation services for the MDs, and especially for the Internet-of-Things (IoT) applications with stringent requirement of latency and reliability [2]. In the edge computing system, as the computing capability of the edge node (EN) is not comparable to the traditional cloud center and one

Supported by organization x.

EN only serves a relative small area where the radio resource is also limited, the offloading decisions of the MDs may have a significant impact on the quality of services (QoS). Accordingly, the usage of the radio resources, such as transmit power and frequency spectrum, and the harvested energy should be carefully coordinated and optimized in line with the offloading decisions. In addition, as the radio environment and the demand for computational resources vary in a fast speed, dynamic scheduling and optimization are more preferred compared to static optimization schemes. However, due to the randomness of radio environment, harvested energy and computation demands, realizing the dynamic optimization is challenging. Therefore, in this paper, our aim is to overcome the obstacles and provide dynamic computation offloading and resource allocation schemes for edge computing system with EH devices.

Most of the researches on the offloading problem focus on designing different and effective static schemes for battery-powered MDs, through optimizing the MD's execution decision, radio resource, and/or computational resource [2–7]. Considering a edge computing system, the authors of [2] apply queuing theory to investigate the delay, energy consumption, and payment cost (E&D&P) of offloading processes. Based on the theoretical analysis, a multi-objective optimization problem is then formulated to minimize the formulated cost functions by finding the offloading decisions and power allocation for each MD. In [3], the authors explore the tradeoff between delay and energy consumption in the edge-cloud hybrid computing system. The associated workload allocation problem is addressed accordingly. In [4], the authors propose an optimization framework of offloading to optimize the task allocation decision and the computational resource allocation.

In this work, to address the offloading problem in edge computing, we consider different queue models at different edge computing devices to provide thorough analysis on the delay and energy consumption performance. At the MD, a $M/M/1$ queue is considered and at the EN, a $M/G/1$ queue is assumed. With the derived analytical results, we are able to formulate the system cost, which consists of service latency and energy consumption. With the objective to minimize the formulated system cost, the offloading strategy, the transmit power, and the subcarrier assignment are jointly optimized in the proposed resource allocation and offloading scheme. Due to the stochastic nature of the radio channel, the request arrival and the amount of harvesting energy, we propose to leverage the advantages of Lyapunov optimization to design an online dynamic algorithm. By minimizing the upper bound of the Lyapunov drift-plus-penalty function from the perspective of different decision variables, the initial problem is divided into several simple sub-problems with low-complexity and can be addressed accordingly.

2 System Model

We consider the system consisting of N single-core MDs, one AP, and one EN. The set of MDs is denoted as $\mathcal{N} = \{1, 2, \cdots, N\}$. Each MD generates a series of homogeneous service requests in order to execute an application. At the MD, a first-in-first-out (FIFO) queue is considered for storing arriving requests, and the radio interface is used for wireless connection. As a single processor is assumed, the process queue at the MD is assumed as a $M/M/1$ queue. The EH capability enables the MD to obtain energy supply from the environment. The harvested energy used for local task execution and data transmission. The AP is responsible for receiving requests from the MD and delivering data to the EN for further processing. The process queue of EN is modelled as a $M/G/1$ queue. The MD offloads (part of) the computation requests to the EN to enjoy a higher level of quality of computation experience. We assume that the time is slotted and the length of each time slot is τ. We denote the time slot set $\mathcal{T} = \{0, 1 \cdots, t \cdots, T-1\}$.

2.1 Local Execution Model

The computation requests generated by MD i, $i \in \mathcal{N}$ is assumed to follow Poisson process with an average arrival rate $A_i(t)$ and within $[A_{i,\min}, A_{i,\max}]$. Each request is of data size θ_i. Note that "at time slot t" means the requests are generated at time slot "t" but executed at time slot "$t+1$".

For MD i, some of the computation requests may be locally executed and the rest will be offloaded to the EN. It may also happen that when neither of these computation modes is feasible, e.g., when MD has insufficient energy, and some of the computation requests have to be dropped. The decision of MD i at time slot t is modeled as a vector $\mathbf{p}_i(t) = \left[p_i^M(t), p_i^F(t), p_i^D(t)\right]$, where $p_i^M(t) + p_i^F(t) + p_i^D(t) = 1$. $p_i^M(t)$ represents the portion that the requests are executed locally at time slot t, $p_i^F(t)$ denotes the portion that the requests are offloaded to the EN, and $p_i^D(t)$ expresses the portion that the requests are dropped.

We denote u_i^M as the computing capability of MD i, which depends on CPU Cycle the MD. Additionally we assume that $l_i^M(t)$ denotes the normalized workload on the MD i at time slot t, which shows the occupation of CPU. For example, $l_i^M(t) = 0$ indicates at time slot t, the CPU is totally idle. When considering a $M/M/1$ queue with request arrival rate λ and service rate u, the response time is $R = \frac{1/u}{1-\rho}$, where $\rho = \frac{\lambda}{u}$ [8]. Then, the average response time $D_i^M(t)$ for local execution of MD i at time slot t is expressed as follows:

$$D_i^M(t) = \frac{1}{u_i^M\left(1 - l_i^M(t)\right) - p_i^M(t) A_i(t)}. \tag{1}$$

Assume that the computing capability of MD i is $u_i^M\left(1 - l_i^M(t)\right)$ and the corresponding CPU-cycle frequency is denoted as $f_i(t)$ at time slot t. As shown in [5], under the assumption of a low CPU voltage, the power consumption of CPU is kf^3, where k is a constant depending on the switched capacitance of MD, and f is the CPU-cycle frequency. Thus, the energy consumption $E_i^M(t)$ of MD i for local execution can be denoted as follows:

$$E_i^M(t) = k_i f^3{}_i(t) D_i^M(t) = \frac{k_i f^3{}_i(t)}{u_i^M\left(1 - l_i^M(t)\right) - p_i^M(t) A_i(t)}. \tag{2}$$

Nevertheless, if some of the requests cannot be executed due to lack of energy, they have to be dropped. We define a cost coefficient μ_i for the task drop, and accordingly the punishment cost for MD i at time slot t can be expressed as follows:

$$C_i^D(t) = \mu_i p_i^D(t) A_i(t) \tau. \tag{3}$$

2.2 Uplink Transmission

The wireless network is assumed to be Orthogonal Frequency Division Multiplexing (OFDM)-based. The set of the subcarrier is denoted as $\mathcal{K} = \{1, 2 \cdots, k, \cdots, K\}$, where $|\mathcal{K}| = K$. The channels are assumed to be independent and identically distributed (i.i.d) block fading during time slots, i.e. the channels remain static within each time slot, but vary among different time slots. Let B denotes the channel bandwidth, N_0 denotes the noise power spectral density at the AP, $h_{i,k}(t)$ denotes the channel gain and $p_{i,k}(t)$ denotes the transmit power of MD i on subcarrier k at time slot t which cannot exceed its maximum value of $p_{i,\max}$. Define $\rho_{i,k}(t) \in \{0,1\}$ as the subcarrier assignment indicator, where $\rho_{i,k}(t) = 1$ indicates that the subcarrier k is assigned to MD i at time slot t. Otherwise, $\rho_{i,k}(t) = 0$. Correspondingly, the uplink data rate $r_{i,k}(t)$ of MD i on subcarrier k at time slot t is expressed as follows:

$$r_{i,k}(t) = \rho_{i,k}(t) B \log_2 \left(1 + \frac{p_{i,k}(t) h_{i,k}(t)}{N_0 B}\right). \tag{4}$$

In this work, we consider one subcarrier can only be assigned to one MD to avoid transmission interference, while one MD can be assigned several subcarriers. The total uplink data rate for MD i at time slot t is denoted as follows:

$$R_i(t) = \sum_{k \in \mathcal{K}} \rho_{i,k}(t) B \log_2 \left(1 + \frac{p_{i,k}(t) h_{i,k}(t)}{N_0 B}\right). \tag{5}$$

Correspondingly, we can obtain the uplink transmission time $D_i^{up}(t)$, as follows:

$$D_i^{up}(t) = \frac{p_i^F(t) A_i(t) \theta_i \tau}{\sum\limits_{k \in \mathcal{K}} \rho_{i,k}(t) B \log_2 \left(1 + \frac{p_{i,k}(t) h_{i,k}(t)}{N_0 B}\right)}. \tag{6}$$

Then the energy consumption $E_i^{up}(t)$ of the uplink transmission can be given as follows:

$$E_i^{up}(t) = \sum_{k \in \mathcal{K}} \frac{\rho_{i,k}(t) p_{i,k}(t) p_i^F(t) A_i(t) \theta_i \tau}{\sum\limits_{k \in \mathcal{K}} \rho_{i,k}(t) B \log_2 \left(1 + \frac{p_{i,k}(t) h_{i,k}(t)}{N_0 B}\right)}. \tag{7}$$

2.3 Fog Execution Model

The EN connecting to the AP can process the offloaded requests and execute the computation task. We consider the connection between the EN and AP is fiber-based with large enough bandwidth and the transmission time from the AP to EN is ignored. We denote the service rate of the EN as u^F. The pending requests of the MDs are pooled together with a total rate $A_{total}(t)$ which also follows the Poisson process. Therefore, $A_{total}(t)$ is given as follows:

$$A_{total}(t) = \sum_{i \in \mathcal{N}} p_i^F(t) A_i(t). \tag{8}$$

We denote the workload of the EN as $l^F(t)$, which presents the occupied percentage of each server and $l^F(t) < 1$. As a $M/G/1$ queue is considered at the EN, the average response time $D^F(t)$ is given as follows [9]:

$$D^F(t) = \frac{2u^F\left(1 - l^F(t)\right) - \left(\sum_{i \in \mathcal{N}} A_i(t)\; p_i^F(t)\right)}{2u^F\left(1 - l^F(t)\right)\left[u^F\left(1 - l^F(t)\right) - \left(\sum_{i \in \mathcal{N}} A_i(t)\; p_i^F(t)\right)\right]}. \tag{9}$$

2.4 Energy Harvesting Model

To model the energy harvesting, a successive energy packet arrival model is considered. The arrival of energy packet follows a Poisson process with an average arrival rate $e_i(t)$, and $0 < e_i(t) \le e_i^{\max}(t)$ where $e_i^{\max}(t)$ is the maximum energy arrival rate in each time slot. The harvested energy is stored in the battery and will be available for further actions. We denote the battery energy level of MD i at the beginning of time slot t as $B_i(t)$. In this work, energy consumed for purposes other than local computation and transmission is ignored for simplicity. The energy consumption $E_{i,total}(t)$ of MD i consists of two parts:

$$E_{i,total}(t) = E_i^M(t) + E_i^{up}(t). \tag{10}$$

where $E_i^M(t)$ is the energy consumption for local processing and $E_i^{up}(t)$ is energy consumption for delivering the requests. Note that $E_{i,total}(t)$ should be smaller than the battery level, i.e., $E_{i,total}(t) \le B_i(t)$. Thus, the battery level of MD i evolves as follows,

$$B_i(t+1) = B_i(t) - E_{i,total}(t) + e_i(t). \tag{11}$$

3 Problem Formulation

The execution cost consists of the execution delay and the task dropping punishment cost. The execution delay $D_i(t)$ at time slot t is derived as follows:

$$D_i(t) = p_i^M(t) D_i^M(t) + p_i^F(t)\left(D_i^{up}(t) + D^F(t)\right). \tag{12}$$

Consequently, the execution cost for MD i can be formulated as follows:

$$EC_i(t) = D_i(t) + \alpha_i C_i^D(t), \tag{13}$$

where α_i is the weight of task dropping cost. The total weighted execution cost of the system at time slot t is denoted as $\Gamma_{total}(t)$, which is given as

$$\Gamma_{total}(t) = \sum_{i \in \mathcal{N}} \omega_i \left[p_i^M(t) D_i^M(t) + p_i^F(t) \left(D_i^{up}(t) + D^F(t) \right) + \alpha_i C_i^D(t) \right], \tag{14}$$

where ω_i is the weight factor, which reflects the relative importance of MD i. Then we derive the average execution cost $\Phi(t)$ of the edge computing system during T time slots, which is given in (15).

$$\Phi(t) = \lim_{T \to +\infty} \frac{1}{T} \sum_{t \in \mathcal{T}} WEC_{total}(t)$$

$$= \lim_{T \to +\infty} \frac{1}{T} \sum_{t \in \mathcal{T}} \sum_{i \in \mathcal{N}} \omega_i \left[p_i^M(t) D_i^M(t) + p_i^F(t) \left(D_i^{up}(t) + D^F(t) \right) + \alpha_i C_i^D(t) \right]. \tag{15}$$

We denote the system decision at time slot t as $\mathbf{V}(t) = [\mathbf{p}(t), \boldsymbol{\rho}(t), \mathbf{p}_{up}(t)]$, $\forall t \in \mathcal{T}$, where $\mathbf{p}(t) = [\mathbf{p}_1(t), \cdots, \mathbf{p}_i(t), \cdots \mathbf{p}_N(t)]$ are execution strategies for all the MDs at time slot t and $\mathbf{p}_i(t) = [p_i^M(t), p_i^F(t), p_i^D(t)]$ is the execution strategy for MD i at time slot t. $\boldsymbol{\rho}(t) = [\boldsymbol{\rho}_1(t), \cdots, \boldsymbol{\rho}_i(t), \cdots, \boldsymbol{\rho}_N(t)]$ is the subcarrier assignment matrix for all MDs at time slot t and $\boldsymbol{\rho}_i(t) = [\rho_{i,1}(t), \cdots, \rho_{i,k}(t), \cdots, \rho_{i,K}(t)]$ is the subcarrier assignment vector for MD i at time slot t. $\mathbf{p}_{up}(t) = [\mathbf{p}_1(t), \cdots, \mathbf{p}_N(t)]$ is the uplink transmit power matrix for all the MDs at time slot t and $\mathbf{p}_i(t) = [p_{i,1}(t), \cdots, p_{i,K}(t)]$ is the set of transmit power for MD i. Thus, the problem can be formulated as shown in **P1**, which is

$$\mathbf{P1} : \min_{\mathbf{V}(t)} \ \Phi(t), \tag{16}$$

s.t.

$$p_i^M(t) + p_i^F(t) + p_i^D(t) = 1, 0 \le p_i^M(t), p_i^F(t), p_i^D(t) \le 1; \tag{17a}$$

$$p_i^M(t) A_i(t) - u_i^M \left(1 - l_i^M(t) \right) < 0; \tag{17b}$$

$$\sum_{i \in \mathcal{N}} p_i^F(t) A_i(t) - u^F \left(1 - l^F(t) \right) < 0; \tag{17c}$$

$$0 < p_{i,k}(t) < p_{i,\max}; \tag{17d}$$

$$\sum_{i \in \mathcal{N}} \rho_{i,k}(t) \le 1, \quad \rho_{i,k} \in \{0, 1\}; \tag{17e}$$

$$E_{i,total}(t) \le B_i(t); \tag{17f}$$

$$i \in \mathcal{N}, t \in \mathcal{T}, k \in \mathcal{K}. \tag{17g}$$

As we can see, the MDs' decisions are coupled among different time slots due to the constraints (17f), which makes the problem difficult to be tackled. As presented in [5], by introducing a reasonable upper bound $E_i^{\max}(t)$ and a non-negative lower bound $E_i^{\min}(t)$ of the battery, the coupling effect is eliminated. Correspondingly, the system operation can be optimized by ignoring (17f). Thus, the problem can be modified as follows:

$$\mathbf{P1} : \min_{\mathbf{V}(t)} \; \varPhi(t)$$

$$(17a) - (17e), (17g) \tag{18}$$

$$E_{i,total}(t) \in \left[E_i^{\min}(t), E_i^{\max}(t)\right] \tag{19}$$

For simplify, we consider $E_i^{\min}(t) = 0$. For $\mathbf{P1}$, a stochastic optimization problem is formulated with decision variables of the execution strategy, the uplink transmit power and the subcarrier assignment. By addressing the deterministic per-time slot problem, we can obtain the total optimal decisions in a stochastic manner.

4   Proposed Solution

Lyapunov optimization is an efficient framework for designing online control algorithm without requiring any prior knowledge [5]. In order to present the proposed solution, we firstly define the Lyapunov function as follows:

$$L(\mathbf{B}(t)) = \frac{1}{2} \sum_{i \in \mathcal{N}} B_i^{\,2}(t), \tag{20}$$

where $\mathbf{B}(t) = [B_1(t), \cdots, B_i(t), \cdots B_N(t)]$. Thus, the conditional Lyapunov drift can be expressed as

$$\varDelta(\mathbf{B}(t)) = E\left[L(\mathbf{B}(t+1)) - L(\mathbf{B}(t)) | \mathbf{B}(t)\right]. \tag{21}$$

The Lyapunov drift-plus-penalty function can be given as follows:

$$\varDelta_V(\mathbf{B}(t)) = \varDelta(\mathbf{B}(t)) + V\mathcal{E}\left[\varGamma_{total}(t) | \mathbf{B}(t)\right], \tag{22}$$

where $V \in (0, +\infty)$ is a control parameter. Then we will find an upper bound of $\varDelta(\mathbf{B}(t))$ under any feasible set of $\mathbf{V}(t)$, which can be found in the following lemma.

Lemma 1. For any feasible set of $\mathbf{V}(t)$, which satisfies (18) and (19), the Lyapunov drift-plus-penalty function $\varDelta_V(\mathbf{B}(t))$ is upper bounded, i.e.,

$$\varDelta_V(\mathbf{B}(t)) \leq \kappa + \sum_{i \in \mathcal{N}} \left\{B_i(t)\left[e_i(t) - E_{i,total}(t)\right]\right\}$$
$$+ VE\left[\varGamma_{total}(t) | \mathbf{B}(t)\right], \tag{23}$$

Algorithm 1. Proposed online algorithm

Step 1: at the beginning of the time slot t, obtain $B(t)$.

Step 2: through solving the problem **P2**, determine the system decision set $V(t) = [p(t), \rho(t), p_{up}(t)]$, to minimize the **P2**.

$$\min_{V(t)} \quad \sum_{i \in \mathcal{N}} \{B_i(t)[e_i(t) - E_{i,total}(t)]\} + V \mathcal{E}[\Gamma_{total}(t) | B(t)|]$$

s.t. (18), (19)

Step 3: set $t = t+1$, update $B(t)$, repeat Step 1 and Step 2, until obtain the system decisions of all the time slots.

---

where κ is a constant, which is denoted as

$$\kappa = \sum_{i \in N} \left[\frac{(e_i^{\max}(t))^2 + (E_i^{\max}(t))^2}{2} \right]. \tag{24}$$

Due to the space limitation, we omit the proof here. The key idea of the proposed algorithm is to minimize the upper bound of $\Delta_V(B(t))$ in the right-hand side of (23). The proposed algorithm is displayed in Algorithm 1.

Due to the high complexity of the considered problem, in the next section, we will divide it into several sub-problems to obtain the optimal system decision.

4.1 Optimal Execution Strategy

Firstly, we seek the optimal execution strategy at each time slot t, while taking the other pending variables as constants, then the problem is translated into the following sub-problem **SP1**, which is denoted as follows:

$$\min_{p(t)} \quad \sum_{i \in \mathcal{N}} -B_i(t) E_{i,total}(t) + V \sum_{i \in \mathcal{N}} \omega_i \left[D_i(t) + \alpha_i C_i^D(t) \right] \tag{25}$$

s.t.

$$(17a) - (17g), (17g), (19)$$

It can be found that (17c) is a coupled constraint, which includes various decision variables of different MDs. Similarly to the ones in [6], we can formulate the proposed problem as a Generalized Nash Equilibrium Problem (GNEP). The exponential penalty function method is applied to transform the original GNEP into a classical NEP and address it by semi-smooth Newton method with Armijo line search.

4.2 Optimal Power Allocation and Subcarrier Assignment

Similarly, the optimal transmit power $p_{up}(t)$ and subcarrier assignment matrix $\rho(t)$ can be obtained by solving the following sub-problem **SP2** through removing some irrelevant parameters from **P2**, which is denoted as follows:

$$\min_{\{\rho(t), p(t)\}} \quad \sum_{i \in \mathcal{N}} -B_i(t) E_i^{up}(t) + V \sum_{i \in \mathcal{N}} \omega_i p_i^F(t) D_i^{up}(t), \tag{26}$$

s.t.

$$0 < p_{i,k}(t) < p_{i,\max},\tag{27a}$$

$$\sum_{i\in\mathcal{N}} \rho_{i,k}(t) \leq 1,\quad \rho_{i,k}\in\{0,1\},\tag{27b}$$

$$E_i^{up}(t) < E_i^{\max}(t),\tag{27c}$$

$$i\in\mathcal{N},k\in\mathcal{K}.\tag{27d}$$

By substituting the specific expressions of $E_i^{up}(t)$ and $D_i^{up}(t)$ into the above problem, we can get an equal form of **SP2**, as shown in **SP2'**. The constraints are the same as those in (27). We can find that the **SP2'** is a mixed-integer programming problem, which involves the joint optimization of both continuous variables $p_{i,k}(t)$ and integer variables $\rho_{i,k}(t)$. Next, we will propose an algorithm to solve the problem. Firstly, we introduce an average offloading priority function [7], and it is defined as follows:

$$\textbf{SP2'}:\quad \min_{\{\rho(t),p(t)\}}\ \sum_{i\in\mathcal{N}} -B_i(t) \sum_{k\in\mathcal{K}} \frac{\rho_{i,k}(t)\,p_{i,k}(t)\,p_i^F(t)\,A_i(t)\,\theta_i\tau}{\sum_{k\in\mathcal{K}}\rho_{i,k}(t)\,B\log_2\left(1+\frac{p_{i,k}(t)h_{i,k}(t)}{N_0 B}\right)}$$

$$+ V\sum_{i\in\mathcal{N}} \omega_i p_i^F(t)\left(\frac{p_i^F(t)\,A_i(t)\,\theta_i\tau}{\sum_{k\in\mathcal{K}}\rho_{i,k}(t)\,B\log_2\left(1+\frac{p_{i,k}(t)h_{i,k}(t)}{N_0 B}\right)}\right)\tag{28}$$

$$\psi_{i,k,t}(\omega_i,\tau,h_{i,k}(t))$$
$$= \begin{cases} \frac{\omega_i N_0 B}{h_{i,k}(t)}\left[v_i(t)\ln v_i(t) - v_i(t) + 1\right], & v_i(t)\geq 1, \\ 0, & v_i(t) < 1, \end{cases}\tag{29}$$

where the constant $v_i(t)$ is defined as $v_i(t) = \frac{Bh_{i,k}(t)\tau c_0}{N_0\ln 2}$ and c_0 is a pre-defined constant. Specifically, with the defined average offloading priority function $\psi_{i,k,t}(\omega_i,\tau,h_{i,k}(t))$ (for simplify, we assume that any two values of $\psi_{i,k,t}(\omega_i,\tau,h_{i,k}(t))$ are not the same), we denote the offloading priority order as $\Psi(t)$ at time slot t, which is composed by $\{\psi_{i,k,t}\}, i\in\mathcal{N}, k\in\mathcal{K}$, and displayed in the descending manner. We denote the sets of assigned and unassigned subcarriers as $\mathcal{K}_1(t)$ and $\mathcal{K}_2(t)$ at the beginning of time slot t. The average channel gain $\tilde{h}_i(t)$ is defined as $\tilde{h}_i(t) = \frac{\sum_{k\in\mathcal{K}_2(t)} h_{i,k}(t)}{|\mathcal{K}_2(t)|}$, where $|\mathcal{K}_2(t)|$ is the number of unassigned subcarriers during the time slot t. For each MD, such as MD i, the assigned subcarrier set is denoted as $\mathcal{Z}_i(t)$ during the time slot t, initialized as $\mathcal{Z}_i(t) = \varnothing$. Additionally, the subcarrier assignment indicators are set as $\{\rho_{i,k}(t) = 0\}$ at the beginning of time slot t. By these definitions, we proposed a subcarrier allocation algorithm, which is displayed in Algorithm 2.

Algorithm 2. Subcarrier allocation algorithm

1: **Input:**
   At beginning of time slot t, obtain $\Psi(t)$, $h_{i,k}(t)$,$\mathcal{K}_1(t)$, $\mathcal{K}_2(t)$, and $\tilde{h}_i(t)$;
2: **Obtain the total integer number of subcarriers:**
   Solving the optimal solution $\{n_i^*(t), \tilde{p}_i^*(t)\}$ of the **SP2''**;
3: **Subcarrier allocation:**
4: **while** $\tilde{\mathcal{N}} \neq \varnothing$, **do**
5:     (1) Let $\rho_{k',n'} = 1$, where $\{i',k'\} = \underset{i' \in N, k' \in K}{\arg\max}\ \psi_{i,k,t}$;
       (2) Update sets:
       $\mathcal{Z}_{i'}(t) = \mathcal{Z}_{i'}(t) \cup \{k'\}$,$\mathcal{K}_1(t) = \mathcal{K}_1(t) \cup \{k'\}$, $\mathcal{K}_2(t) = \mathcal{K}_2(t) \setminus \{k'\}$;
       (3) if $|\mathcal{Z}_{i'}(t)| = \tilde{n}_{i'}^*(t)$, then $\tilde{\mathcal{N}} = \tilde{\mathcal{N}} \setminus \{i'\}$;
6: **end while**
7: **Transmit power allocation**
   Solving the optimal solution of **SP2'''**.
8: **return** $\{\rho_{i,k}^*(t), p_{i,k}^*(t)\}$

In the proposed algorithm, we need to find the optimal power allocation, which involves addressing the following **SP2''**, which is

$$\textbf{SP2''}: \min_{\{n_i(t), \tilde{p}_i(t)\}} \sum_{i \in \mathcal{N}} \left\{ \frac{-B_i(t)\,\tilde{p}_i(t)\,p_i^F(t)\,A_i(t)\,\theta_i\tau}{B\log_2\left(1 + \frac{\tilde{p}_i(t)\tilde{h}_i(t)}{N_0 B}\right)} \right.$$
$$\left. + \frac{V\omega_i\left[p_i^F(t)\right]^2 A_i(t)\,\theta_i\tau}{n_i(t)\,B\log_2\left(1 + \frac{\tilde{p}_i(t)\tilde{h}_i(t)}{N_0 B}\right)} \right\}, \tag{30}$$

s.t.

$$\sum_{i \in \mathcal{N}} n_i(t) \leq |\mathcal{K}_2(t)|, \tag{31a}$$

$$\tilde{p}_i(t) \leq p_{i,\max}, \tag{31b}$$

$$\frac{\tilde{p}_i(t)\,p_i^F(t)\,A_i(t)\,\theta_i\tau}{B\log_2\left(1 + \frac{\tilde{p}_i(t)\tilde{h}_i(t)}{N_0 B}\right)} \leq E_i^{\max}(t), \tag{31c}$$

where $n_i(t)$ is the total integer number of subcarriers that allocated to MD i at time slot t. We can also find that **SP2''** is a mixed integer programming including a coupled constraint (31a). Thus, we can address it with semi-smooth Newton method, which is similar with [6]. Then with the branch-and-bound procedure, we can obtain the integer solution $n_i^*(t)$.

We denote the set of MDs that still require subcarriers as $\tilde{\mathcal{N}}$, where $\tilde{\mathcal{N}} = \{i \,|\, n_i^*(t) > 0\}$. We allocate subcarriers for each MD with the highest offloading priority principle. After searching for the highest offloading priority $\psi_{i',k',t}$ over unassigned subcarriers $\mathcal{K}_2(t)$ for the remaining offloading-required users $\tilde{\mathcal{N}}$ and then allocates subcarrier k' to user i'. Such a sequential subcarrier assignment follows the descending offloading priority order. Then the remaining sets can be updated until all subcarriers are assigned. At last, the optimal transmit power for

MD i at time slot t over the assigned subcarriers $\mathcal{Z}_i(t)$ is obtained by minimizing the problem **SP2"'**

$$\textbf{SP2"'} : \min_{p_{i,k'}(t),k'\in\mathcal{Z}_i(t)} \sum_{k'\in\mathcal{Z}_i(t)} \frac{-B_i(t)\,p_{i,k'}(t)\,p_i^F(t)\,A_i(t)\,\theta_i\tau}{\sum\limits_{k'\in\mathcal{Z}_i(t)} B\log_2\left(1+\frac{p_{i,k'}(t)h_{i,k'}(t)}{N_0B}\right)}$$

$$+\frac{V\omega_i\left(p_i^F(t)\right)^2 A_i(t)\,\theta_i\tau}{\sum\limits_{k'\in\mathcal{Z}_i(t)} B\log_2\left(1+\frac{p_{i,k'}(t)h_{i,k'}(t)}{N_0B}\right)}, \tag{32}$$

s.t.

$$0 < p_{i,k'}(t) \leq p_{i,\max}, k' \in \mathcal{Z}_i(t), \tag{33a}$$

$$\sum_{k'\in\mathcal{Z}_i(t)} \frac{p_{i,k'}(t)\,p_i^F(t)\,A_i(t)\,\theta_i\tau}{\sum\limits_{k'\in\mathcal{Z}_i(t)} B\log_2\left(1+\frac{p_{i,k'}(t)h_{i,k'}(t)}{N_0B}\right)} \leq E_i^{\max}(t), \tag{33b}$$

We can see that the formulated problem **SP2"'** is similar with the problem investigated in [2]. Then, we can solve it with Interior Point Method (IPM), the details of which can be found in [2].

5   Performance Evaluations

In this section, extensive simulations are conducted to illustrate the effectiveness of the proposed algorithm. The simulation parameters are similar to the one used in [2] and [6]. First, we illustrate the relationship of the average execution cost of the system versus the number of subcarriers with 6 MDs in Fig. 1. It can be observed that with the optimal subcarrier allocation strategy, the average execution cost of the system is the smallest among all three schemes. Moreover, as shown in this figure, with the increasing of the number of subcarriers, the average execution cost becomes smaller, as the MDs have sufficient choices to offload the requests to the EN to reduce the execution delay. In this way, the dropped requests would also be reduced.

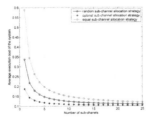

Fig. 1. The effect of subcarrier allocation

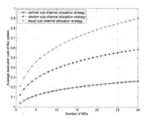

Fig. 2. The effect of the number of MDs

Then we show the total execution cost of the system versus the number of MDs in the system when the number of subcarriers is fixed in Fig. 2. It can be observed that the average execution costs are increasing when the number of MDs increases, which means that the execution delay or the punishment cost become larger under the condition of fixed number of subcarriers. As more and more users compete for the radio and computational resources with each other, longer transmission time and fog execution delay can be induced. Thus, the MDs have to execute more requests locally or drop them, which leads to a larger execution cost.

6   Conclusion

In this paper, we propose a dynamic optimization scheme for an edge computing system with multiple users, where the radio and computational resources, and offloading decisions, can be dynamically allocated with the variation of computation demands, radio channels and the computation resources. Specifically, with the objective to minimize the energy consumption of the considered system, we propose a joint computation offloading, radio and computational resource allocation algorithm based on Lyapunov optimization. Through minimizing the derived upper bound of the Lyapunov drift-plus-penalty function, the main problem is divided into several sub-problems at each time slot and are addressed separately. The simulation results demonstrate the effectiveness of the proposed scheme.

References

1. Guerrero-Contreras, G., Garrido, J.L., Balderas-Diaz, S., Rodriguez-Dominguez, C.: A context-aware architecture supporting service availability in mobile cloud computing. IEEE Trans. Serv. Comput. **10**(6), 956–968 (2017)
2. Liu, L., Chang, Z., Guo, X., Mao, S., Ristaniemi, T.: Multi-objective optimization for computation offloading in fog computing. IEEE Internet Things J. **5**(1), 283–294 (2018)
3. Deng, R., Lu, R., Lai, C., Luan, T.H., Liang, H.: Optimal workload allocation in fog-cloud computing towards balanced delay and power consumption. IEEE Internet Things J. **3**(6), 1171–1181 (2016)

4. Dinh, T.Q., Tang, J., La, Q.D., Quek, T.Q.S.: Offloading in mobile edge computing: task allocation and computational frequency scaling. IEEE Trans. Commun. **65**(8), 3571–3584 (2017)
5. Mao, Y., Zhang, J., Letaief, K.B.: Dynamic computation offloading for mobile-edge computing with energy harvesting devices. IEEE J. Sel. Areas Commun. **34**(12), 3590–3605 (2016)
6. Liu, L., Chang, Z., Guo, X.: Socially-aware dynamic computation offloading scheme for fog computing system with energy harvesting devices. IEEE Internet Things J. **5**(1), 283–294 (2018)
7. You, C., Huang, K., Chae, H., Kim, B.H.: Energy-efficient resource allocation for mobile-edge computation offloading. IEEE Trans. Wirel. Commun. **16**(3), 1397–1411 (2017)
8. Lazar, A.: The throughput time delay function of an M/M/1 queue (Corresp.). IEEE Trans. Inf. Theory **29**(6), 914–918 (1983)
9. Machol, R.E.: Queue theory. IRE Trans. Educ. **E-5**(2), 99–105 (2007)

Intelligent Orchestration of End-to-End Network Slices for the Allocation of Mission Critical Services over NFV Architectures

Bego Blanco[1]([✉])[iD], Rubén Solozabal[1][iD], Aitor Sanchoyerto[1][iD],
Javier López-Cuadrado[1][iD], Elisa Jimeno[2][iD], and Miguel Catalan-Cid[3][iD]

[1] University of the Basque Country, Bilbao, Spain
{begona.blanco,ruben.solozabal,aitor.sanchoyerto,javilo}@ehu.eus
[2] Atos, Madrid, Spain
elisa.jimeno@atos.net
[3] i2CAT Foundation, Barcelona, Spain
miguel.catalan@i2cat.net

Abstract. The challenge of deploying mission critical services upon virtualised shared network models is the allocation of both radio and cloud resources to the critical actors who require prioritized and high-quality services. This paper describes the design and deployment of an intelligent orchestration cycle to manage end-to-end slices on a NFV architecture. This novel tool includes the monitoring of the network elements at different levels and the processing of the gathered data to produce the corresponding alert mitigation actions.

Keywords: Network slicing · Orchestration · NFV · Mission-critical

1 Introduction and Related Work

5G networks are expected to bring a new disrupting ecosystem, prompting the creation of innovative next generation vertical applications. To that end, one of the most awaited features is the provisioning and management of network slices tailored to the needs of each particular vertical industry and specific deployment. In particular, Network Function Virtualization (NFV) is embraced as one of the key technologies that will allow the creation of customized network slices to meet different service requirements.

The public safety sector will be one of the major beneficiaries of this technological development. Traditional mission critical applications expose tight QoS requirements, which find difficulties to be fulfilled by traditional network models. In consequence, traditional public safety networks have demanded private and dedicated network models, which eventually lead to an inefficient use of resources

© IFIP International Federation for Information Processing 2020
Published by Springer Nature Switzerland AG 2020
I. Maglogiannis et al. (Eds.): AIAI 2020 Workshops, IFIP AICT 585, pp. 74–83, 2020.
https://doi.org/10.1007/978-3-030-49190-1_7

and spectrum. But now, network slicing through proper resource orchestration is making the network sharing model a reality.

The concept of network slicing was introduced by the Next Generation Mobile Network (NGMN) alliance within its whitepaper [8]. Later, the 3GPP took the responsability of standardising this technology, defining the entities and the functionality required to manage network slicing [2]. Presently, network slicing is integrated in the ETSI-NFV architecture [4]. Current NFV standards [5] define the interaction between the network slice management functions defined by the 3GPP and the NFV Management and Orchestration (MANO) module, establishing the required connection between the network controllers and the NFV orchestration unit in order to perform the dynamic assignment of network resources.

However, the implementation of the concept of orchestrating a service slice within this standardized network architecture is still in a development phase. In this sense, there are some independent initiatives as [3,6,7,9] that are contributing to the creation of modules that complement the current MANO capabilities in order to orchestrate E2E slices.

In this paper, we present an NFV-based intelligent orchestration cycle with the capability of providing a set of shared resources to deal with the dynamic reconfiguration challenge. This orchestration cycle has been developed in the scope of H2020 5G ESSENCE project [1]. The slice concept introduced in 5G, along with the highly virtualised and software-based deployments, enables the automatic on-the-fly adjustment of the resource assignment to the changeable environment. This feature is of utmost importance in mission critical applications where sudden events can instantly alter the network requirements and priorities. For this reason, this work provides a comprehensive approach to demonstrating dynamic End-to-End (E2E) slices reconfiguration and service adaptation in a mission critical deployment.

The paper is organised as follows: Sect. 2 describes the orchestration cycle defined to dynamically adjust the end-to-end network slices in a NFV-based deployment. Next, Sect. 3 describes the validation scenario to later discuss the obtained results. Finally, Sect. 4 summarizes the main contributions and poses new research challenges that will be addressed in the future.

2   NFV-Based Intelligent Orchestration Cycle

NFV comes up driven by the telecommunications industry in order to enhance the deployment flexibility, foster the integration of new services within operators and also attain CAPEX/OPEX drawdowns.

However, the dynamic allocation of resources to separated and customised network slices still remains a challenge. This section describes a novel orchestration cycle providing new tools for automated E2E network slicing. The proposed orchestration cycle involves the monitoring system, the alert mitigation module and the execution of the mitigation actions.

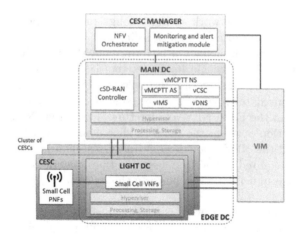

Fig. 1. 5G ESSENCE network architecture.

2.1   Network Architecture

The 5G ESSENCE approach, depicted in Fig. 1, takes the existing 5G architectures as a reference point, combining the 3GPP framework for network management in Radio Access Network (RAN) sharing scenarios and the ETSI NFV framework for managing virtualised network functions. Our architecture allows multiple network operators (tenants) to provide services to their users through a set of Cloud-enabled Small Cells (CESCs) deployed, owned and managed by a third party (i.e., the CESC provider). The CESC offers virtualised environment with computing, storage and radio resources at the edge of the mobile network. This cloud can also be 'sliced' to enable multi-tenancy.

Besides, the two-tier architecture of 5G ESSENCE is well aligned with the 5G architecture described by 5G-PPP, where the infrastructure programmability is identified as one key design paradigm for 5G. First, 5G ESSENCE achieves infrastructure programmability by leveraging the virtualised computation resources available in an Edge Datacenter (Edge DC). These resources are used for hosting VNFs tailored according to the needs of each tenant, on a per-slice basis. Second, the Main Datacenter (Main DC) allows centralising and softwarising the control plane of small cell functions to enable a more efficient utilisation of the radio resources coordinated among multiple CESCs.

We propose to enhance the orchestration functionalities adding more intelligence into the CESC Manager (CESCM) together with the NFV Orchestrator (NFVO). In particular, 5G ESSENCE provides a network monitoring and alert mitigation mechanism that supports and improves both the NFVO and RAN controlling functions. The event flow for the management of end-to-end slicing for a Mission-critical Push-to-talk (MCPTT) service is depicted in Fig. 2, and each component is further described in the following sections.

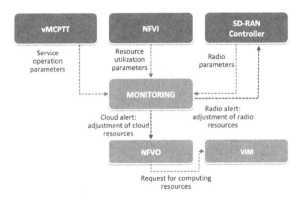

Fig. 2. End-to-end slicing event flow.

2.2   System and Service Monitoring and Alert Mitigation

The main objective of the Monitoring and Alert Mitigation system shown in Fig. 3 is to access the available information about the network elements and process it in order to conclude if and when a network reconfiguration is needed.

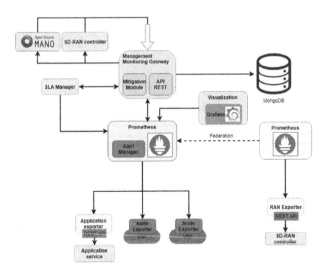

Fig. 3. Monitoring and alert mitigation architecture.

The orchestration cycle begins with the collection of the monitored data through the **exporters** in each monitoring-enabled building block. The monitored data is stored in Prometheus, which is on charge of triggering the alerts as defined according to the different services and their Service Level Agreement

(SLA). These alerts are defined to notify about an unexpected behaviour in the system and SLA violations.

It must be also noted that the monitoring of the Wi-Fi RAN controller relies on the **federation** of the Prometheus server installed in the component. Federation allows Prometheus to have a heritage of some targets monitored from another Prometheus. The main idea for using Federation is to have a decentralised system in order to monitor the Wi-Fi RAN metrics through another Prometheus for other tasks.

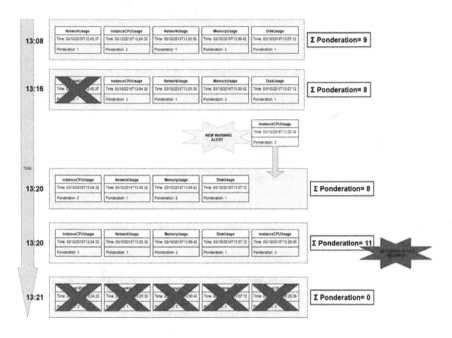

Fig. 4. Flow for mitigation warning alerts.

The alerts raised are picked by the **Alert Mitigation Module (AMM)**, which is part of the **Management Monitoring Gateway**. The purpose of AMM is to manage the configuration of the architectural components responsible of the behavior of the E2E slice. To that aim, AMM contains the mitigation logic based on a ponderation of the rules defined in the **Rulebook**. When an alert is triggered, AMM differences between different severity levels. If the severity is critical, the mitigation module must mitigate the alert with higher priority without considering further alerts following the configuration defined in the Rulebook. For warning severities, the Mitigation module saves the alert in a time window, which is configured by the Rulebook (Fig. 4). The window (or queue), groups the alerts by the specific mitigation required by it. Every warning alert has a ponderation in the Rulebook. The warning alert is added in the queue with its correspondent ponderation. If the sum of the ponderations in the mitigation queue exceeds the mitigation ponderation, configured in the Rulebook, a mitigation action composed with all the warning severity alerts is triggered, emptying the mitigation queue and silencing the alert.

Finally, within the scope of this paper, we have defined two endpoints to forward the mitigation actions and close the monitoring and mitigation loop: the NFVO orchestrator to manage the scaling options of the Network Service, and Wi-Fi RAN controller to manage the resources used by the Wi-Fi slice. These two blocks are further described in the next sections.

2.3 MCPTT Service Architecture

Mission Critical Push-To-Talk (MCPTT) is a mission critical communication standard that allows half duplex one-to-many and one-to-one voice services in order to coordinate emergency teams. Users request permission to transmit pressing a button. Additionally, the MCPTT service provides a means for a user with higher priority (e.g., MCPTT Emergency condition) to override (interrupt) the current speaker. As it appears, the management of this type of half-duplex communication is not trivial, since it requires an appropriate management of priorities and privileges to allow communication.

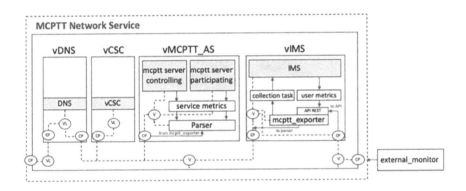

Fig. 5. MCPTT service architecture.

The MCPTT Network Service is composed of one VNF that completes the mission critical push to talk service. This service is defined in multiple Virtual Deployment Units (VDU) to optimise the usage of the resources: a DNS server, an IMS (IP Multimedia Subsystem) service for session management, a CSC (Common Service Core) for service status information, and the MCPTT AS (Application Server) providing centralised support for MCPTT services and call control. Figure 5 depicts the deployment of the described MCPTT network architecture.

In order to integrate the described MCPTT network service within the orchestration cycle detailed above, we must include a tailored exporter to extract

the required metrics for the monitoring tasks. It appears as *mcptt_exporter* in
Fig. 5. This component is responsible for collecting the metrics from the MCPTT
service to later expose them for the analysis in the monitoring system. It is implemented as a REST API: when the mcptt_exporter receives a status request from
the Prometheus in the Monitoring module, it queries the involved components
of the NS (mainly IMS and *MCPTT_AS*) to gather the metrics and format them
properly.

2.4 RAN Controller Architecture

Figure 6 depicts the components of the RACOON Wi-Fi RAN slicing solution.

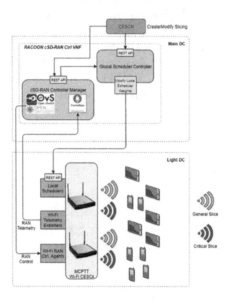

Fig. 6. RACOON SD-RAN controller architecture.

The **Controller Manager** is the core of RACOON. It is in charge of Open-
DayLight SDN controller, Open vSwitch database server and the Netconf Manager by means of the different implemented clients (REST APIs) and controls the
CESCs according to the deployed slices and services. It also gathers telemetry
from the Wi-Fi RAN by means of its Prometheus server. Moreover, through its
REST API, the RAN Controller exposes the management of the infrastructure
and the slices to the CESCM.

The **Global Scheduler Controller** manages the weights/quotas of the
instantiated slices in the Wi-Fi RAN. It allows enabling, modifying and dis-
abling the local schedulers of the different Wi-Fi CESCs, which locally manage
the percentage of airtime or channel time assigned to each slice. It implements
a REST API to allow its control via the CESCM.

Finally, the **Wi-Fi CESC** is composed by Single Board Computers (SBCs) with a Linux distribution. The main software used in order to deploy Wi-Fi connectivity is Hostapd, which has been modified in order to deploy, monitor and control multiple virtual Access Points (vAPs) on top of a single physical interface, according to the desired Wi-Fi slices. By means of these modifications, the Local Scheduler is able to manage the MAC-scheduler which controls the airtime or channel time assigned to each slice (which is then fairly distributed among all the user terminals of each slice). Also, it hosts a Prometheus Exporter (Hostapd Exporter[1]) in order to gather RAN telemetry.

3   Orchestration Cycle for MCPTT Deployments

This section shows the results of the integration of the described enhanced orchestration tools developed within the 5G ESSENCE project to deploy a MCPTT service slice. To that aim, we first declare the metrics collected from the network elements and the mitigation actions defined when an emergency event is detected. Then, we describe the validation scenario and show the results of the complete deployment.

3.1   Monitoring Metrics and Mitigation Action Definition

The monitoring system collects network status information from network elements at different levels: NFVI through *node_exporter*, MCPTT service through a tailored exporter and RACOON cSD-RAN controller through Prometheus federation. The information collected from the NFVI that is involved in this experiment includes CPU, memory and disk usages, VM port throughput and availability of VMs (if they are up). The information collected from the MCPTT service includes the number of registered and active users, the number of private calls, group calls, private emergency calls, group emergency calls that have been started/ongoing/terminated and the number of users involved in each of the calls. Finally, the system collects information from RACOON about the number of users per slice per cell, transmitted bit rate and quality of the signal. For each identified metric, the measurement framework and the alarms it can trigger is included. Two alarm thresholds are defined. The first alarm threshold provides a warning, whereas the second threshold is considered a critical situation.

3.2   Scenario Definition and Deployment Results

The demonstration of the dynamically orchestrated MCPTT deployment cannot be based on a static scenario, since one of its objectives to be proven is the elastic allocation of resources attending to different levels of emergency conditions detected by the monitoring system. We propose a deployment topology in three main stages.

---

[1] http://bitbucket.i2cat.net/users/miguel_catalan/repos/hostapd_prometheus_exporter/browse.

Fig. 7. Orchestration cycle screenshots.

Under normal circumstances, the system instantiates the network slices that correspond to a default service agreement. Here, the first responder only needs a reduced amount of access capacity and communication features for its normal operations. Then, triggered by an emergency incident that is detected through a private emergency call, the first responder requires increased capacity in terms of edge computing resources, in order to serve a higher number of incoming communications and/or public safety users. This implies the scaling of the MCPTT VNF and it may involve a deterioration of the service for legacy users, since their network slice(s) must be reduced in order to appropriately allocate the higher priority MCPTT service. Finally, in the third stage triggered by a group emergency call, the system responds with an expansion of the MCPTT radio slice up to the 75% of the available bandwidth in the cell where the emergency events are happening (detected by the increasing number of users in the cell). Again, this situation may involve an impairment of the service provided to civilians in favor of the communications for first responders, which require higher priority.

Figure 7 shows some screenshots that illustrate the operation of the orchestration process. The upper screen shows the monitoring of MCPTT calls during the experiment. It can be observed how the different events are detected over time. The screenshot in the middle shows the result of an alert mitigation action in the second stage that leads to the MCPTT VNF scale. Finally, the lower screenshot shows the reconfiguration of the radio slice as a result of the mitigation action in the third stage.

4   Conclusions and Future Work

This paper has described the intelligent orchestration cycle that proves that the 5G ESSENCE context provides a solution for an efficient and elastic E2E network slicing and the efficient orchestration of the radio and cloud resources. The results highlight the value of the shared network model, demonstrating the capacity of the 5G ESSENCE architecture to autonomously allocate resources to first responders whenever they are required, but giving them up to the commercial services when the requirements are low. The elastic allocation of resources is performed automatically, leveraging the monitoring and alert mitigation functionalities that complement the orchestration processes in the CESCM.

Our research work will continue to further develop orchestration tools to enhance the E2E slicing capabilities of NFV environments. New research trends include the use of machine learning techniques in the decision-making process, the migration and placement of VNFs and the analysis of the possibilities of multi-RAT access.

Acknowledgement. This work has been partly funded by the EU funded H2020 5G-PPP project 5G ESSENCE (Grant Agreement No 761592).

References

1. H2020 5G ESSENCE project. https://www.5g-essence-h2020.eu
2. 3GPP: Study on management and orchestration of network slicing for next generation network. TR 28.801, 3GPP, January 2018
3. Chien, H.T., Lin, Y.D., Lai, C.L., Wang, C.T.: End-to-end slicing as a service with computing and communication resource allocation for multi-tenant 5G systems. IEEE Wirel. Commun. **26**(5), 104–112 (2019)
4. ETSI: Network Function Virtualization (NFV). Architectural Framework. GR GS NFV 002, ETSI, October 2013
5. ETSI: Report on Network Slicing Support with ETSI NFV Architecture Framework. GR NFV-EVE 012, ETSI, December 2017
6. Khalili, H., et al.: Network slicing-aware NFV orchestration for 5G service platforms. In: 2019 European Conference on Networks and Communications (EuCNC), pp. 25–30. IEEE (2019)
7. Montero, R., Agraz, F., Pagès, A., Spadaro, S.: End-to-end network slicing in support of latency-sensitive 5G services. In: Tzanakaki, A., et al. (eds.) ONDM 2019. LNCS, vol. 11616, pp. 51–61. Springer, Cham (2020). https://doi.org/10.1007/978-3-030-38085-4_5
8. NGMN: Description of network slicing concept (2016)
9. Ni, R., et al.: An end-to-end demonstration for 5G network slicing. In: 2019 IEEE 89th Vehicular Technology Conference (VTC2019-Spring), pp. 1–5. IEEE (2019)

On the Prediction of Future User Connections Based on Historical Records in Wireless Networks

Seyedeh Soheila Shaabanzadeh and Juan Sánchez-González[✉]

Universitat Politècnica de Catalunya (UPC),
c/Jordi Girona, 1-3, 08034 Barcelona, Spain
juansanchez@tsc.upc.edu

Abstract. Recent developments of data monitoring and analytics technologies in the context of wireless networks will boost the capacity to extract knowledge about the network and the users. On the one hand, the obtained knowledge can be useful for running more efficient network management tasks related to network reconfiguration and optimization. On the other hand, the extraction of knowledge related to user needs, user mobility patterns and user habits and interests can also be useful to provide a more personalized service to the clients. Focusing on user mobility, this paper presents a methodology that predicts the future Access Point (AP) that the user will be connected to in a Wi-Fi Network. The prediction is based on the historical data related to the previous APs which the user connected to. Different approaches are proposed, according to the data that is used for prediction, in order to capture weekly, daily and hourly user activity-based behaviours. Two prediction algorithms are compared, based on Neural Networks (NN) and Random Forest (RF). The methodology has been evaluated in a large Wi-Fi network deployed in a University Campus.

Keywords: Wi-Fi network · Supervised learning · Length of stay prediction · Neural Network (NN) · Random Forest (RF)

1 Introduction

The demand of new multimedia services (i.e. online multimedia applications, high quality video, augmented/virtual reality, etc.) has dramatically increased in the last years. A solution to cope with the high bandwidth and strict Quality of Service (QoS) requirements associated to these new services consists on network densification through the deployment of Small Cells (SC) operating cellular technologies (e.g. 4G/5G), complemented with Wi-Fi hotspots using the unlicensed spectrum. In fact, Wi-Fi technology is a competitive option for serving multimedia demands due to its popularity among mobile users. In the last years, a dramatic increase in the amount of IEEE 802.11 (i.e. Wi-Fi) traffic has been observed. It is estimated that by 2021, 63% of the global cellular data traffic will be offloaded to Wi-Fi or small cell networks [1]. Globally, there will be nearly 549 million public Wi-Fi hotspots by 2022, up from 124 million in 2017, a fourfold increase.

I. Maglogiannis et al. (Eds.): AIAI 2020 Workshops, IFIP AICT 585, pp. 84–94, 2020.
https://doi.org/10.1007/978-3-030-49190-1_8

In the last years, we have witnessed a widespread use of powerful (Big) Data monitoring and analytics technologies in many areas of our lives. In particular, in the context of cellular and Wi-Fi networks, the use of these technologies will be one of the main pillars to cope with the above-mentioned challenges. The monitoring system provides the ability to collect information about the users and the network, while the analytics system allows to extract knowledge of the collected data by means of Artificial Intelligence (AI) mechanisms [2]. There are different ways to extract knowledge (e.g. by using classification, clustering and prediction mechanisms) [3].

Multiple applicability examples of data monitoring and analytics in the context of Wi-Fi or cellular networks can be found in the literature. As an example related to mobile cellular networks and concerning the characterization of user habits, the collection of the Base Station and the mobile terminal communication activity (messages, calls, etc.) has been used for urban and transportation planning purposes to identify daily motifs, given that human daily mobility can be highly structural and organized by a few activities essential to life [4]. Similarly, [5] proposed a methodology to partition a population of users tracked by their mobile phones into four predefined user profiles: residents, commuters, in transit and visitors. Applications envisaged are traffic management, to better understand how traffic is affected by the residents mobility compared to the commuters, or studying how the city is receiving people from outside and how their movements affect the city. [6] proposed an agglomerative clustering to identify user's daily motifs according to the cells in which the user is camping during the day. Real measurements obtained from a 3G/4G network were used.

The obtained knowledge related to the network status, the performance of the services, user habits, user requirements, etc. can also be useful for supporting different decision-making processes over the network (e.g. adjusting the usage of the network resources) which will lead to more efficient network management tasks related to network reconfiguration and optimization. As an example, the use of prediction methodologies for identifying the future SC/AP which the user will be connected to, together with an estimation of the future user traffic volume and perceived user performance may provide a more accurate future user characterization. This can be useful for carrying out a more proactive network reconfiguration approach. In the context of mobility management in 5G cellular networks, anticipating the cell to which users will be connected in the future is useful to facilitate handover procedures [7]. In the context of Wi-Fi networks, the prediction of APs to which a client will connect in the future can be useful for a more efficient Pairwise Master Key (PMK) caching or Opportunistic Key Caching (OKC) techniques which can reduce the time for re-authentication when roaming to a new AP [8]. Concerning the AP selection in Wi-Fi networks, [9] proposed a mobility prediction methodology based on a Hidden Markov Model that is used to forecast the next AP that users will connect to, based on current and historical user location information. On the other hand, from the point of view of traffic offloading from cellular to Wi-Fi systems, length of stay prediction at an AP can be useful for user bandwidth allocation e.g. giving higher priority to soon-to-depart Wi-Fi users so that the larger amount of traffic is sent through the Wi-Fi before performing the handover to the cellular system [10].

The extracted knowledge related to user location and mobility, user habits and interests, etc. can also be useful for companies for commercial purposes. As an example, a reliable prediction of future user location and length of stay connected to the different SC/AP enables the use of Location Based Advertising (LBA) mechanisms. This presents the possibility for advertisers to personalize their messages to people based on their location and interests [11].

Within this context, this paper proposes a methodology that predicts the future user connections to the different APs of a Wi-Fi network according to historical user records. The main contribution of the paper is the proposal of a prediction methodology that is able to extract user periodical patterns at different time-levels in order to capture weekly, daily and hourly user activity-based behaviours. Two prediction algorithms based on a supervised learning process are compared, one using a Neural Network (NN) and the other one based on Random Forest (RF). The proposed methodologies are evaluated for a large Wi-Fi network deployed in a University Campus. The remaining of the paper is organized as follows. Section 2 presents the proposed AP prediction methodology, while Sect. 3 describes the considered prediction tools. The results are presented in Sect. 4, while Sect. 5 summarizes the conclusions.

2   Proposed Methodology

The proposed prediction methodology is shown in Fig. 1 and assumes a Wi-Fi Network with monitoring capabilities for the collection of measurements reported by the users when connected to the different APs. The *Collection of Network Measurements* process collects a list of metrics for each u-th user ($u = 1, \dots , U$) when connected to each AP (e.g. the instants of time when the user begins and ends a connection to each AP, the average SNR -Signal to Noise Ratio-, the average RSSI -Received Signal Strength Indicator-, the amount of bytes transmitted/received during the connection of the user to each AP, etc.). All this information is stored in a database. Then, for each user, a pre-processing of the collected data is done so that the measurements collected during each d-th day (with $d = 1, \dots , D$) are grouped in M time periods with equal duration T. In particular, the *pre-processing* step generates a matrix A for each user, so that each term $a_{d,m}$ (with $m = 1, \dots , M$ and $d = 1, \dots D$) represents the AP identifier to which this user was connected during the m-th time period of the d-th day. In case that the user connects to more than one AP at the same m-th time period, it is assumed that the term $a_{d,m}$ will correspond to the AP with the highest connection duration.

For the prediction of the AP to which the user will be connected in a specific m^*-th time period of a specific d^*-th day in the future ($a_{d*,m*}$), the proposed methodology makes use of some historical information of the AP to which the user was connected in the past and a prediction function $f(\cdot)$ that is obtained by means of a supervised learning. For that purpose, the *Selection of historical data* process selects some specific terms in matrix A. Different approaches are presented below:

Prediction Based on Time-Period Patterns (PBTP): In this case, the prediction of $a_{d*,m*}$ is based on the APs to which the user was connected in the last N previous time periods (i.e. $a_{d*,m*-N}, \dots , a_{d*,m*-n}, \dots , a_{d*,m*-1}$). In order to obtain the prediction function $f(\cdot)$, a vector $\boldsymbol{B} = (b_1, \dots , b_f, \dots b_F)$ is built from all the $F = D \cdot M$ previous time periods in the last D days, i.e. $\boldsymbol{B} = (a_{1,1}, \dots , a_{1,m}, \dots ,$

$a_{1,M}, \ldots, a_{d,1}, \ldots, a_{d,m}, \ldots, a_{d,M}, \ldots, a_{D,1}, \ldots, a_{D,m}, \ldots, a_{D,M})$. Then, $\boldsymbol{B}$ is split into I different training tuples $\boldsymbol{B}^i$, each one composed of the i-th element and its N previous elements. This split is done by applying a sliding window of length N over the set of F measurements, resulting in a training set of F-N training tuples of the form $\boldsymbol{B}^i = (b_{i-N}, \ldots, b_{i-n}, \ldots, b_i)$ with $i = 1, \ldots, F - N$. The $f(\cdot)$ function is learnt by a supervised learning that consists on observing the relationship between b_i and its N previous elements $(b_{i-N}, \ldots, b_{i-1})$ for all the $I = F - N$ tuples. The rationale of this approach is to identify user frequent AP connectivity patterns in N consecutive time periods.

Prediction Based on Daily Patterns (PBDP): In this case, the prediction of $a_{d*,m*}$ is done according to the APs to which the user was connected in the previous N days at the same time period of the day (i.e. $a_{d*-N,m*}, \ldots, a_{d*-n*,m*} \ldots, a_{d*-1,m*}$). In order to obtain the prediction function $f(\cdot)$, a set of M vectors $\boldsymbol{B}_m = (b_{1,m}, \ldots, b_{f,m} \ldots, b_{F,m})$ is built. Each $\boldsymbol{B}_m$ consists on the AP to which the user connected in the last $F = D$ days at the m-th time period of the day, i.e. $\boldsymbol{B}_m = (a_{1,m} \ldots, a_{D-d,m} \ldots, a_{D-1,m}, a_{D,m})$. Then, each $\boldsymbol{B}_m$ is split into I different training tuples $\boldsymbol{B}^i_m$, each one composed of the i-th element and its N previous elements, i.e. $\boldsymbol{B}^i_m = (b_{i-N,m}, \ldots, b_{i-n,m}, \ldots, b_{i,m})$ with $i = 1, \ldots, D - N$. Then, a total of $(D - N) \cdot M$ tuples with size $N + 1$ are generated. The rationale of this is to identify user periodical AP connectivity patterns in N consecutive days at the same time of the day.

Prediction Based on Weekly Patterns (PBWP): In this case, the prediction of $a_{d*,m*}$ is done according to the APs to which the user was connected in the N previous weeks at the same day of the week and time period of the day (i.e. $a_{d*-7N,m*}, \ldots, a_{d*-7n,m*}, \ldots, a_{d*-7,m*}$). Again, a set of M vectors $\boldsymbol{B}_m = (b_{1,m}, \ldots, b_{f,m} \ldots, b_{F,m})$ is built, each one consisting on the AP to which the user connected in the last $F = W$ weeks at each m-th time period of a specific day of the week, i.e. $\boldsymbol{B}_m = (a_{d-7W,m}, \ldots, a_{d-7w,m} \ldots, a_{d-7,m}, a_{d,m})$. Then, each $\boldsymbol{B}_m$ is split into different I training tuples $\boldsymbol{B}^i_m$, each one composed of the i-th element and its N previous elements, i.e. $\boldsymbol{B}^i_k = (b_{i-N,m}, \ldots, b_{i-n,m} \ldots, b_{i,m})$ with $i = 1, \ldots, W - N$. In this case, the total number of tuples is $(W - N) \cdot M$. The rationale of this is to identify weekly AP connectivity patterns at the same day of the week and time of the day.

Joint Based Prediction (JBP): It consists on the same methodology but doing a combination of the three approaches described previously. In this case, the prediction of $a_{d*,m*}$ is done according to the APs to which the user connected in the last N time periods (i.e. $a_{d*,m*-N}, \ldots, a_{d*,m*-n}, \ldots, a_{d*,m*-1}$), the APs at the same m-th time period for the last N days (i.e. $a_{d*-N,m*}, \ldots, a_{d*-n,m*}, \ldots, a_{d*-1,m*}$) and the APs at the same day of the week and time period of the day for the last N weeks (i.e. $a_{d*-7N,m*}, \ldots, a_{d*-7n,m*}, \ldots, a_{d*-7,m*}$). The prediction function $f(\cdot)$ is learnt in a similar way as before by observing the relationship of specific $a_{d,m}$ and the observations in the last N time periods, the last N days at the same time period and the last N weeks at the same day of the week and time period of the day. A total number of $(W - N) \cdot M$ tuples with size $3N + 1$ are obtained.

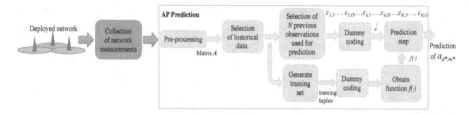

Fig. 1. Proposed prediction methodology.

It is worth noting that all these terms $a_{d,m}$ in matrix A correspond to categorical values (e.g. an AP identifier). For both the training and prediction, these terms are converted into numerical attributes by means of the so-called dummy coding process [11]. A dummy variable is a binary variable coded as 0 or 1 to represent the absence or presence of some categorical attribute. Therefore, each of the N elements used for prediction a_λ ($\lambda = 1, \dots , N$) are converted into a set of G dummy variables $c_\lambda = (c_{\lambda,1},$ $\dots , c_{\lambda,g}, \dots , c_{\lambda,G})$, where G is the number of different APs in the set of N measurements, so that the term $c_{\lambda,g} = 1$ if a_λ corresponds to the g-th AP and $c_{\lambda,g} = 0$ otherwise. Then, the resulting number of dummy variables $D = N \cdot G$ are used for the prediction of $a_{d*,m*}$ according to (1). Before the training, the same dummy coding is also done for all the training tuples of the training set.

$$a_{d*,m*} = f\left(c_{1,1}, \dots, c_{1,G}, \dots, c_{\lambda,1}, \dots, c_{\lambda,G}, \dots, c_{N,1}, \dots, c_{N,G}\right) \tag{1}$$

3   Considered Supervised Learning Algorithms

In this paper, a supervised learning algorithm based on Neural Networks and Random Forest are compared. A brief description of them is provided below.

Neural Networks (NN): In this case, the prediction is done by means of a feedforward Neural Network that consists on an input layer, one or more hidden layers and an output layer [12]. Each layer is made up of processing units called neurons. The inputs are fed simultaneously into the units of the input layer. Then, these inputs are weighted and are fed simultaneously to the first hidden layer. The outputs of the hidden layer units are input to the next hidden layer, and so on. A supervised learning technique called backpropagation is used for training. Back propagation iteratively learns the weights of the Neural Network by comparing the inputs and outputs of the training set.

Random Forest (RF): Ensemble methodologies are used to increase the overall accuracy by learning and combining a series of individual classifier models. Random Forests is a popular ensemble method. RF is based on building multiple decision trees, generated during the training phase, and merge them together in order to obtain a more accurate and stable prediction [3]. Different from the single decision tree methodology, where each node of the tree is split by searching for the most important feature, in random forest, additional random components are included (i.e. for each node of each tree the algorithm searches for the best feature among a random subset of features). Once all the trees are built, the result of the prediction corresponds to the most occurred prediction from all the trees of the forest.

4   Results

The considered scenario consists on a large Wi-Fi network with 429 APs deployed in a University Campus with 33 buildings with four floors per building. The reported user measurements are collected by the Cisco Prime Infrastructure tool [13]. The users' measurements were collected during $D = 84$ consecutive days (i.e. $W = 12$ weeks). The prediction methodology was run for $U = 967$ users. According to the methodology described in Sect. 2, the matrix A is built for each user by determining the AP to which the user is connected in each of the $M = 96$ periods of $T = 15$ min for each of the $D = 84$ days. According to this data, the proposed prediction methodology is run in order to predict the AP which each user will be connected to in all the $M = 96$ time periods of $T = 15$ min in the subsequent week. The obtained predictions are compared to the real APs which the user connected to. The prediction accuracy is calculated as the percentage of time periods that have been predicted correctly in the range between 6:00 h and 22:00 h for all the weekdays (from Monday to Friday) for all the users that connected to the Wi-Fi network at least one time every day. The prediction methodology has been implemented by means of Rapidminer Studio [14]. The parameters of each supervised learning algorithm have been tuned to obtain the maximum prediction accuracy. In particular, the Neural Network is configured with learning rate 0.05, momentum 0.9, 100 training cycles and 1 hidden layer of size 20 and the Random Forest has been configured with 100 trees, gain_ratio criterion and maximal depth 10.

4.1   Example of the AP Prediction Methodology

In order to illustrate the performance of the proposed prediction methodology, let first focus on the AP prediction for a specific user for all the time periods on a Wednesday. Assuming here the PBWP approach, the AP prediction at the m-th time period is based on the APs to which the user connected to in the previous $N = 6$ Wednesdays at the same m-th time period of the day. The training set is built by using the last $F = 12$ weeks. For validation purposes, the predictions are compared to the real AP where the user connected to during this Wednesday. According to this, Fig. 2 presents this comparison when using the Neural Network algorithm. As shown, for this particular user, the methodology is able to correctly predict the AP in 60 out of 64 periods of 15 min (i.e. a 93.75% of prediction accuracy). In general, most of the transitions between AP are correctly predicted. In fact, only an error of one period of 15 min is observed in predicting the user time of arrival while a slightly higher error is also observed for the prediction of departure.

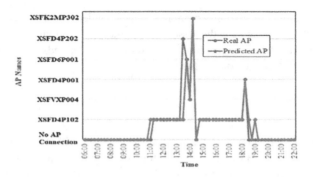

Fig. 2. Comparison of real and predicted AP for a specific user for Wednesday with NN.

During lunch time, the connection to AP XSFD4P202 is not correctly-predicted, but the prediction was AP XSFD4P102 that is located just in the lower floor of the same building. This indicates that, although the AP is not well predicted in this case, the methodology predicted correctly the region where the user was located.

4.2   Comparison of the Different Proposed Approaches

In order to gain insight in the performance of the proposed methodology, the prediction process has been run for all the set of users in all the time periods of 15 min during a whole week. Then, the predictions were compared to the AP to which each user connected at each time period. Table 1 presents the percentage of users in which each approach provides the best prediction accuracy for PBWP, PBDP and PBTP. As shown for both NN and RF predictors, PBTP approach provides better prediction accuracy than PBWP or PBDP for most of the users. This indicates that the AP to which a user was connected in the most recent time periods is the most useful information for prediction. However, it is worth noting that, for a relatively high percentage of users, the best approach is obtained with PBWP or PBDP (e.g. around 30% and 18% for NN and RF, respectively). This result indicates that the daily or weekly periodical behavior of some users can be captured better by PBDP or PBWP approaches, respectively.

Table 1. Percentage of users in which the different approaches provide the best accuracy.

	NN	RF
PBWP	24.07	18.62
PBDP	6.01	0
PBTP	69.90	81.37

Figure 3 presents the Cumulative Distribution Function of the prediction accuracy for the different prediction approaches with Neural Network. For comparison purposes, in all the approaches, the prediction is based on the 6 previous observations. Therefore, in PBWP, PBDP and PBTP, the sliding window is set to $N = 6$. In JBP approach, the sliding window is set to $N = 2$, i.e. the prediction is based according to the APs to which the user connected to in the last $N = 2$ time periods (i.e. $a_{d*,m*-2}$, $a_{d*,m*-1}$), the APs at the same m-th time period for the last $N = 2$ days (i.e. $a_{d*-2,m*}$, $a_{d*-1,m*}$) and the APs at the same day of the week and time period of the day for the last $N = 2$ weeks ($a_{d*-14,m*}$, $a_{d*-7,m*}$). As shown in Fig. 3, the JBP approach is able to provide a better prediction accuracy than the rest of the approaches separately. The reason is that the JBP is able to jointly capture the hourly, daily and weekly user behavior.

In Table 2, the average prediction accuracy and the average computation time, required for running the methodology for each user, are compared for the different approaches for both NN and RF. The methodology was executed in a computer with a Core i5-3330 processor at 3.00 GHz and RAM memory of 8 GB running Microsoft Windows 10. It has been observed that the computation time is mainly due to the process of training while the time for the prediction step is negligible. As shown in Table 2, the PBTP and PBDP approaches exhibit higher computation time per user since they make use of larger number of training tuples, leading to longer training times. As shown in Table 2, the JBP approach provides the best prediction accuracy with a relatively low computation time.

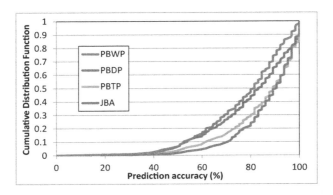

Fig. 3. CDF of the prediction accuracy the different approaches.

Table 2. Comparison of the different approaches.

	Average prediction accuracy (%)		Computation time per user (s)	
	NN	RF	NN	RF
PBWP	77.16	79.29	0.87	0.22
PBDP	79.88	79.64	33.33	3.74
PBTP	84.84	84.53	38.95	3.94
JBP	86.73	84.26	3.21	0.64

It is worth noting that the computation time required for the training may impose some restrictions in the maximum number of users that can included in the AP prediction or the frequency in which the training is updated. The values of the average computation time per user obtained in Table 2 may be excessively high in a Wi-Fi network that may have several thousands of simultaneous user connections. As a consequence, running the proposed methodology for such a high amount of users may require the parallelisation of the proposed methodology using multiple processors, each of them to run the prediction of a group of users.

4.3   Impact of the Amount of Data Used for Training

This section presents the impact of the amount of historical data used for building the training set. In particular, Fig. 4a presents a comparison of the prediction accuracy for JBP with $N = 2$ for Neural Network and Random Forest as a function of the number of days with measurements considered for generating the training set. On the other hand, Fig. 4b shows the average computation time required per user. As shown in Fig. 4a, the Neural Network predictor provides higher average prediction accuracy than Random Forest. Figure 4a also shows that the use of larger amount of data for generating the training set provides higher prediction accuracy. However, processing larger amount of data requires higher computation time, especially for the Neural Network, as shown in Fig. 4b.

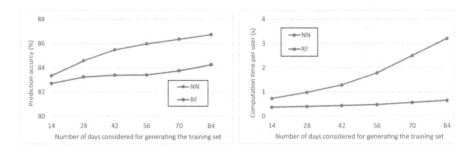

Fig. 4. a. Average prediction accuracy. b. Average Computation Time per user.

4.4   Impact of the Size of the Sliding Window

This section evaluates the impact of the size of the sliding window for the JBP approach when $D = 84$ days of measurements are considered for generating the training set. In particular, Table 3 presents the average prediction accuracy and the computation time per user for different values of the sliding window N. As shown in Table 3, a too low value of the sliding window reduces the capability to detect weekly, daily and hourly user periodical behaviour, which leads to a lower prediction accuracy. However, when setting a too high sliding window, the number of the tuples for generating the training set will become lower and, as a consequence, a worse training process is done, which reduces the prediction accuracy.

Table 3. Impact of the size of the sliding window

	Average prediction accuracy (%)		Computation time per user (s)	
	NN	RF	NN	RF
$N = 2$	86.73	84.26	3.21	0.64
$N = 6$	90.71	84.75	4.75	0.79
$N = 10$	88.79	82.96	2.54	0.71

5 Conclusions

This paper has proposed a methodology for the prediction of future APs to which users will be connected in a Wi-Fi network. The proposed methodology is based on a supervised learning that makes use of historical user connectivity to build a prediction model. Different approaches have been defined depending the historical data that is used. In general, the PBTP approach, in which the prediction is based according to the most recent APs to which the user connected, provides the best prediction accuracies. However, PBDP or PBWP perform better for users that follow some daily or weekly periodical behavior. As shown, a joint approach (JBP) is able to provide better prediction accuracy than the rest of the approaches separately with a relatively low computation time per user. The impact of the training set size has been illustrated for the JBP approach in terms of prediction accuracy and computation time. As shown, higher amount of days with measurements considered for generating the training set provides higher prediction accuracy at expenses of higher computation time, especially for Neural Networks. The impact of the size of the sliding window has been also evaluated. A too low value of the sliding window results in a worse capability to detect weekly, daily and hourly user periodical behavior while a too large value leads to a too low number of tuples for training. The results indicate that the prediction based on the Neural Network provides a higher prediction accuracy than the prediction based on Random Forest at expenses of an increase in the computation time.

Acknowledgements. This work has been supported by the Spanish Research Council and FEDER funds under SONAR 5G grant (ref. TEC2017-82651-R).

References

1. Cisco Visual Networking Index: Forecast and Trends, 2017–2022. Cisco White Papers, November, 2018
2. Chih-Lin, I., Liu, Y., Han, S., Wang, S., Liu, G.: On big data analytics for greener and softer RAN. IEEE Access **3**, 3068–3075 (2015)
3. Nisbet, R., Miner, G., Yale, K.: Handbook of Statistical Analysis and Data Mining Applications, 2nd edn. Academic Press, Cambridge (2017)
4. Jiang, S., Ferreira, J., González, M.C.: Activity-based human mobility patterns inferred from mobile phone data: a case study of Singapore. IEEE Trans. Big Data **3**, 208–219 (2015)
5. Furletti, B., Gabrielli, L., Rinzivillo, S., Renso, C.: Identifying users' profiles from mobile calls habits. In: International Workshop on Urban Computing (2012)

6. Sánchez-González, J., Sallent, O., Pérez-Romero, J., Agustí, R.: On extracting user-centric knowledge for personalised quality of service in 5G Networks. International Symposium on Integrated Network Management (2017)

7. 3GPP TR 23.791: Technical Specification Group Services and System Aspects. Study of Enablers for Network Automation for 5G, Release 15 (2017)

8. Kumar, A., Om, H.: A secure seamless handover authentication technique for wireless LAN. In: International Conference on Information Technology (2015)

9. Khong-Lim, Y., Yung-Wey, C.: Optimised access point selection with mobility prediction using hidden Markov model for wireless networks. In: International Conference on Ubiquitous and Future Networks (ICUFN) (2017)

10. Manweiler, J., Santhapuri, N., Choudhury, R.R., Nelakuditi, S.: Predicting length of stay at WiFi hotspots. In: IEEE International Conference on Computer Communications (INFOCOM), April 2013

11. Yan, C., Wang, P., Pang, H., Sun, L., Yang, S.: CELoF: WiFi dwell time estimation in free environment. In: Amsaleg, L., Guðmundsson, G., Gurrin, C., Jónsson, B., Satoh, S. (eds.) MMM 2017. LNCS, vol. 10132, pp. 503–514. Springer, Cham (2017). https://doi.org/10. 1007/978-3-319-51811-4_41

12. Han, J., Kamber, M., Pei, J.: Data Mining: Concepts and Techniques. Morgan Kaufman (MK), Elsevier (2006)

13. Cisco Prime Infrastructure 3.5 Administrator Guide. www.cisco.com

14. RapidMiner Studio. http://www.rapidminer.com

Programmable Edge-to-Cloud Virtualization for 5G Media Industry: The 5G-MEDIA Approach

Stamatia Rizou[1(✉)], Panagiotis Athanasoulis[1], Pasquale Andriani[2],
Francesco Iadanza[2], Panagiotis Trakadas[3], David Griffin[4],
Morteza Kheirkhah[4], David Breitgand[5], Avi Weit[5], Refik Fatih Ustok[6],
Selcuk Keskin[6], Francesca Moscatelli[7], Giacomo Bernini[7], Gordana Macher[8],
Javier Serrano[9], and David Jimenez[9]

[1] Singular Logic S.A., Athens, Greece
srizou@singularlogic.eu, pathanasoulis@ep.singularlogic.eu
[2] Engineering, Rome, Italy
{pasquale.andriani,francesco.iadanza}@eng.it
[3] National and Kapodistrian University of Athens, Athens, Greece
ptrakadas@uoa.gr
[4] University College London, London, UK
{d.griffin,m.kheirkhah}@ucl.ac.uk
[5] IBM Israel Ltd Haifa, Haifa, Israel
{davidbr,weit}@il.ibm.com
[6] Netas, Istanbul, Turkey
{fustok,selcukk}@netas.com.tr
[7] Nextworks, Pisa, Italy
{f.moscatelli,g.bernini}@nextworks.it
[8] Institut für Rundfunktechnik, Munich, Germany
gordana.macher@irt.de
[9] Universidad Politecnica de Madrid, Madrid, Spain
{jsr,djb}@gatv.ssr.upm.es

Abstract. To ensure high Quality of Experience (QoE) for end users, many media applications require significant quantities of computing and network resources, making their realization challenging in resource constrained environments. In this paper, we present the approach of the 5G-MEDIA project, providing an integrated programmable service platform for the development, design and operations of media applications in 5G networks, facilitating media service management across the service life cycle. The platform offers tools to service developers for efficient development, testing and continuous correction of services. One step further, it provides a service virtualization platform offering horizontal services, such as a Media Service Catalogue and accounting services, as well as optimization mechanisms to flexibly adapt service operations to dynamic conditions with efficient use of infrastructure resources. The paper outlines three use cases where the platform was tested and validated.

© IFIP International Federation for Information Processing 2020
Published by Springer Nature Switzerland AG 2020
I. Maglogiannis et al. (Eds.): AIAI 2020 Workshops, IFIP AICT 585, pp. 95–104, 2020.
https://doi.org/10.1007/978-3-030-49190-1_9

Keywords: Network function virtualization · Service Virtualization Platform · Cognitive network optimizer · Quality of experience

1   Introduction

Media applications are among the most demanding applications in terms of QoS, since they require the near real-time delivery and processing of media content across dispersed geographical locations. Recent advancements in 5G technologies [19, 23, 24] can provide valuable solutions for the realization of complex demanding media-related scenarios enabling the timely media content delivery and processing though intelligent and flexible service orchestration [15, 20, 22].

The 5G PPP 5G-MEDIA Phase 2 project has worked in the design and implementation of a platform that supports the media services lifecycle management providing a holistic solution encompassing mechanisms and tools for the development, testing and continuously-optimized deployment of media services. The main innovations of the proposed platform lie in the following parts: i) the offering of a complete Service Development Kit (SDK), encompassing tools for the media service validation and emulation as well as for the testing of optimization algorithms in emulation environment and the continuous corrective sizing of resources required after the media service deployment; ii) the development of two auxiliary services, the 5G-MEDIA Service Catalogue and the AAA mechanisms facilitating the media service management as well as accounting and billing mechanisms; iii) the introduction of a multi-hierarchical cognitive network optimizer catering for the continuous optimization of media services during and after deployment and iv) the enablement of traditional as well as serverless orchestration allowing event-driven orchestration of services at run time. While the main innovation aspects of the 5G-MEDIA solution can be applied to other application domains beyond the media industry, the 5G-MEDIA project has focused on the validation and evaluation of its solution in the media vertical, providing promising results for the value and use of the platform.

In this paper, we present the 5G-MEDIA technical solution and we discuss the functionalities of its technical components. We provide a brief overview of the main benefits achieved in the context of the use cases addressed in the project, although a deeper analysis of the results of the validation and trials testing of the solution is beyond the scope of this paper. Section 2 provides an overview of the refined high level 5G-MEDIA architecture and explains its main components comprised by the 5G-MEDIA Service Development Kit (SDK) and the Service Virtualization Platform (SVP). Section 3 explains the benefits achieved during pilot testing, before concluding the paper in Sect. 4.

2   5G-MEDIA High Level Architecture

In this Section, the main components of the 5G-MEDIA architecture shown in Fig. 1 are presented.

2.1 Service Development Kit

The SDK can be considered as a sandbox where the service developers can develop, emulate and test their NFV-based services, integrating both development and operational aspects together.

The main tools offered to the service developers within the 5G-MEDIA SDK are as follows: i) **Packaging Tools:** These collect the component software artefacts (e.g. required libraries) and generate software packages to be uploaded to the Private Catalogue. A range of packaging options are supported to equip the SDK to harmonize various VNF types such traditional plain ISO-based, unikernel-based and container-based VNFs; ii) **Validator:** This tool is the main interface for the developers to write/edit both NSDs and VNFDs, and validate them against TOSCA-based [8] and/or OSM-IM based [5] schemas. Validated TOSCA-based descriptors are then onboarded to the private catalogue via the validator web user interface (UI); iii) **Editor:** The editor is a web-based application whose main purpose is to assist with creating and editing of applications and their descriptors; iv) **Emulator:** The emulator in 5G-MEDIA SDK facilitates local prototyping and testing of real network functions in emulated network

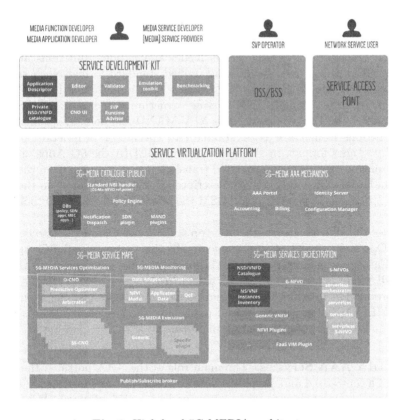

Fig. 1. High-level 5G-MEDIA architecture

topologies running on developers' machines. It leverages the vim-emu for non-FaaS VNFs [14] and the FaaS-vim for the FaaS VNFs [14]; **Benchmarking:** The 5G-MEDIA SDK benchmarking tool supports load-testing under several resource constraints on VNFs that are deployed on the emulation environment. Application developers can benefit from these tests for finding bugs, detecting congestions or investigating issues in their applications; **CNO Training:** Using this tool, the developer can configure a training model based on reinforcement learning, view the training performance and if the model achieves desirable performance, the developer can deploy it to SVP in order to have it utilized by the CNO; **SVP Runtime Advisor:** The SVP Runtime Advisor aims to feed the developer with necessary information about how their services are working in the operational environment. This is particularly necessary when the emulation environment capabilities are significantly different from those in the operational environment.

2.2 5G-MEDIA Service Virtualization Platform

This subsection provides further details on the design and implementation for the core components of the SVP [16].

5G-MEDIA Public Catalogue. The 5G Apps and Services Catalogue is a structured repository of heterogeneous media applications, functions and service descriptors based on a generic and unified standard format, such as VNF Descriptor (VNFD) and NS Descriptor (NSD) data models based on ETSI GS NFV SOL001 v2.5.1 [3] and VNF Package structure based on ETSI GS NFV SOL004 v2.5.1 [4]. The catalogue offers NFV MANO and domain-specific translation functions from ETSI NFV standard to specific or proprietary descriptors and packages format. In the context of 5G-MEDIA the 5G Apps and Services Catalogue provides an automated translation and mapping from the ETSI NFV standard TOSCA based VNF Descriptor and NS Descriptors to the ETSI OSM [5] specific data models, being OSM the reference NFV MANO tool in the project.

Besides the above features, the 5G App and Service Catalogue also connects the DevOps and production environments. To this end a private 5G App and Service Catalogue instance running in the local developer environment within the 5G-MEDIA SDK is connected through a dedicated catalogue-to-catalogue plugin to the production (public) 5G App and Service Catalogue instance running in the 5G-MEDIA SVP with the aim of publishing the designed validates media services and VNFs in the production platform.

5G-MEDIA AAA Services. The main role of the AAA portal is the provisioning of a centralised and simplified view to administrators of resource utilisation and the associated costs for services running on the platform. It has been designed to allow future extensibility through a plug-in architecture. It currently supports OpenID Connect protocol to facilitate the integration of additional resources and the two login profiles [12] for UI and API access, "Authorisation Code Flow" and "Resource Owner Password Grant Code Flow". The inner AAA architecture comprehends an Identity Server based on KeyCloak [9] that provides the access and refresh tokens to the authorised users. All the configuration is managed by the AAA portal that takes in charge the setup on the different resources involved: Identity Server, NFVO/VNFM, VIM, Catalogue, SDK, MAPE.

5G-MEDIA Service MAPE. The Media Service Monitoring, Analysis, Planning and Execution (MAPE) components provide the intelligence to dynamically manage and provide infrastructure resources for the deployed media services according to observed changes in user demand patterns, availability and performance of network and computational resources.

QoE Monitoring. Besides the collection of resource consumption data, the 5G-MEDIA project has defined application-specific metrics, relevant to media use cases for quantifying the Quality of Experience (QoE). In order to measure the performance of the service in terms of perceived quality, the platform deploys a QoE probe as a VNF close to the end user, which provides a Mean Opinion Score (MOS) through a statistical model fed by Non-Referenced (NR) video metrics. The goal is achieved by using different ML algorithms in order to obtain the estimated QoE from different data coming from the parameterisation of video services such as bitrate, intrinsic video features as temporal and spatial complexity, the aforementioned NR metrics as blurring. Finally, video quality losses are obtained by applying specific indicators proposed by AGH University [13]. The resulting QoE data are considered in the MAPE optimization to maximize perceived quality at application level.

Cognitive Network Optimizer. For the analysis of monitoring data, 5G-MEDIA adopts a hierarchical Cognitive Optimizer model to allocate and distribute resources across its services. Without loss of generality, we categorize this hierarchy into two broad levels and we name them as follows: (1) Overarching-CNO (O-CNO); and (2) Service Specific-CNO (SS-CNO). In a nutshell, the former optimises resources across all services while the latter optimises the allocated resources to a service (granted by the O-CNO). O-CNO conducts two separate but complementary tasks, each of which may follow separate optimisation algorithm. First task is an offline task related to planning, predicting and allocating resources to *all* services periodically (potentially with a long interval, e.g., in the order of hours or days). In 5G-MEDIA this has been implemented with a genetic algorithm which tries to optimally allocate resources to services based on their predicted resource consumption/demand [21]. We refer to this component of O-CNO as the predictive optimizer. The second task allocates resources on demand from a pool of resources shared across all services (or at least shared across a subset of all services). This is implemented as a utility based optimization algorithm which also considers service priorities, constraints and service level agreements.

The latter algorithm is mainly responsible to dynamically allocate shared-pool resources between individual services under the control of the lower-level SS-CNO. Unlike the predictive optimizer side of O-CNO, this is a run-time online algorithm that reacts to requests in real-time.

5G-MEDIA Service Orchestration. In 5G-MEDIA, we adopt an approach that combines traditional VNF orchestration with a novel approach that we term *Serverless Orchestration*. This resulted in an integrated 5G-MEDIA Service Orchestration platform that uses existing VIMs supporting OpenStack and implementing new VIM to support OpenNebula integration. Serverless VNFs are characterised by being invoked in response to service-specific events rather than being instantiated as part of the traditional network service instantiation flows. There are no provisions in the current ETSI standards for orchestrating serverless VNFs. To handle these complex run-time orchestration flows the project has developed a novel event-driven serverless orchestrator (based on Argo Workflows [2] and Argo Events [1] projects) – resulting in a full serverless management and orchestration stack in 5G-MEDIA Service Virtualization Platform. This stack is interoperable with OSM and complements its functionality allowing to unleash the full potential of a serverless computing paradigm for media applications.

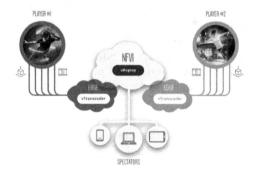

Fig. 2. Tele-immersive gaming scenario

3   5G-MEDIA Use Cases

In the following, we outline the scope of the 5G-MEDIA use cases [17] and the main benefits achieved.

3.1   Tele-Immersive Gaming

This use case demonstrates a real-time interactive immersive media application [18] in which the two players are volumetrically reconstructed and interact with each other in a common virtual gaming environment through their digitized virtual representations (i.e. textured 3D shapes). The application allows for the

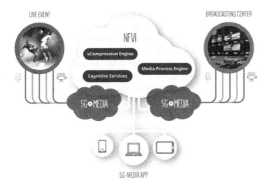

Fig. 3. Remote production scenario

live spectating of each gaming session by remote third party users. The high-level scenario is illustrated in Fig. 2. The role of the 5G-MEDIA platform in this use case lies in the flexible real-time adaptive streaming service, through the use of serverless orchestration that enables the on-demand deployment of transcoding services upon the start of a game session or for the delivery of replay clips to spectators. This use case has tested the efficacy of the CNO considering two different scenarios: i) the optimized selection of transcoding profile to ensure QoE satisfaction; ii) the optimization of the cost efficiency of each session in order to eventually maximize profits, while also retaining the serviced QoE levels relying on the interactions between O-CNO and SS-CNO. The latter approach demonstrated the adoption of a finer-grained service cost analysis opening up new opportunities for application centric optimization.

3.2 Mobile Contribution, Remote and Smart Media Production

This use case enables two media production scenarios. Scenario 1) is a remote production of an event without the need for dedicated infrastructure to be specifically deployed in the event venue as shown in Fig. 3. Scenario 2) considers the streaming of live events via smartphones or tablets by spectators or journalists for enhancing the program stream of an event. The role of the 5G-MEDIA Platform in this use case is to ensure that the media processing functions are efficiently deployed in cloud infrastructure enabling low latency and high throughput as required by live streaming and media processing. This is achieved by using the 5G-MEDIA Service MAPE to optimize bitrate/compression levels of media streams and ensure QoE for the realization of the remote production scenario. In addition, this use case demonstrates the use of FaaS orchestration by automatically deploying media services upon the start of a mobile contribution session. Serverless VNFs implementing cognitive services (captions production and face recognition) for mobile contribution as well as video stream vSplitter and sink are being deployed on demand at the edge where and when they are needed.

During the project the "Remote Production" scenario was approved by supporting a real production of RTVE's Radio3. A time difference of around t = 500 ms, i.e. around 12 frames, was measured in the pretest and could be decreased to 10 frames during the final remote production. The work of the CNO was approved in a "Multi-Instance" scenario, where UC1 and the "Mobile Contribution" scenario shared resources (e.g. GPUs) in the same Edge. In this scenario, the resources where allocated by the CNO.

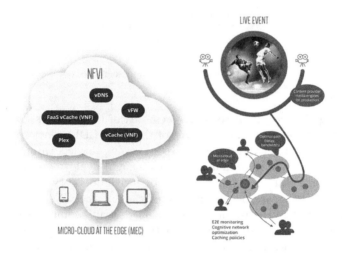

Fig. 4. UHD over vCDN scenario

3.3   Ultra HD over Content Delivery Networks

The focus of this scenario is enabling Media Service Providers (MSPs) to build flexible and adaptable media distribution service chains, made up of virtualized functions, and deliver UHD media contents while users are moving in a geographically distributed 5G network, as shown in Fig. 4. The 5G-MEDIA SDK and Services Catalogue are used for the design, dimensioning, creation and onboarding of the media services, such as the media caching VNFs building the vCDN service. In practice, this service is realized as a multi-NFVI scenario, where regular VM-based media caches (running in Openstack [10]) are integrated in the same media service instance with FaaS based media caches (running in Kubernetes [6]) to create a hierarchical media delivery chain. At the root, a media origin server (based on Plex [11]) hosts all of the media contents that can be accessed by end-users from their fixed (e.g. using a Nextworks Symphony entertainment platform audio/video client [7]) or mobile devices. The 5G-MEDIA SVP is used for the instantiation and application configuration of UHD media delivery services as NFV Network Services. Here, the coordinated configuration of the media caches and load balancing functions is applied by the 5G-MEDIA SVP to re-direct users to proper media content delivering caches (e.g. based on load). Moreover, the 5G-MEDIA MAPE module monitors the running services and predicts through online ML algorithms operation anomalies (at both network and media service level) due to service congestion (e.g. caused by flash crowds). Upon such predictions, optimization events are generated to dynamically scale the media caches hierarchy (with the option of creating either regular VM-based or serverless virtualized caches) and properly reconfigure the load balancing function for maintaining user perceived quality.

3.4 Cross-Cutting Scenarios

To validate the efficacy of the 5G-MEDIA platform, the project has considered two cross-cutting scenarios mixing more than one sessions or service in the same infrastructure. In particular, to showcase the behaviour of 5G-MEDIA Service MAPE in a multi-tenant environment, the use of O-CNO and SS-CNO was tested in the presence of multiple sessions of the same use case (e.g., parallel remote production sessions sharing the same edge and the same infrastructure) or different use cases (e.g., co-existence of mobile contribution use case and Tele-immersive use case) competing for limited resources such as GPUs in the same NFVI. These test scenarios show the applicability of the proposed approach and in particular of the CNO architecture in multi-tenant environments.

4   Conclusions

This paper presents the 5G-MEDIA high level architecture presenting the role and functionalities of its components. Overall, the 5G-MEDIA approach supports the management of media services across their life cycle, by providing a Service Development Kit for the development and validation of services and a Service Virtualization platform for their continuous optimized deployment. The paper also provides a brief description of the media use cases and the role of the 5G-MEDIA platform in optimizing their performance.

References

1. Argo Events. https://argoproj.github.io/projects/argo-events
2. Argo Workflows. https://argoproj.github.io/argo
3. ETSI GS NFV-SOL 001 V2.5.1: Protocols and data models; NFV descriptors based on Tosca specification. ETSI NFV ISG
4. ETSI GS NFV-SOL 004 V2.5.1. Protocols and data models; VNF package specification. ETSI NFV ISG
5. ETSI Open Source Mano. https://osm.etsi.org/
6. Kubernetes. https://kubernetes.io
7. Nextworks Symphony Entertainment Platform. http://www.nextworks.it/en/products/brands/symphony
8. Oasis Tosca: Tosca simple profile for network functions virtualization. http://docs.oasis-open.org/tosca/TOSCA-Simple-Profile-YAML/v1.0/TOSCA-Simple-Profile-YAML-v1.0.pdf. Accessed 2 Mar 2020

9. Open Source Identity and Access Management. https://www.keycloak.org. Accessed 2 Mar 2020
10. Openstack. https://www.openstack.org
11. Plex Media Server. https://www.plex.tv
12. The OAuth 2.0 Authorization Framework Section 1.3. https://tools.ietf.org/html/rfc6749#section-1.3. Accessed 2 Mar 2020
13. Video Quality Indicators - AGH University. http://vq.kt.agh.edu.pl/metrics.html
14. Acar, U., Ustok, R., Keskin, S., Breitgand, D., Weit, A.: Programming tools for rapid NFV-based media application development in 5G networks. In: IEEE Conference on Network Function Virtualization and Software Defined Networks (NFV-SDN), Verona, Italy, pp. 1–5 (2018)
15. Alemany, P., et al.: Network slicing over a packet/optical network for vertical applications applied to multimedia real-time communications. In: 2019 IEEE Conference on Network Function Virtualization and Software Defined Networks (NFV-SDN), pp. 1–2. IEEE (2019)
16. Alvarez, F., et al.: An edge-to-cloud virtualized multimedia service platform for 5G networks. IEEE Trans. Broadcast. **65**(2), 369–380 (2019)
17. Caruso, G., et al.: Embedding 5G solutions enabling new business scenarios in media and entertainment industry. In: 2019 IEEE 2nd 5G World Forum, pp. 460–464. IEEE (2019)
18. Karakottas, A., Papachristou, A., Doumanoqlou, A., Zioulis, N., Zarpalas, D., Daras, P.: Augmented VR. In: 2018 IEEE Conference on Virtual Reality and 3D User Interfaces (VR), p. 1. IEEE (2018)
19. Peuster, M., et al.: Introducing automated verification and validation for virtualized network functions and services. IEEE Commun. Mag. **57**(5), 96–102 (2019)
20. Pol, A., et al.: Advanced NFV features applied to multimedia real-time communications use case. In: 2019 IEEE 2nd 5G World Forum (5GWF), pp. 323–328. IEEE (2019)
21. Rocha, M., Phan, T.K., Reis, J., Griffin, D., Rio, M.: Triptych: multi-objective optimisation of service deployment costs, application delay and bandwidth usage. In: 2019 IFIP Networking Conference (IFIP Networking), pp. 1–9 (2019)
22. Shekhawat, Y., et al.: Orchestrating live immersive media services over cloud native edge infrastructure. In: 2019 IEEE 2nd 5G World Forum (5GWF), pp. 316–322. IEEE (2019)
23. Soenen, T., et al.: Insights from Sonata: implementing and integrating a microservice-based NFV service platform with a DevOps methodology. In: 2018 IEEE/IFIP Network Operations and Management Symposium, NOMS 2018, pp. 1–6. IEEE (2018)
24. Trakadas, P., et al.: Comparison of management and orchestration solutions for the 5G era. J. Sens. Actuator Netw. MDPI **9**(1), 1–4 (2020)

Protocol Deployment for Employing Honeypot-as-a-Service

Alexandros Kostopoulos[1](✉) ⓘ, Ioannis P. Chochliouros[1],
Constantinos Patsakis[2], Miltos Anastasiadis[3],
and Alessandro Guarino[4]

[1] Hellenic Telecommunications Organization (OTE) S.A., 99 Kifissias Avenue,
15124 Maroussi, Athens, Greece
{alexkosto,ichochliouros}@oteresearch.gr
[2] University of Piraeus, Piraeus, Greece
kpatsak@gmail.com
[3] Motivian Eood, Sofia, Bulgaria
manastasiadis@motivian.com
[4] StagCyber, Cavazzale, Italy
a.guarino@stagcyber.eu

Abstract. The YAKSHA project aims at reinforcing EU-ASEAN cooperation and building partnerships in cybersecurity domain by developing a solution tailored to specific national needs leveraging EU know-how and local knowledge. YAKSHA enhances cybersecurity readiness levels for its end-users, helps better prevent cyber-attacks, reduces cyber-risks and better governs the whole cybersecurity process. The EU-ASEAN cooperation also helps to mitigate some of the weaknesses identified in the cybersecurity ecosystem. In this paper, we consider the protocol deployment process for employing honeypot-as-a-service, with focus on the Internet of Things (IoT) use case.

Keywords: ASEAN-EU cooperation · Cybersecurity · Data analytics · Honeypots-as-a-service · ICT · Malware · Protocol deployment

1 Introduction

Informatisation is widely recognized as a "key" enabling factor for developing economies and society. ASEAN (Association of Southeast Asian Nations), and in particular low- and middle-income countries in this region, have long been subject to several cybersecurity issues and are exposed to specific risks, ranging from data breaches to intentional intrusions by adversaries. Security is a common element buttressing all other ICT technologies [1, 2], and without which ICT can be considered as much of a risk than an opportunity for organisations, businesses and governments [3].

YAKSHA [4] aims at reinforcing EU (European Union) - ASEAN cooperation and building partnerships in the cybersecurity domain by developing a solution tailored to specific user and national needs, leveraging EU know-how and local expertise. YAKSHA develops and introduces the innovative concept of "honeypot-as-a-service" which greatly enhances the process of gathering threat intelligence [5, 6]. Many

© IFIP International Federation for Information Processing 2020
Published by Springer Nature Switzerland AG 2020
I. Maglogiannis et al. (Eds.): AIAI 2020 Workshops, IFIP AICT 585, pp. 105–115, 2020.
https://doi.org/10.1007/978-3-030-49190-1_10

companies and organisations desire to test the systems they deploy in terms of security, however they are not always able to do it "appropriately". Moreover, since the developments in this field are continuous, many end-users would like to be informed about zero-day exploits for their systems. YAKSHA enables organisations to handle this challenge in an automated way, allowing different modalities of processing and features, whether this is access to sample of other nodes or more advanced algorithms.

YAKSHA develops innovative methods for malware detection, collection and analysis [7, 8], as well as designs a specialized ontology to be used for long-term storage and analysis of the information, and deploys standard information formats and interfaces to facilitate interoperability. The YAKSHA software solution is validated in real-world pilot projects in both regions, focusing on Vietnam, Malaysia and Greece. The test cases are represented by complex end-users with articulated cybersecurity risks and allows the consortium to gather feedback to be used later to bring the solution to the market. YAKSHA develops a comprehensive business plan for the transition of the solution and complementary services to Technology Readiness Level 9 (TRL9), leveraging the very strong ASEAN partners that are members of the consortium - including governmental organisations and leading end-users communities and associations with regional scope. As part of this effort, YAKSHA builds a whole ecosystem of partners around its solutions. This contributes to enhancing cybersecurity skills in Europe and creating new positions for cybersecurity specialists in ASEAN. Moreover, the direct access to the all-important ASEAN market provided to partners will positively impact the competitiveness of European security industry.

The paper is organised as follows: Sect. 2 presents the overall architecture of the YAKSHA platform. Section 3 provides the pilots' deployment protocol for the YAKSHA data flow compliance. Section 4 focuses on the protocol deployment for the Internet of Things (IoT) use case. In Sect. 5 we conclude our remarks and present our future work.

2   Architecture

YAKSHA is a distributed system which allows the automated deployment of honeypots, data collection and analysis as well as reporting and information sharing with affiliated YAKSHA installations. Honeypots despite the fact that they provide a very good insight on the actual attacks that can be launched against a system [9, 10], they are rather difficult to be properly deployed and in many occasions, require a lot of effort and dedicated personnel to integrate them [11]. Moreover, most honeypots are focusing specific systems, with Windows and Linux dominating the field. As a result, many companies and organisations are discouraged to deploy their custom honeypots to monitor possible attacks on their systems [12]. Furthermore, it is quite often that these systems are not properly configured to monitor the attacks properly, or perform maintenance procedures for the continuation of these efforts. YAKSHA aims to advance current state-of-the-art and practice, by providing an easy mechanism for the automated deployment and management of honeypots, so that organisations and companies can easily create custom honeypots with the integrated sensors properly configured and sending all the collected information to a central repository that they manage [13].

Currently, most honeypots and sandboxes might be able to collect a lot of valuable information about an attack [14, 15], however, this information is reported in the form of logs, and require a dedicated analyst to go through them and understand the attack pattern and impact [16]. The latter is something that cannot be expected in many "actors" (such as companies and organisations), as in many occasions they would need a simple report that states that their system is vulnerable to, for example, a denial of service (DoS) or privilege escalation attack, where the attacker was able to perform a list of actions, using the collected piece of code.

In this regard, YAKSHA advances current state-of-the-art by extracting actual knowledge from the log files in a human readable format, so that the attack analysis can be simplified and partially automated. In addition, YAKSHA makes honeypots more stealth, and collects even more important information, when this is possible. Finally, YAKSHA advances existing knowledge by providing machine learning tools and Artificial Intelligence (AI) algorithms able to detect malware more accurately, correlates the information with other samples, and extracts attack vectors and patterns.

The modular and distributed nature of YAKSHA allows it to cater for both opportunistic and continuous sample collection, and selective information sharing with other entities when deemed necessary. YAKSHA, therefore, enables organisations, companies and government agencies to upload custom honeypots that "meet" their own specifications, monitor attacks in real time and analyse them. However, since some of these honeypots may expose corporate or organisation specific vulnerabilities, each YAKSHA node may specify policies for information sharing per honeypot, attack pattern, affiliated nodes or even user roles of users in affiliated nodes. To this end, initially each YAKSHA installation is an independent instantiation of the system which has its own users (e.g.: admins, auditors, analyzers, backup managers, integrators, etc.), its own honeypots, and performs its processing locally. Clearly, a YAKSHA node, due to processing requirements would consist of more than one computer, but in what follows is considered as a single system.

The conceptual architecture of a YAKSHA node is illustrated in Fig. 1. On top, the installed honeypots which are exposed to the Internet so that attackers will try to penetrate them. YAKSHA apart from typical Linux and Windows honeypots aims to provide hooks for IoT devices, as well as for Android and for SCADA (Supervisory Control and Data Acquisition) systems [17]. YAKSHA takes into consideration tools to provide a sandbox for automating the analysis of the collected samples [18], nonetheless, YAKSHA strives to extend them, not only in terms of integrating them in a honeypot, but hooking other operating systems, extracting more information, but more importantly, processing the extracted information.

In the following, we briefly discuss the various distinct Engines/Modules included in the original YAKSHA architecture.

Firstly, the *Maintenance and Integration Engine* which allows the configuration of a new honeypot, uploading and exposing it to the Internet and data wipe. Therefore, this engine enables the node admin to deploy a honeypot from scratch, share it and, if deemed necessary, drop back to initial settings to collect more data. The critical point of this module is to automate the procedure of creating hooks to the system for a range of operating systems, so that end-users can assess the risk to which several of their systems are exposed to. Apart from making the procedure seamless and automatic, this module must make the procedure transparent, so that the hooks cannot be traced by an adversary who penetrated the system. The integration for systems beyond desktop and server environments is not easy nor straightforward, as core and undocumented changes have to be made to the underlying operating system. The architecture of a YAKSHA node is illustrated in Fig. 2, as appearing below.

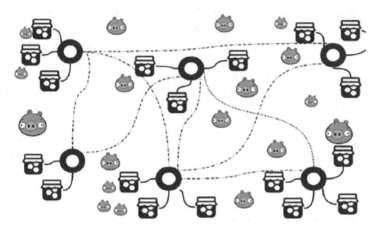

Fig. 1. YAKSHA overall architecture.

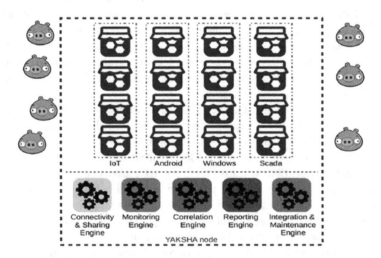

Fig. 2. The architecture of a YAKSHA node.

The *Monitoring Engine* performs sanity checks to determine whether the honeypot is properly working and records all changes in memory, processes and filesystem as well as network connections to detect anomalies that an adversary performs during an attack. The core goal of this module is to monitor everything that happens in the system so that:

- Its presence cannot be traced by the attacker. If the attacker understands that s/he is being monitored, then the honeypot loses its value, as the attacker is expected to quit.
- Collect all the information so that the actions can be replicated.
- Maintain all the actions in a sandboxed environment so that no malicious actions can escape the honeypot and infect the rest of the system.

The *Correlation Engine*, on receiving the data from the monitoring engine, tries to find how significant is the penetration and propagation of the sample, that is: what privileges did the malware manage to gain, did it manage to add users, did it manage to write to protected folders or shut down the system. Then it tries to correlate the attack patterns with input from older samples. For instance, it finds whether changes in the registry, filesystem, system calls etc., have already been made by another sample. The Correlation Engine is the most crucial part of YAKSHA as it is the selling point of the platform since it automates the evaluation of the risks a system is exposed to. Many systems may enable the deployment of a honeypot, however, without taking into consideration the amount of effort for installation and customisation, at the end of the day, one has to go through each attack independently and evaluate it. YAKSHA does not make this analysis obsolete by making it completely automated; instead, it provides a set of filters which significantly reduces the amount of manual work and ranks it according to the impact on the system. In addition, attacks are clustered to extract further attack patterns in terms of tools, methods and results.

The *Reporting Engine* is the module charged with presenting the information in a readable form to the users. On one hand, it is in charge of issuing alerts and aggregating information for specific documents targeted to technical personnel; on the other hand it has the task of providing management with meaningful input on the organisation's cybersecurity current posture and risk levels. For the non-technical audience inside the organisation, the Reporting Engine provides dashboard presenting in real-time the status of the node, the level of risk for each asset, type of attacks, threat vectors, as well as an estimation of the possible impacts. The latter is presented both in financial and operational terms. The dashboard also presents in real-time the areas where the risk of attack is higher and propose controls to apply to mitigate them; for example, patches to apply, firewall and IDS (Intrusion Detection System) configurations [19] to be updated, etc. In short, YAKSHA's Reporting Engine supplies the decision-makers with a continuous risk assessment tool, as well as the IT personnel with detailed technical reports while acting as a recommender system, when this is possible.

Finally, the role of *Connectivity and Sharing Engine* is to allow the exchange of information with other YAKSHA nodes. Each node has its own users, with their respective roles and can connect with other nodes to exchange malware samples. Each node can select which samples to share and with which nodes, for instance node A has some SCADA honeypots [20] that wants to share only with node B and not with node C. These policies can be further tuned so that, *for example*, only auditors from node B can access this information.

3 Pilots' Deployment Protocol for YAKSHA Data Flow Compliance

This section describes the identified baseline of activities that form part of the pilots' deployment protocol. These activities ensure that the YAKSHA platform deployed in the pilots' premises is compliant with the dataflow principles and legal grounds for data processing defined for proper operation and results of the platform [21]. The protocol activities for data flow compliance are essential and required to take place for all pilots.

The protocol's activities for organisational data flow compliance include:

- *Node installation and administrative access flow:* A pilot organisation appoints YAKSHA administrators (persons), assisted by the YAKSHA technical team to install and administrate a YAKSHA node for the given organisation. A YAKSHA node instantiation with all administrative data access/data flow is properly set up and configured for the given organisation.
- *End-users access flow:* Relevant employees of the pilot organisation (security officers, managers, executive positions) are given access to the YAKSHA node to receive cybersecurity repots and alerts on the status of the cybersecurity analyses. All YAKSHA end-users' access is properly set up according to roles established.

The protocol's activities for technical data flow compliance include:

- *Honeypot-to-Node Affiliation:* A pilot organisation technically affiliates (sets, configures and deploys) all needed honeypots to an organisation's own and instantiated (operational) YAKSHA node. The pilot organisation ensures each honeypot is affiliated to only one operational YAKSHA node of that organisation. For the sake of separation of administration and data flow management, each honeypot reports results to one affiliated node only while the node policy may allow sharing reports from honeypots with other affiliated nodes (within or outside the organisation).
- *Honeypot-to-Node Data Flow:* The pilot organisation ensures adequate level of the Quality of Service (QoS) for the network connection between a honeypot and its affiliated node. The data flow between a honeypot and its node has to be reliable and timely (e.g., soft real-time restriction is desirable) to ensure adequate analysis and alerts triggering when an attack is taking place. This protocol activity must entail pilot organisation guarantee reliable honeypot-to-node data flow. Any misconfiguration or connection unavailability (e.g., due to low QoS) may degrade the results of YAKSHA analytics and the overall results/evaluation of the pilot. This protocol activity defines reliable data flow not only between a honeypot and the node, but also between a honeypot and its associated (external) tools for malware analysis, such as the Cuckoo Sandbox[1], and also between those tools and the affiliated YAKSHA node.
- *Node-to-Node Data Flow:* A pilot organisation affiliates with other pilot organisations to automatically exchange collected malware data. To do so, the pilot organisation, upon organisation-level decision making, sets and configures a data

---

[1] More details can be found at: https://cuckoosandbox.org/.

sharing policy of the YAKSHA node of that organisation to enable such sharing with other organisations' nodes. Importantly, the pilot organisation must ensure no business-sensitive data is shared with other organisations.

- *Data protection compliance:* A pilot organisation guarantees all technical means of data protection are properly enabled -or set- as part of the YAKHSA platform solution, both for the data flows from the honeypots to the affiliated nodes and for the data flows from a YAKSHA node to other YAKSHA nodes affiliated for such data sharing. Any improper security settings -or no security means for those data flows- imply incorrect or distrusted analysis or reports by the YAKSHA node. For instance, data from honeypots to an affiliated node may be tampered in transit so that an attacker may influence on the analysis of the platform. The pilot organisation ensures all personally identifiable data from honeypot collection, such as IP addresses, must be treated according to the regulations or laws of each country the pilot takes place. Particularly, legal ground compliance must be ensured for data collection, retention and sharing as discussed in [22].

4   Deployment Protocol for the IoT Use Case

The goal of the smart home IoT use case is to use a YAKSHA node within a pre-commercial environment (infrastructure and settings) provided by a telecom operator (i.e., the Hellenic Telecommunications Organization S.A. (OTE)) to collect real data of potential attacks against the smart home IoT platform (pre-commercial) product. YAKSHA analytics capability is used to raise awareness and provide decision support in strengthening the cybersecurity posture of the product.

Using YAKSHA in a pre-commercial environment makes OTE aware of potential attacks in the wild against OTE's products and services. OTE has developed, completely "in-house", an end-to-end (E2E) platform/solution for building energy monitoring and management. The solution is based entirely on open source technologies and it is modular by design. As such, it is vendor- and technology-agnostic, capable of integrating numerous and heterogeneous sensors, modules and devices to a common ecosystem.

The IoT testbed layout is depicted in Fig. 3 and includes the following parts:

- A wide range of end-devices/sensors, such as air-quality, temperature, humidity, pressure, activity, luminance, fire and for power/energy communicate with the backend (cloud) infrastructure over a wide range of short/long range technologies (i.e.: Ethernet, WiFi, z-wave[2] BLE (Bluetooth Low-Energy), LoRaWAN (Long-Range Wide Area Network), NB-IoT (Narrow-Band IoT)).
- IoT hubs/gateways (local and remote-based on LoRaWAN) for facility automation and energy management/control (based on events/rules) supporting multiple HAN (Home Area Network)/BAN (Body-Area Network)/LAN (Local Area Network)/

---

[2] More details can be found at: https://www.z-wave.com/.

WAN (Wide Area Network) technologies/interfaces; over 150 Techs/protocols are currently supported.

- A (common) backend infrastructure (including storage, monitoring/data visualization, command exchange, etc.).

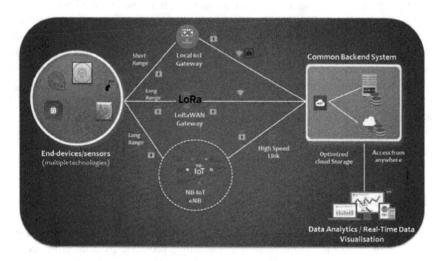

Fig. 3. OTE's IoT testbed layout.

Monitoring data are sent to a common backend system with optimised cloud storage via a gateway. The gateway could be either a local IoT (e.g.: UP Board[3] Raspberry Pi), a LoRaWAN, or an NB (NodeB)/eNB (evolved NodeB) IoT gateway.

The IoT service is accessible via any end-device (e.g.: phone, tablet, laptop), from any network. Two user interfaces are available. The first interface is via a mobile application installed in end-users' devices, which enables users to monitor the measurements of the sensors, or manage their devices. The second interface communicates with web server via http requests, which also enables users to define specific automations for their devices.

Next, the identified baseline of activities that form part of the OTE's pilot deployment protocol are described. The protocol's activities for technical data flow compliance related to the *development of the testing environment* include:

- *Storage and computational resources' definition:* The required storage and computational resources were defined in order to develop a testing environment to host the IoT service.
- *Virtual Machine Creation for hosting MQTT in the YAKSHA testing environment:* A virtual machine is created within OTE's cloud environment in order to host the Message Queuing Telemetry Transport (MQTT) broker. MQTT is a machine-to-machine (M2M)/"Internet of Things" connectivity protocol, which is designed for

---

[3] More details can be found at: https://up-board.org/.

connections with remote locations where a "small code footprint" is required or the network bandwidth is limited.

- *Virtual Machine Creation for hosting database in the YAKSHA testing environment:* A virtual machine (VM) is created within OTE's cloud environment in order to host the database, where all the data sent by the sensors are to be stored.
- *Virtual Machine Creation for hosting data visualization services in the YAKSHA testing environment:* A VM is created within OTE's cloud environment in order to host services related to data analytics and real-time data visualisation, as well as enable users to create customised figures.
- *Network configuration support for the YAKSHA testing environment:* A separate VLAN is configured for testing purposes. An IP (Internet Protocol) address is assigned to each virtual machine, gateway and sensor device in order to enable communication among each IoT platform component.

The protocol's activities for technical data flow compliance related to *data transmission* include:

- *Gateway configuration to enable connectivity with the back-end system:* The gateway is configured in order to support a plethora of WAN wireless/wired connectivity options (e.g.: Ethernet, direct VGW-to-VGW (virtual private gateway) communications, 2G/3G/4G/4G+, RF@ 433/868/2400 MHz).
- *Gateway configuration to enable connectivity with the sensors/IoT devices:* The gateway is configured in order to be hardware agnostic (vendor independent) and protocol/technology agnostic. It also supports a plethora of HAN/BAN/LAN communication technologies/protocols (e.g.: modbus, z-wave, KNX[4], BACnet/IP[5], BLE, WiFi, unlicensed bands such as RF@433/868 MHz, etc.).
- *Sensors/IoT devices:* A subset of the available sensors/IoT devices is selected in order to be used for the YAKSHA pilot (e.g.: air-quality, temperature, humidity, pressure, soil moisture, PIR/activity, luminance, distance, fire, rain, sound, GPS, cameras, gyroscopes, accelerometers, etc.).
- *Data collection and transmission:* Data from a wide range of energy and non-energy related measurements (such as weather data either from a local weather station or from "external" weather operators, temperature, humidity and barometer data from sensors, fire/CO2/water/activity related data from sensors, etc.) are collected, processed, controlled, stored, and pushed.

The protocol's activities for technical data flow compliance related to the *end-users* include:

- *End-user interaction with the IoT platform:* Users are enabled to connect to the IoT service, as well as receive push notifications (and/or e-mail) to their device (iOS and/or Android, wearables) on specific user/system related events (e.g.: "dryer is done", turn device on upon activity detection, alarm), and enable voice commands.

---

[4] https://www.knx.org/knx-en/for-professionals/What-is-KNX/A-brief-introduction/index.php.

[5] More details can be found at: http://www.bacnet.org/Tutorial/BACnetIP/index.html.

5 Conclusion

Information systems, regardless of whether they are mobile or not, have penetrated our everyday lives, automating many procedures but also creating huge dependencies. Moreover, modern information systems are highly heterogeneous and due to networking, especially connection to the Internet, they are exposed to far too many risks [23]. Corporations and organisations need to know these risks and assess them, as in many occasions they may constitute the core part of their lifecycle or because they need these systems to operate. Apart from several measures, like auditing, penetration tests etc., security analysts need to know how adversaries try to hack their systems and study their behavior, knowledge, etc. Cybersecurity capabilities are essential for achieving individual organisations' and societies' goals, even more so in the globalized and connected world.

This vital knowledge demands a lot of manual work to deploy such a system, but most importantly, a lot of knowledge and analysis to extract the attack patterns and determine their impact [24–26]. YAKSHA aims to automate a big part of this procedure and distribute this information to peers. For many reasons, most companies and organisations are not able to create such analytics for their systems, so YAKSHA can become the first such system to automatically provide such features. Therefore, the technological experience and knowhow of the EU is "matched" with the wide deployments of ASEAN countries to develop and field test the solution.

In addition, YAKSHA intends to provide an automated framework for deploying honeypots and correlating the collected information. The essential goal is to enable end-users, whether they are governments, organisations or companies, to easily setup customised honeypots, which will allow them to understand how their systems are being attacked on the wild, in an autonomous way.

Acknowledgments. The paper has been based on the context of the *"YAKSHA" ("Cybersecurity Awareness and Knowledge Systemic High-level Application")* Project, funded by the EC under the Grant Agreement (GA) No. 780498.

References

1. Symantec: 2019 Internet Security Threat Report (ISTR), vol. 24. Symantec Corporation (2019)
2. Trustwave: 2019 Trustwave Global Security Report. Trustwave (2019)
3. European Union Agency for Network and Information Security: Threat Landscape Report 2018: 15 Top Cyberthreats and Trends. ENISA (2018). https://www.enisa.europa.eu/publications/enisa-threat-landscape-report-2018
4. YAKSHA (Cybersecurity Awareness and Knowledge Systemic High-level Application) H2020 Project, GA No. 780498. http://project-yaksha.eu
5. Spitzner, L.: Honeypots: Tracking Hackers. Addison-Wesley Reading, Boston (2003)
6. Balamurugan, M., Poornima, S.C.B.: Honeypot as a service in cloud. In: Proceedings of the 9th International Conference on Web Services Computing (ICWSC) 2011, pp. 39–43. IEEE (2011)

7. Mokube, I., Adams, M.: Honeypots: concepts, approaches, and challenges. In: Proceedings of the 45th ACM Southeast Conference (ACM-SE), pp. 321–326. ACM (2007)

8. Gandotra, E., Bansal, D., Sofat, S.: Malware analysis and classification: a survey. J. Inf. Secur. **5**(02), 56–64 (2014)

9. Kumar Jain, Y., Singh, S.: Honeypot based secure network system. Int. J. Comput. Sci. Eng. **3**(2), 612–620 (2011)

10. McGrew, R.: Experiences with honeypot systems: development, deployment, and analysis. In: Proceedings of the 39th Hawaii International Conference on Systems Science (HICSS 2006), vol. 9, p. 220a. IEEE (2006)

11. Zhang, F., Zhou, S., Qin, Z., Liu, J.: Honeypot: a supplemented active defense system for network security. In: Parallel & Distributed Computing Applications and Technologies, pp. 231–235 (2003)

12. Parker, M.: Why honeypot technology is no longer effective, CSO (2015). https://www.cso.com.au/article/576966/why-honeypot-technology-no-longer-effective/

13. Chin, W.Y., Markatos, E.P., Antonatos, S., Ioannidis, S., et al.: HoneyLab: large-scale honeypot deployment and resource sharing. In: Proceedings of the 3rd International Conference on Network and System Security (NSS), pp. 381–388. IEEE (2009)

14. Bringer, M.L., et al.: A survey: recent advances and future trends in honeypot research. Int. J. Comput. Netw. Inf. Secur. **10**, 63–75 (2012)

15. Mitchell, A.: An intelligent honeypot. Thesis, Cork Institute of Technology, May 2018

16. Holz, T.: Learning more about attack patterns with honeypots. In: Proceedings of Sicherheit 2006, pp. 30–41. Informatik e.v. (GI) (2006)

17. Kovaliuk, D.O., Huza, K.M., Kovaliuk, O.O.: Development of SCADA system based on web technologies. Int. J. Inf. Eng. Electron. Bus. **10**(2), 25–32 (2018)

18. Sun, B., Fujino, A., Mori, T., Takahashi, T., Inoue, D.: Automatically generating malware analysis reports using sandbox logs. IEICE Trans. Inf. Syst. **E101D**(11), 2622–2632 (2018)

19. Liao, H.-J., et al.: Intrusion detection system: a comprehensive review. J. Netw. Comput. Appl. **36**(1), 16–24 (2013)

20. Jicha, A., Patton, M., Chen, H.: SCADA honeypots: an in-depth analysis of Conpot. In: Proceedings of the IEE 19th International Conference on Intelligent and Security Informatics (ISI), pp. 196–198. IEEE (2016)

21. YAKSHA project: Deliverable 2.1: Data Collection Methodology, June 2018

22. Commission of the European Communities: Horizon 2020 Work Programme 2016–2017. http://ec.europa.eu/research/participants/data/ref/h2020/wp/2016_2017/main/h2020-wp1617-intro_en.pdf

23. European Union Agency for Network and Information Security: Threat Taxonomy. ENISA (2016). https://www.enisa.europa.eu/topics/threat-risk-management/threats-and-trends/enisa-threat-landscape/threat-taxonomy/at_download/file

24. Mairh, A., Barik, D., Verma, K., Jena, D.: Honeypot in network security: a survey. In: Proceedings of the 2011 International Conference on Communication, Computing & Security (ICCCS), pp. 600–605. Elsevier (2011)

25. Shamsi, J.A., Zeadally, S., Sheikh, F., Flowers, A.: Attribution in cyberspace: techniques and legal implications. Secur. Commun. Netw. **9**(15), 2886–2900 (2016)

26. Egele, M., Scholte, T., Kirda, E., Kruegel, C.: A survey on automated dynamic malware-analysis techniques and tools. ACM Comput. Surv. (CSUR) **44**(2), 6, 1–42 (2012)

Threat Landscape of Next Generation IoT-Enabled Smart Grids

Theodoros Mavroeidakos$^{(\boxtimes)}$ and Vasilis Chaldeakis

Hellenic Telecommunications Organization S.A., 99 Kifissias Avenue, Athens, Greece
tmavroeid@ote.gr, vchaldeak@cosmote.gr
http://www.ote.gr

Abstract. The Smart Grids (SGs) consist of an emerging paradigm that pave the way for the power grids' modernization and seek novel techniques for improving the transmittion and distribution of power to consumers, as well as achieving end- to-end real-time governance. Thus, the prospect of SGs are to behave intelligently, through the deployment of advanced technologies, applications and standards. A subset of such technologies and applications consists of Software Defined Netowrks (SDNs), Cloud Computing (CC), Machine-to-Machine (M2M) communications, Big Data applications, Internet-of-Things (IoT), 5G and wireless standards such as IEEE 802.15.4g and IEEE 802.16.1. The SGs, the CC and the IoT paradigms' convergence lie on satisfying the clients' needs, improving efficiency and in the same time maintaining overall control. However, the coupling of diverse technologies under a unified architecture raise multiple interdependencies which pose new challenges, ranging from the reliability of the whole power system to novel cyber-security risks. This paper sheds new light in the overall definition of the threat landscape that emerges by the convergence of CC and IoT in a SG.

Keywords: Smart Grid · IoT · Cloud Computing · Threat landscape

1 Introduction

Electricity is the most valuable resource of social structure supporting the operation of health care, banking, means of transportation and the provision of public utilities such as natural gas and water. Electricity is generated on large power plants consisting of steam, hydro and combustion turbines which require energy sources such as water, oil, coal, gas and thereupon the produced energy is routed into an interconnected high voltage transmission network. Following its generation, it is transferred through a series of distribution transformers to the consumers. The power transmission network has progressively developed for over a century, from the original design of local low-voltage DC networks, to AC three-phase high voltage networks deployed over Supervisory Control and Acquisition (SCADA) System and eventually to modern massive interconnected networks with various voltage levels and complex electrical components such as

© IFIP International Federation for Information Processing 2020
Published by Springer Nature Switzerland AG 2020
I. Maglogiannis et al. (Eds.): AIAI 2020 Workshops, IFIP AICT 585, pp. 116–127, 2020.
https://doi.org/10.1007/978-3-030-49190-1_11

substation transformers and Phasor Measurement Units (PMUs). Throughout the power grid's evolution, several industrial challenges have been dealt in view of provisioning power to the customer premises fast and uninterruptedly. In light of the SG's technological innovations and novel communication links amongst its architectural components, the security risk is increased due to the expansion of the points of interests from the attackers' perspective.

Nowadays, the complexity of power grid is multifaceted and depends on the interconnection of heterogeneous electrical and electronic components, the integration of Renewable Energy Resources (RES), the Energy Management System (EMS), the Distribution Management System (DMS), the Intelligent Electronic Devices (IEDs) and systems operations. Furthermore, in view of encountering periods of peak demand, the Transmission System Operator (TSO) balances supply and demand across the transmission network by deploying automation systems. The automation and control capabilities of transmission and distribution networks, add a new layer of complexity that burdens the power grid with new challenges concerning reliability and performance.

By exploiting the emergence of telemetry technologies, the already deployed conventional static networks controlled so far by SCADA systems, evolve into modern and dynamic smart grids. The SGs' telemetry technologies, lead to the deployment and control of energy sources such as wind, solar, geothermal, which pave the way for disburdening the strained power grid suffering from serious problems such as power outages, voltage drops and overloads, leading to greatly reduce power quality. To this end, SGs are comprised of many moving parts leading to the challenge that the exposure of a component may result to cascading failures across the power grid.

The correlation of SDNs, CC, M2M, IoT, 5G and Big Data on SGs, as well as the insufficiencies residing on previous conventional cyber-security models that are utilized on power grids compel the industry and the relevant national authorities to advise upon safeguards and best practices to encounter vulnerabilities and security risks. On the grounds that the power grid's role is very important for the social structure, the SGs' security safeguards and measures, should be treated with caution and be placed high in the priority hierarchy set by the organizational operations. To this end, security challenges, threats and requirements should be classified side by side with performance and functionality issues prior the SG's deployment.

2   Background

In recent years there has been growing interest in threat analysis and security model propositions in support of SG infrastructure. The current threat landscape of SGs is largely addressed by standards and solutions both by the academia and the industry, as described below. However, the next generation SGs are characterized by the addition of new technologies that introduce novel threats.

A systematic study on cyber security guidelines for smart grid was conducted by the National Institute of Standards and Technology (NIST) aiming to close the gaps, scrutinizes security requirements, a framework for assessing risks, an evaluation of privacy issues, and additional information about strategies to protect the modern power grids from their attack surface. This study was later reviewed due to the emergence of novel technologies and standards [11]. Following the initial approach of NIST, the European Network and Information Security Agency (ENISA) puts forward 10 recommendations, in order to resolve concerns about cyber-security in modernized power grids consisting of a SGs [14]. These recommendations provided practical advice aimed at improving current initiatives, raising awareness, developing new countermeasures and good practices with scope to reduce barriers, which are encountered amidst the sharing of information intelligence. More work on securing SGs has been carried out by ENISA in [6,19], where the cyber security certification process of the SG is analysed and several aspects of it are scrutinized such as, architectural guidelines, recommendations and good practices.

In a cutting edge survey, Mahmud et al. [13], presented a classification of attacks on the communication networks of SGs and henceforth proposed a security framework for the SG's metering infrastructure which consists of a variety of requirements that ensure effective preservation of the Confidentiality, Integrity and Availability (CIA) triad. A more recent survey, Tong et al. [22], highlights the role of Intrusion Detection Systems on Advanced Metering Infrastructure (AMI) by analysing the attack surface, penetration techniques and consequences in AMI components. Then, security recommendations and guidelines are proposed on the basis of designing an IDS architecture suitable for AMI.

According to [8], a cyber-physical security framework that incorporates Cyber-Physical System (CPS) aspects into the security aspects is proposed for the protection of SGs. The framework captures the methodology behind attacking scenarios and their consequences on the physical domain of a CPS and accordingly effective controls and solutions can be deployed to eliminate cyber-physical attacks. With regards to [2], a breakdown of security and energy big data analytics issues is carried out with scope to determine critical attacks based on malware targeting metering data and big data from the distributed databases. Over and above this, Pour et al., argue in [18] about the vulnerabilities of SG infrastructure (i.e. the lack of standards and regulations), different kinds of attacks in the system (i.e. false data injection attack) and countermeasures (i.e. IP fast hopping mechanism) to increase the security level of the future power grid.

3   Next Generation Smart Grid Apparatus

3.1   Smart Grid Infrastructure

The SG apparatus upon which the core idea of this paper is illustrated, has developed on the basis of the Smart Grid Architecture Model (SG-AM) framework which is the reference architecture of SG use cases. The SG-AM framework consists of five interoperability layers namely, Business, Functions, Information, Communications and Components. Each one of these layers address different aspects of SG and encompass services, operations, assets and devices in support of the power grid's functionality.

Across the SG, the main architectural element is the communication infrastructure which interconnects the interoperability layers of the SG-AM framework architecture and comprises of four networking sectors as indicated in Fig. 1 the core or backbone network, the middle-mile or backhaul network, the last-mile or access network and the Premises Area Network (PAN). The four interconnected sectors are supported by various technologies and substantially aggregate the communication infrastructure of SG.

- The core network supports the link between the numerous substations and the seats of public utilities.
- The backhaul network bridges data concentrators to the AMI with distribution automation systems and control centers related to the operation of public utilities. This sector provides broadband following a cost-efficient economy concerning its deployment and operation. In addition, the communication paths through which operational and sensorial data traverse, must be flexible and uninterrupted. To that end, this network may be owned and managed by operators and may utilize wired or wireless technologies such as Wi-Fi, WiMAX and mobile networks such as LTE and 5G.
- The last-mile network is supported by Neighborhood Area Network (NAN) and the Field Area Network (FAN), as well as the AMI. This network facilitates the collection of data from smart energy meters and their propagation to the concentrators back to the control center of AMI.
- The PAN is implemented by Home Area Networks (HANs), which are based on IEEE 802.15.4, IEEE 802.11 and PLC standards. The HAN regulate several components such as thermostats, HVAC (heating, ventilation and air conditioning), smart devices, lighting control, home automation and PHEV/EV (Plug-in Hybrid Electric Vehicle/Electric Vehicle).

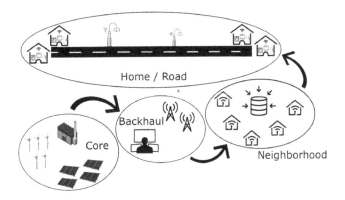

Fig. 1. Smart grid infrastructure

3.2   Cloud Computing Infrastructure

By virtue of the distributed nature of SG's communication infrastructure and the multiple data generation sources, it is required a highly scalable and elastic computing infrastructure in order to support the deployment of industrial applications. The CC infrastructure is the best computing structure in the case of SG due to the fact that provides scalable storage, appropriate processing capabilities for data analysis and cost-efficient services throughout the SG's operation. Moreover, this paradigm can handle the data generation rhythm of sensors, actuators and IoT devices in general.

The most useful applications in the context of SG, are big data analytics and remote control of components such as PMUs. The CC paradigm offers ideal conditions for the deployment of big data applications. The integration of CC applications in the operations of SGs, is comprised by development of big data Application Programming Interfaces (APIs), implementation of interoperability standards that will link the already deployed computing infrastructure with the CC applications, as well as configuration of the SG's components.

3.3   IoT Infrastructure

Cellular technology has been continually evolving with the aim of unlocking new possibilities to the industry. The advent of the Low-Power Wide-Area Network (LPWAN) technologies serve the IoT paradigm; therefore this paradigm's integration in a SG architecture is supported by LPWAN equipment and protocols.

The IoT infrastructure resides at the edge of the SGs and consists of four layers [1], namely the perception, the network, the processing and the application. The network layer is the SG's PAN, which facilitates governance over IoT devices deployed in houses. Across the SG, the intermediate link between the IoT devices and the SC controller, is the smart meter. Beyond the time-based consumption data, billing interval data and data related to the clients' usage history resulted by the smart meters operation, the IoT devices generate huge streams of data daily. Thus, many measurements and logs may be concentrated in Data Lakes residing in the backend CC environment.

4   Threat Landscape

4.1   Smart Grid Attacks

The attack vectors and threats that emerge in the Next Generation SG apparatus can be classified in the following categories as illustrated also in Fig. 2: [5,14,15, 17,20,24]:

- *Physical Layer Attacks:* The interference channel is one of the most effective ways to initiate a physical-layer DoS attack, especially for wireless communications. The intruders only need to connect to communication channels where it is easy to unleash DoS attacks on the physical layer. In SGs, where wireless technologies are used, the main objective is to achieve wireless interference.

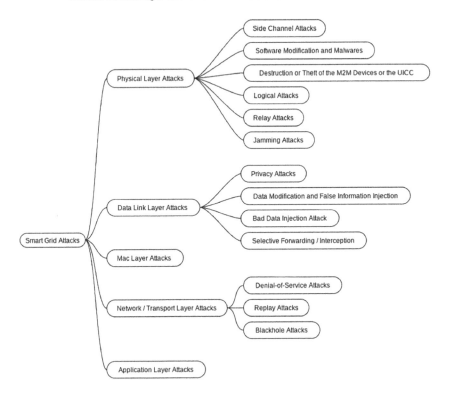

Fig. 2. Smart grid attacks

- *Side Channel Attacks:* M2Ms are located in accessible locations that attackers can easily access and perform attack on the channel side. These attacks could be based on any power consumption, timing information, error or electromagnetic leakage and allow the recovery of secret keys.
- *Software Modification and Malwares:* Software modifications can be performed by an attacker, or even a malicious user, affecting the expected operation of M2M devices. Malicious users can do so in order to reduce the amount of fees they have to pay. But the impact of these threats is even worse when it comes to e-health or automotive applications.
- *Destruction or Theft of the M2M Device or the Universal Integrated Circuit Card (UICC):* M2M or UICC devices can be easily stolen because they are placed in accessible locations. However, this is somewhat solved by welding the integrated UICC known as eUICC to the M2M.
- *Logical Attacks:* Targeting the correct operation of the system without changes to the device software when dealing with M2M communications, an intruder may forge the identity of a back-end server, an M2M device or a gateway, and so on. These attacks can lead to significant economic and human losses. For example, an attacker who manages to forge a smart gauge identity can make his owner pay for the charges himself without

his permission. In the case of electronic health, such attacks can pose a threat to human life.

- *Relay Attacks:* An attacker can carry out an attack and disguise an entity to make others believe it is in the sender or receiver area. This attack can target the device, gateway or network domain.
- *Jamming Attacks:* This attack is channel-based in which the legitimate signal is overwhelmed by noise [21].
- *Data Link Layer Attacks:* In this layer, the attackers target the exchange of intra-operational information.
  - *Privacy Attacks:* Because of the deployment models followed on M2M architecture concerning the utilized equipment in its device domain, malicious users can invade M2M devices and thus infer user habits, but also tamper with Personally Identifiable Information (PII).
  - *Data Modification and False Information Injection:* The data may be violated during transport, as well as in a resting state of an application's device or server. Taking into account the case of e-Health or e-Call, modifying the measured values of information tracking can endanger the lives of people. On the other hand, in some applications, the introduction of false data can cause financial losses.
  - *Bad Data Injection Attacks:* This attack aims at making inferences of the power network topology from the correlations in line measurements using independent component analysis. The inference results can then be utilized to design stealth attacks [7].
  - *Selective Forwarding/Interception:* An attacker can track and delay or intercept the received packets. The impact of such a threat depends on the content of rejected packages. Such attacks are launched from the network infrastructure, but they could also be carried out by the M2M gateway.
- *Mac Layer Attacks:* Through the Mac Layer, reliable point-to-point communication is achieved. An attacker (e.g., a dangerous device) can deliberately modify MAC parameters and have better opportunities for network access and downgrading the performance of others who share the same communications channel. Therefore, Mac Layer can lead to a weak version of DoS attacks. In Smart Grid, spoofing is a relatively harmful threat to the MAC layer because it targets both availability and integrity. An attacking spoofing, can be disguised as another device and send false information to other devices.
- *Network/Transport Layer Attacks:* Under the TCP/IP protocol, these two layers must provide audit reliability for providing information on a multi-hop communications network. Due to the fact that SGs are comprized by multiple internal and external networks (e.g. core, backhaul, last-mile, etc.), attacking methodology can be realized remotely or localy.
  - *Denial-of-Service (DoS):* DoS attacks targeting the network and transport layers can significantly degrade the end-to-end communication between the systems and the end-users, by flooding the network with illegitimate network traffic.

- *Replay Attacks:* The Killerbee framework can be utilized to target security vulnerabilities existing in ZigBee and IEEE 802.15.4 networks. This framework enables exploitation of in-band signaling mechanisms in digital radio protocols. To stage a replay attack, interception of network traffic should be implemented in order to delay or misdirect it; therefore the networks deployed closer to the clients are far more susceptible to this type of attack.
- *Blackhole Attacks:* This attack threatens the smart meters; following it, several measurements gathered in the clients' premises never reach the SG core infrastructure leading to billing or logistics inconsistencies.
- *Application Layer Attacks:* These attacks focus primarily on damaging the bandwidth of communication channels. However, over and above their primary goal, they also intend to exhaust computing resources, such as CPU or Input/Output (I/O) bandwidth. Moreover, attacks against integrity and confidentiality generally occur in the application layer and enable the manipulation of information. Attacks to data integrity can be considered less violent than DoS. These attacks attempt to disclose data in order to disturb the exchange of information across the SG.
  - *Social Network Misinformation:* This attack focuses on diffusing misinformation in social networks in order to damage the SG's operations as illustrated in [16] by leveraging the Misinformation Attack Problem in Social-smart grid (MAPSS).

4.2   Cloud Attacks

The most daunting CC threats are associated to data loss, interception and tampering with the network traffic, insecure Application Programming Interfaces (APIs), malicious insiders, hijacking of virtualization technologies and threats against the end-services confidentiality, integrity and availability.

Due to the existence of multiple abstraction layers on any given CC infrastructure, the cloud consumers acquire access in-depth for the purpose of the end-services utilization. In the context of this paper, the cloud consumers are the personnel of the SG provider but also the IoT devices. To this end, the attackers leverage a huge number of attacks, aiming to target different points of the CC infrastructure. Despite the large number of attacks against CC, the impact and the risk of successful penetrations in SG assisted by CC and IoT, is greater.

Overall, following the initial stages of any attack (e.g. passive and active information gathering), the attackers are in position to coordinate their penetration methodology by exploiting vulnerabilities across the whole infrastructure. To this end, new attack vectors emerge due to the conjunction of these technologies and as a result the threats' impact on the end-service, is hazardous.

A taxonomy of threats [9,10] targeting the industrial environment of SGs where CC solutions are utilized is the following:

- *SQL Injection:* In this attack, malicious queries target the production database aiming to gain unauthorized access.

- *Malware Injection:* In this attack, malicious code is implanted in legitimate software or systems aiming to give remote Control & Command to the attacker in order to control services and extract data.
- *XML Signature Wrapping:* The SOAP protocol facilitates communication amongst different systems. The communication is secured by XML signatures where vulnerabilities can be exploited.
- *Deep Packet Inspection:* In this attack, analysis of internal and external network traffic is performed with scope to acquire sensitive network information about the data circulating the network architecture.
- *Denial of Service:* In this attack, the policies of CC services concerning scalability and elasticity are leveraged maliciously in order to misuse the CC resources and exhaust them.
- *Eavesdropping:* In this attack, network information is captured and malicious actions such as interruption of network packets propagation to reach their destination.

4.3   IoT Attacks

The security issues and concerns surrounding the IoT, occur as a consequence of threats emerging due to unaccounted vulnerabilities and 0-day exploits extended both on hardware and software, sensitive data circulating the IoT architecturte (i.e. clinical health data, spatial data) and weak communication paths facilitating interconnection of sensors and devices through a diversity of protocols and standards.

The majority of IoT attacks are based on the weaponization of Proof of Concepts (PoC) exploits with malicious payloads against known vulnerabilities. Many vulnerabilities are left unpatched due to performance, cost related issues, or because of the fact that the implementation of proper security controls on IoT devices is a costly process requiring part of the limited energy resources.

The most dangerous IoT attacks, focusing on vulnerabilities laying on the paradigm itself, are classified in the following categories:

- *Malware:* is malicious software that hijacks the sensors' functions and spreads in the IoT infrastructure in order to gather operational intelligence, which can be leveraged to exploit critical components linked to the IoT devices such as smart meters. Having integrated IoT devices in the SG, several malwares capable to damage both the clients and the SG provider. For example, the IoT reaper was a malware botnet that gathers and assesses information in order to use ideal exploits with regard to the discovered vulnerabilities. Already infected two million devices and growing at rate of 10,000 new devices per day.
- *Botnet:* is a network of infected devices spread across the world and controlled remotely from a master following the client-server architecture. For example, the Mirai was a self-replicating and self-propagating botnet worm based on telnet scanning, which launches Distributed Denial-of-Service (DDoS) attacks and targets Linux-based embedded systems such as IP cameras, home routers

and home automations simiral to those, which are met in an industrial environment such as SGs, where the same principles are applied. Since its source code publication, many blackhat groups utilize it in the midst of malware development. The Botnets can be utilized by the master not only for DDoS, but also to achieve cascading failures in the SG, leading even to physical damages (i.e. stuxnet).

- *Ransomware:* targets data storage both in the IoT and CC paradigm and blocks access to the collected data by encrypting them. A good example of ransomware is CryptoWall that generates and stores a key on the backend IoT infrastructure and then sends the key to Command-and-Control (C&C) server which is behind a proxy chain and controlled by the attacker. Moreover, the Curve-Tor-bitcoin Locker (CTB-Locker) uses AES encryption by compression step using ZLib and communicates with the C&C server through proxy websites (Tor2web).

Having overviewed these attacks, there are several threats that emerge by the adoption of Narrowband 5G and the mesh topology of IoT devices. A synopsis of threats and attacks is presented.

- *Physical Layer Attacks on 5G:* In this layer several threats exist [12], which exploit vulnerabilities of the physical channel over which the communication paths between devices are established.
  - *Selectively Jamming PSS/SSS:* Similar to the Long-Term Evolution (LTE) standard, the 5G also consists of the Primary Synchronization Signal (PSS) and the Secondary Synchronization Signal (SSS) which can be interrupted by a jammer transmitting fake signals with greater power immitating those.
  - *Sniffing and Spoofing Vulnerability of the PBCH:* The Physical Broadcast Channel (PBCH) is utilized by the System Information Block (SIB) messages, which overlay information about the power thresholds responsible for the handover process of a device from a cell to another. The information that the SIB messages carry, is transmitted unencrypted, leaving it vulnerable to malicious acivities.
- *Network Attacks [3]:*
  - *Traffic Analysis:* In this attack, network information is captured and analysed in order to acquire useful information about the operation of the IoT architecture.
  - *Sleep Deprivation:* This type of attack targets to the power reserves of wireless nodes by keeping them busy with useless request which are broadcasted recursively by the perpetrator.
  - *Sybil:* This attack lies on exploiting the identity verification process of Wireless Sensor Networks (WSNs) where the malicious node disguises its identity with multiple others.
  - *Resource Consumption:* In this attack, the main aim is to degrade the network's latency and capacity by broadcasting Route Request (RREQ) packets.

- *Key Reinstallation Attacks (KRACKs)*: In this series of attacks, the propagated network packets are captured and then are decrypted [23]. Most of
  WiFi devices are vulnerable of installing zero encryption key, this is feasible due to a fault in the WPA2 protocol. Upon this fault, the KRACKs
  are enabled during 4-way handshakes of IoT devices with the network
  Access Point (AP).
- *Man in the Middle:* In this attack, interception of data flowing from a
  source to a destination is implemented by the attacker in order to read
  them and extrack useful knowledge. In several occasions, the attacker
  focuses on modifying the data in-transit from the source to the destination.
- *Kr00k*: This attack leverages a bug in order to decrypt the WiFi network
  traffic [4]. Many IoT devices are equiped with Broadcom and Cypress wifi
  chips', which are affected by this bug. According to this bug, a short wifi
  disconnection, called disassociation, is enforced by the attackers leading
  the devices to reset the session key which can be all-zero.

5   Conclusion and Future Work

This work scrutinizes the threat landscape that exist in next generation SGs.
The main point to focus is that there is a huge number of attack vectors against
a next generation SG due to its architectural components and its distributed
functionality. By summarizing the majority of threats, proper security guidelines
would be possible to be set up in order to protect modern applications on top of
SGs. Future reaserch should focus on analysing the majority of these attacks in
depth for the purpose of formulating ideal security measures that will mitigate
this landscape.

References

1. Ali, I., Sabir, S., Ullah, Z.: Internet of things security, device authentication and
   access control: a review. arXiv preprint arXiv:1901.07309 (2019)
2. Chin, W.L., Li, W., Chen, H.H.: Energy big data security threats in IoT-based
   smart grid communications. IEEE Commun. Mag. **55**(10), 70–75 (2017)
3. Deogirikar, J., Vidhate, A.: Security attacks in IoT: a survey. In: 2017 International
   Conference on I-SMAC (IoT in Social, Mobile, Analytics and Cloud) (I-SMAC),
   pp. 32–37. IEEE (2017)
4. ESET INTERNET SECURITY: a serious vulnerability deep inside Wi-Fi encryption. https://www.eset.com/int/kr00k/. Accessed 28 Feb 2020
5. European Union Agency for Network and Information Security (ENISA): Ad-
   hoc & sensor networking for M2M communications - threat landscape and good
   practice guide. https://www.enisa.europa.eu/publications/m2m-communications-
   threat-landscape. Accessed 27 Feb 2020
6. European Union Agency for Network and Information Security (ENISA): Smart
   grid security certification in Europe challenges and recommendations. https://
   www.enisa.europa.eu/publications/smart-grid-security-certification-in-europe.
   Accessed 27 Feb 2020

7. Huang, Y., et al.: Bad data injection in smart grid: attack and defense mechanisms. IEEE Commun. Mag. **51**(1), 27–33 (2013)
8. Humayed, A., Lin, J., Li, F., Luo, B.: Cyber-physical systems security–a survey. IEEE Internet Things J. **4**(6), 1802–1831 (2017)
9. Islam, T., Manivannan, D., Zeadally, S.: A classification and characterization of security threats in cloud computing. Int. J. Next-Gener. Comput. **7**(1) (2016)
10. Khan, N., Al-Yasiri, A.: Cloud security threats and techniques to strengthen cloud computing adoption framework. In: Cyber Security and Threats: Concepts, Methodologies, Tools, and Applications, pp. 268–285. IGI Global (2018)
11. Lee, A.: Guidelines for smart grid cyber security. NIST Interagency/Internal Report Revision 1, pp. 15–26 (2016)
12. Lichtman, M., Rao, R., Marojevic, V., Reed, J., Jover, R.P.: 5G NR jamming, spoofing, and sniffing: threat assessment and mitigation. In: 2018 IEEE International Conference on Communications Workshops (ICC Workshops), pp. 1–6. IEEE (2018)
13. Mahmud, R., Vallakati, R., Mukherjee, A., Ranganathan, P., Nejadpak, A.: A survey on smart grid metering infrastructures: threats and solutions. In: 2015 IEEE International Conference on Electro/Information Technology (EIT), pp. 386–391. IEEE (2015)
14. Mattioli, R., Moulinos, K.: Communication network interdependencies in smart grids. In: EUA FNAI Security, (ed.) EU: ENISA (2015)
15. Nazir, S., Patel, S., Patel, D.: Assessing and augmenting scada cyber security: a survey of techniques. Comput. Secur. **70**, 436–454 (2017)
16. Pan, T., et al.: Threat from being social: vulnerability analysis of social network coupled smart grid. IEEE Access **5**, 16774–16783 (2017)
17. Pidikiti, D.S., Kalluri, R., Kumar, R.S., Bindhumadhava, B.: Scada communication protocols: vulnerabilities, attacks and possible mitigations. CSI Trans. ICT **1**(2), 135–141 (2013)
18. Pour, M.M., Anzalchi, A., Sarwat, A.: A review on cyber security issues and mitigation methods in smart grid systems. In: SoutheastCon 2017, pp. 1–4. IEEE (2017)
19. Ruland, K.C., Sassmannshausen, J., Waedt, K., Zivic, N.: Smart grid security–an overview of standards and guidelines. e&i Elektrotech. Informationstechnik **134**(1), 19–25 (2017)
20. Sanjab, A., Saad, W., Guvenc, I., Sarwat, A., Biswas, S.: Smart grid security: threats, challenges, and solutions. arXiv preprint arXiv:1606.06992 (2016)
21. Tazi, K., Abdi, F., Abbou, M.F.: Review on cyber-physical security of the smart grid: attacks and defense mechanisms. In: 2015 3rd International Renewable and Sustainable Energy Conference (IRSEC), pp. 1–6. IEEE (2015)
22. Tong, W., Lu, L., Li, Z., Lin, J., Jin, X.: A survey on intrusion detection system for advanced metering infrastructure. In: 2016 Sixth International Conference on Instrumentation & Measurement, Computer, Communication and Control (IMCCC), pp. 33–37. IEEE (2016)
23. Vanhoef, M., Piessens, F.: Key reinstallation attacks: forcing nonce reuse in WPA2. In: Proceedings of the 2017 ACM SIGSAC Conference on Computer and Communications Security, pp. 1313–1328 (2017)
24. Wang, W., Lu, Z.: Cyber security in the smart grid: survey and challenges. Comput. Netw. **57**(5), 1344–1371 (2013)

Towards a Smart Port: The Role of the Telecom Industry

Christos-Antonios Gizelis[1]([⊠]) [iD], Theodoros Mavroeidakos[1] [iD],
Achilleas Marinakis[2] [iD], Antonis Litke[2] [iD], and Vrettos Moulos[2] [iD]

[1] Hellenic Telecommunications Organization S.A.,
99 Kifissias Avenue, Athens, Greece
cgkizelis@cosmote.gr, tmavroeid@ote.gr
[2] National (Metsovian) Technical University of Athens,
Patision Complex, Athens, Greece
{achmarin,litke,vrettos}@mail.ntua.gr
http://www.ote.gr, http://www.ece.ntua.gr

Abstract. Transformation is not only today's trend but also a reality.
Ports could not be excluded from that change. A transformation process
has been initiated in order to change their operational structure, and the
services they offer. Artificial Intelligent and Data oriented services push
the services's landscape beyond the traditional ones that are currently
used. The scope of this paper is to analyze and scrutinize the opportunities that are risen for Telecommunications/Information and Communication Technology (ICT) providers at ports. These opportunities are the
stepping stone towards the transformation of ports for the future. This
work in progress is under the DataPorts project that is funded by the
European Union's Horizon 2020 Research and Innovation Programme
under grant agreement No. 871493.

Keywords: Ports · Smart Ports · Data platforms · AI · Blockchain ·
Privacy

1 Introduction

"DataPorts project aims to boost the transition of European seaports from connected and digital to smart and cognitive, by providing a secure environment for
the aggregation and integration of data coming from different sources existing
in the digital ports and owned by diverse stakeholders, so that the whole port
community could benefit from this data in order to improve their processes, offer
new services and devise new AI based and data driven business models" [10]. For
this purpose, the technological innovation is destined to transform the business
as usual, therefore more and more companies hop on that huge wave in order to
avoid to be forgotten in the near future as it happened in well branded companies
in the past that did not see the need for change [16,20]. This massive transformation of the businesses has become more data-driven. Inevitable data owners

© IFIP International Federation for Information Processing 2020
Published by Springer Nature Switzerland AG 2020
I. Maglogiannis et al. (Eds.): AIAI 2020 Workshops, IFIP AICT 585, pp. 128–139, 2020.
https://doi.org/10.1007/978-3-030-49190-1_12

or those that can produce data have become the new major actors. The port industry is no exception and data-driven services is what they should offer, not in the future but today to their end-user, customers, stakeholder (many names exist to define them). According to Deloitte Port Services [3], Smart Ports is the fourth technological priority in improving and evolving the Shipping/Maritime Industry. By making a port smart, then AI-based services will offer cognitive services that will offer opportunities to Port owners, visitors, customers, etc.

Smart and Cognitive Ports is the newest trend and like the Smart Cities is a creation of a new emerging data market. It is a term that expands the traditional stakeholders' ecosystem with limitless opportunities for new entries. A multi-actor and very diverse ecosystem is created with many opportunities for market expansion, revenue increase, new services, especially data-driven ones such as Internet of Things (IoT) [30] and AI-based services. This rapid growing ecosystem with many actors and many roles creates the need for new and dynamic Business Models to fulfill the also rising needs. This opportunity was early identified by European Union in 2014 [29] and a special chapter was included within the Smart Cities one. "Ports are considered a special case of a Smart Community, then they have to meet the same requirements that are asked for a Smart City, adapted to the port situation".

Ports operate on a certain basis by following a number of models. They can be Public, where the administration is operated by a central authority at a national, regional or city level, or Private, a model that is run by a port company, or even a port (local) society and Hybrid where in this case, public-private partnerships govern the port administration and the provided services. Therefore, Port Authorities whether are Private, Public, or Hybrid, are "forced" to transform and create the Ports of the future, not only by creating an interconnection grid between them but offering new innovative services to their existing "customers" like companies in shipping, supply-chain and logistics, tourism, but also many more from a wide diversity areas, that they can take advantage from the new services. Therefore, Port Authorities create synergies with research community, data owners and providers, software-houses, startups and SMEs in order to, together create new innovative services and expand the list of the potential beneficiaries.

The need of Port Authorities has become an opportunity for port-oriented companies to experiment their wide range of services, algorithms, and data that they own and monetize their offerings in this new emerging market. It is an opportunity, which could be beneficial for numerous stakeholders. This opportunity increases the dynamics of the Smart Ports or Ports of the Future transformation.

The basis for port transformation lays within the co-operation that takes place between strategic partnerships at national and international level. To that we should add partnerships with port-oriented service 3rd parties. The new ecosystem that is created around the ports is highly competitive in order to increase their market share, and ports are trying to get an advantage by implementing smart technologies and services in order to optimize their operations in many areas such as energy, security, transport, logistics and more. Local Port Authorities gather around, numerous entities. Organizations, Associations, Companies that may be stakeholders and potentially beneficiaries of a data-oriented platform provided by DataPorts. The list can be endless if attempt to put everyone in the frame, but trying to pin-point the main ones we can identify synergies within Academia and Research Community, Shipping companies, SMEs and Startups, Public Authorities and Policy Makers, Data Providers, and Local Community Associations (Commercial, Tourism, Culture, etc.)

On the port transformation journey, the Telecommunication industry (also involved in ICT services) can have a significant role and perhaps become a key player towards the transformation success. Telecom (wired and wireless) hold the backbone of the data-driven environment [1, 2, 7] through their networks. Therefore, it is on their hand to become leaders in this rapidly increased emerging market. A Telecom/ICT Provider in order to enter this emerging ecosystem and potentially benefit from its growth should firstly address real-life data market use cases in Ports that are related to its areas of operations. The data that a Telecom Provider owns might not be directly usable by Ports' community and interoperability issues should be prior investigated. Data may be provided/shared through advanced AI-based services that are scalable, resilient and using a semantic approach. Data should be designed and provided in a matter that can be governed and maintained in a business manner. For these reasons, new business models and a standardized methodology like [21] should be defined and adopted respectively. Policies should be also taken under consideration so that a reliable data sharing and trading platform to be established. These design patterns should be obtained under a secure and trusted environment between stakeholder and beneficiaries, internal or external to the Port. Telecommunication industry owns, due to its field of operations, owns, handles and process large volumes of data, real and non-real time. Data that collected and stored from many different services. A Telecom Provider has the largest availability of customers' personal data, network data, mobility tracking, billing location, and so on. The correlation of such datasets, as well as the combination of them with external publicly available data, may potentially create a great value for solving problems and serving future needs. Since it is a new field of operations and due to the fact that until now such data sharing wasn't available for many different reasons, the value or what needs data can solve may be uncertain yet. According to the EU [29], it is estimated that the open data market is expected to increase by 37% by 2020, reaching €75.7 billion, with the cumulative figure of €325bn. Open data in Greece can generate an additional €3.2bn. GDP and approximately €12 billion in cumulative benefits within 5 years. That led researchers, and other related entities to be highly involved, in order benefit from these numbers.

2   Related Work

Every Port transformation was focused on different elements. From the Freight loading and uploading in the 1960s, the industrial port and the logistics in the

1980s. Today even with a tighter regulatory environment from the data sharing point of view, the element of transformation is the interoperability and how the ports of the future will become smart and cognitive. The research community and the port related actors are relative active during the last few years. European Authorities turned their attention into three points of action that could potentially affect and transform a Port; the supply, the Platform and the Demand. Various Port Management Platforms/Services/Applications/Systems, where created in order to cover these elements. Supply in order to monitor and handle the operations with the logistics companies, the shipping companies and the freight carriers. Port operations are monitored both for inbound and outbound activities, both equally demanding with different actors in each value chain. Several initiatives in European level, have taken place in the past and some of them are very active even today in order to create an ecosystem around the Ports. Actions of European Organizations and Associations such as ESPO [13], IAPH [15] and AIVP [28] aim to interconnect and represent Port Authorities and their relationships with EU and other States. They played a vital role in the global trade and practically can be considered as the pioneers of the Smart Ports. In addition to that, ENISA [11] developed - in collaboration with several EU ports - a report that intends to provide a useful information regarding the cybersecurity strategy of port authorities and terminal operators.

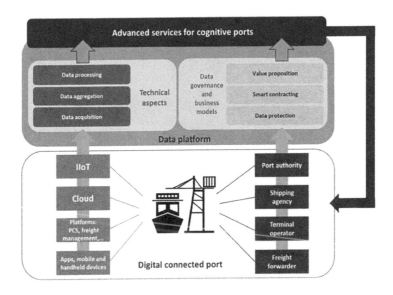

Fig. 1. DataPorts concept

Moreover, EU - especially through Horizon2020 programs - has funded numerous projects, that aim to create management platforms [17] for maritime and port environments, in order to create interoperability and eventually the ports to become cognitive and smart. Projects like SmartCities, among others, became The Marketplace of the European Innovation Partnership on Smart Cities and Communities [27]. The projects e-Mar, FLAGSHIP, and INMARE [9] handle maritime transport related issues, MASS [9] deals with ways to improve human behavior on board ships with special attention to emergency situations, MARINE-ABC [9] demonstrates the opportunities of the mobile ship-to-shore communication, BigDataStack [5] attempts to optimize cluster management for data operations, SmartShip [25] develops data analytics decision support systems and a circular economy based optimization platform. All the aforementioned and other projects prove that research community, port authorities, shipping and supply companies are aligned with a common objective which is the creation of a new ecosystem with advanced data-driven services for the benefit of the ports and the local communities. On top of that, European maritime sector through new calls is planning to offer efficient quality services integrated to the overall European transport system.

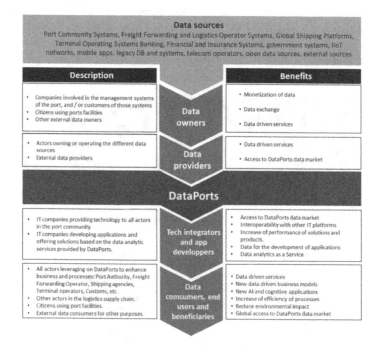

Fig. 2. DataPorts value-chain and stakeholders

DataPorts since January 2020 is planning to implement a data management platform to be operated by Port Authorities in order to provide advanced services (Fig. 1) and create a value-chain between stakeholders, internal and external ones (Fig. 2).

3   DataPorts Conceptualization

Data in the maritime domain is growing at an unprecedented rate, e.g., ter-
abytes of oceanographic data are collected every month as well as petabytes
of data are already publicly available. Big data from different sources such as
sensors, buoys, vessels, and satellites could potentially feed a large number of
interesting applications regarding environmental protection, security, shipping
routes optimization or cargo handling [18]. Although many projects [24,25] are
trying to develop data management platforms in various application domains,
not many of them have addressed integration in port environments with the
possibility of including cognitive services and extending their platform to whole
transportation routes around Europe.

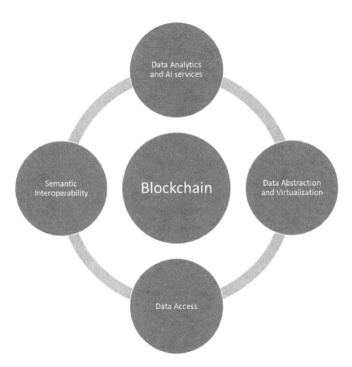

Fig. 3. DataPorts architecture

To this end, Fig. 3 presents the main building blocks of the DataPorts platform's proposed solution:

– Data Access: the platform will ensure access to the heterogeneous data
  sources of the port - including relational and NoSQL databases, object storage, publish/subscribe streams - in a common manner. To achieve this goal,
  the project will rely on widely adopted data formats and interface specifications, such as JSON [26] and OpenAPI [22] respectively.

- Semantic Interoperability: the project will develop a framework for semantic interoperability of diverse data platforms, autonomous systems and applications. Acting as a unifier, the framework will provide business level interoperability, in addition to data interoperability at the level of common spatial and temporal semantics.
- Data Abstraction and Virtualization: the platform will provide an abstraction layer that takes care of retrieving, processing and delivering the data with the proper quality level, while in parallel putting special emphasis on data security, performance, privacy and protection. This layer, acting as a middleware, will let the data consumers simply define their requirements on the needed data - expressed as data utility - and will take the responsibility for providing these data timely, securely and accurately by hiding the complexity of the underlying infrastructure. The latter could consist of different platforms, storage systems, and network capabilities. The orchestration of those (micro)services could be implemented via flow-based programming tools like Node-RED [23].
- Data Analytics and AI services: the project will develop a set of data analytics services for supporting the development of descriptive, predictive, prescriptive models using the different datasets available to the platform. Since the project will have to deal with big data technologies, the defined services should be scalable enough to process huge data volumes. Appropriate State-of-the-Art machine learning algorithms will be identified for supporting the development of cognitive applications in the context of the smart ports domain.
- Blockchain: the platform will provide all the tools for data sharing and trading in a secure and trusted manner. The specific building block should take into consideration the rules defined from data providers to data consumers. On top of that, it has to offer a clear value proposition to data owners. Data access mechanisms, based on purpose control, will also be established. As a result, the solution has to keep provenance of the data entering the platform and implement the functionalities of data governance. The project will exploit permissioned blockchain technology such as Hyperledger [14], in order to address all these requirements.

4 Challenges and Opportunities

As mentioned earlier in this paper, the emerging data market within ports is very appealing for a telecommunications provider due to the wide diversity and the large volumes of data that it owns or handles. Although a Telecom Company can benefit in many ways from being involved in such ecosystem and eventually create a new revenue stream [7,12], considerations should be taken into account, regarding the risks that come in front. Since it is a new marketplace, the legal and regulatory environment cannot be considered as stable. Entering a new area always demands careful business approaches. Since a main involvement contains data sharing, trust should also be taken into account, not only technological but also ethical which might cause otherwise losing a competitive advantage. Towards that direction, DataPorts project aims at designing a trusted marketplace in order to lower privacy barriers associated with the development of innovative data-intensive applications that consume personal data. The scope is to develop mechanisms that will encourage more and more people (travelers, employees, workers etc.), who so far seem to be reluctant, to share their personal utility and behavioral data. This is very likely to be achieved by keeping data subjects fully informed, including them as actual stakeholders and co-owners of the data archive. The goal is to find the balance between the level of risk the people are willing to take and the benefit they expect as users of a personal data platform; in other words, *data privacy versus data utility*. The fundamental concern of privacy protection is to prevent confidential data from being leaked. However, in the area of IoT and Big Data, some information about the dataset is desired to be revealed by design. Consequently, the quest is to quantify and control the leakage of sensitive information, so that it remains within a tolerated threshold, while allowing certain types of analytics to be performed. In the following paragraphs indicative techniques to fulfill the privacy requirements are presented:

Privacy and Compliance by Design

In fact, legislation and privacy norms are becoming increasingly strict, but IT solutions for addressing these issues are lacking. Part of the research in DataPorts project will be to provide solutions for logging and auditing access to sensitive data, modeling, managing and enforcing privacy and consent policies, as well as providing the ability to anonymize sensitive data. With such a solution in place, trust becomes a differentiator while auditing and compliance overhead is decreased for both the data processor and controller. As a result, the business challenge addressed is twofold; (i) the need to prove compliance to privacy and security laws, directives and norms in a more automated and systematic manner with less overhead and (ii) the desire to gain end user trust, encouraging the sharing of personal data and improving the quality of the data shared. The approach aims at providing tools and libraries for privacy and compliance by design and also offering such kind of solutions for existing applications without requiring changes to them. The goal is to make privacy and compliance part of the IT infrastructure and to ensure close coupling of all data with relevant consent and policies.

Privacy Through Data Fuzzification

In many occasions, people want to share not their actual data but (slightly) different one, trying to balance privacy and accuracy [8]. For example, residents do not wish to expose their exact location, for a variety of purposes, including privacy considerations and risk data leakage that could aid e.g. criminals to understand the occupancy pattern of their house. In the case of utility and behavioral data, the fuzzification could be multidimensional, in terms of space, time and aggregation of the data that are produced from all the smart devices.

Privacy-Enhanced Decentralized Blockchain-Based Storage System
The initial idea of the blockchain framework was a permissionless distributed database based on the Bitcoin Peer-2-Peer open-source protocol [6], maintaining a growing list of data records hardened against tampering and revision, even by its own operators. This network model protects users from most prevalent frauds like chargebacks or unwanted charges. DataPorts project aims at moving one step forward in the context of a data marketplace, strengthening the integrity of the framework in terms of privacy. In a decentralized blockchain architecture as such, a full copy of the blockchain contains - at any time - all records of every transaction ever completed in the network and in addition every block contains a hash of the previous block. This enables the blocks to be traced back even to the first one, known as "the genesis block", which makes computationally prohibitively difficult and impractical to modify a block once it is created, especially as the chain of subsequent blocks gets generated [4]. This will protect the privacy-restrictions defined by data subjects, against any possible alternation attempts.

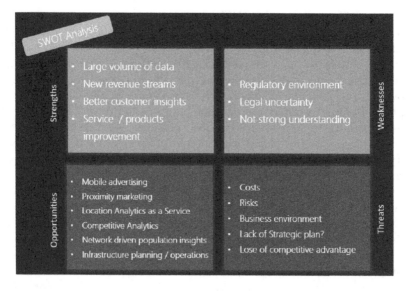

Fig. 4. Challenges & opportunities for telecom industry – a SWOT analysis

The data that is owned along with their process mechanisms, require Intellectual Property protection, especially within a regulatory complexity. Moreover, the development of data agreements and privacy concerns, as well as, a different than it is used so far, pricing model should be taken under consideration. Risks and potential harms of sharing corporate data, as well as, collecting inaccurate, old or "dirty" data might affect data quality. Since to most of the actions concerning data, the GDPR should be applied, collecting unauthorized data or intrusive collection from individuals and organizations could be a complex process. Therefore, improper or unauthorized access to shared data could cause conflicting legal jurisdictions and different security levels and in some cases loss of regulatory licenses, standards and certifications, reputational and industrial damages, as well as, drop in share price and/or increase in cost of capital. Moreover, incomplete or non-representative sampling, or insufficient, outdated or incompatible data sets can be disastrous, especially in the case where there are many recipients of this new data-sharing/trading platform.

Although someone might say that from all the above described parameters, the risk for a Telecom Provider is forbidding enough to enter this new data sharing/trading market, there is equally amount of opportunities to enter these Open data marketplaces [12, 19].

Business model opportunity	Example
1	**Product innovators** enhance their products and services with data	Incorporating smart lighting networks in ports through using data from motion sensors
2	**Systems Innovators** use data to integrate multiple product types	Creating a transport management system using diverse sources of data (weather sensors, motion sensors, etc.) and applying insights to multiple devices like bridges, quays, etc.
3	**Data Providers** gather and sell raw data without adding too much value to it	Data services like the Automatic identification System linked to GPS which offers insights in multiple aspects of ship movements like origin, destination, cargo, etc.
4	**Data Brokers** gather and combine data from multiple sources, create additional value with analytics and sell insights	Create market reports using multiple sources like order books and scrapping forecasts
5	**Value Chain Integrators** share data with system-integrator partners to extend product offerings or reduce costs	Improve the internal port supply chain with data shared by the port users
6	**Delivery Network Collaborators** share data to drive deal making, foster marketplaces and enable advertising	Foster the marketplace and drive deal making to a new level through novel insight driven business models

Fig. 5. Business opportunities [3]

As it is described in Figs. 4 and 5, it can be an opportunity for new business and increase in customer/subscribers base. In addition, can create an increased availability of vast and heterogeneous data ecosystems for AI and innovative data-driven business models, as well as, a way to tap into 'safe' personal data. Opportunities can also exist for the Telecom subscribers as well, by obtaining control over personal data. It is considered that the well-being and the quality of life benefits from personal data sharing in key sectors. Moreover, opportunities exist by accessing personalized and cross-sectoral B2C services and increasing the potential of personal data monetization. The entry of a Telecom data owner in this emerging data-driven market, creates opportunities for third parties as well. For academia, by increasing the socio-economic impact of research data across domains and borders, it creates an open innovation access through data marketplaces. Last but not least opportunities can be created in general for Government and Public Bodies thus improving the local economy. These bodies could include, among others, the Municipalities and the Regions that host the Ports. Common use of data through platforms can lead to improved governmental services, especially AI-enhanced digital services. These local and regional opportunities can also lead to an integrated real-time European analytics system exposing annual statistics of the ports ecosystem.

5   Conclusion and Future Work

A Telecom Provider can benefit from entering such rapidly evolving data market. As in every case, there are considerations and risks that should be taken into account. These parameters will be investigated during the Pilots' execution within DataPorts H2020 Project, where various data sets will be provided and used for cognitive applications. During the Piloting Phase, the value of the data and their governance methods will be thoroughly investigated.

References

1. Agarwal, V., Mittal, S., Mukherjea, S., Dalal, P.: Exploiting rich telecom data for increased monetization of telecom application stores. In: 2012 IEEE 13th International Conference on Mobile Data Management. IEEE, July 2012. https://doi.org/10.1109/mdm.2012.28
2. Banerjee, A.: Big data & advanced analytics in telecom: a multi-billion-dollar revenue opportunity. Heavy Reading, pp. 1–24 (2013)
3. Berns, S., Dickson, R., Vonck, I., Dragt, J.: Smart Ports (2017). https://www2.deloitte.com/content/dam/Deloitte/nl/Documents/energy-resources/deloitte-nl-er-port-services-smart-ports.pdf. Accessed 27 Feb 2020
4. Bheemaiah, K.: Why business schools need to teach about the blockchain. SSRN Electron. J. (2015). https://doi.org/10.2139/ssrn.2596465
5. BigDataStack H2020 Project. https://www.bigdatastack.eu. Accessed 27 Feb 2020
6. Bitcoin. https://bitcoin.org/en/. Accessed 27 Feb 2020
7. Bonneau, V.: Data monetisation: opportunities beyond OTT: finance, retail, telecom and connected objects. Commun. Strat. (97), 123 (2015)
8. COSMOS EU Project: End-to-end security and privacy: design and open specification (Final). https://cordis.europa.eu/project/id/609043/reporting. Accessed 27 Feb 2020
9. Danaos Shipping Co., Ltd. https://web2.danaos.gr/research/eu-projects/. Accessed 27 Feb 2020
10. DataPorts H2020 Project. http://dataports-project.eu. Accessed 27 Feb 2020
11. Drougkas, A., Sarri, A., Kyranoudi, P., Zisi, A.: Port cybersecurity - good practices for cybersecurity in the maritime sector, November 2019. https://www.enisa.europa.eu/publications/port-cybersecurity-good-practices-for-cybersecurity-in-the-maritime-sector. Accessed 27 Feb 2020
12. Ducruet, C. (ed.): Advances in Shipping Data Analysis and Modeling. Routledge, London (2017). https://doi.org/10.4324/9781315271446
13. European Sea Ports Organisation. https://www.espo.be/. Accessed 27 Feb 2020
14. Hyperledger Fabric. https://www.hyperledger.org/projects/fabric. Accessed 27 Feb 2020
15. International Association of Ports and Harbors. https://www.iaphworldports.org. Accessed 27 Feb 2020

16. Jovic, M., Kavran, N., Aksentijevic, S., Tijan, E.: The transition of croatian seaports into smart ports. In: 2019 42nd International Convention on Information and Communication Technology, Electronics and Microelectronics (MIPRO). IEEE, May 2019. https://doi.org/10.23919/mipro.2019.8757111

17. Kim, J., Son, J., Yoon, K.: An implementation of integrated interfaces for telecom systems and TMS in vessels. Int. J. Eng. Technol. **10**(2), 195–199 (2018). https://doi.org/10.7763/ijet.2018.v10.1058

18. Lytra, I., Vidal, M.E., Orlandi, F., Attard, J.: A big data architecture for managing oceans of data and maritime applications. In: 2017 International Conference on Engineering, Technology and Innovation (ICE/ITMC). IEEE, June 2017. https://doi.org/10.1109/ice.2017.8280019

19. Miele, S., Shockley, R.: Analytics: the real-world use of big data. Retrieved from IBM Institute for Business Value, Said Business School (2013)

20. Molavi, A., Lim, G.J., Race, B.: A framework for building a smart port and smart port index. Int. J. Sustain. Transp., 1–13 (2019). https://doi.org/10.1080/15568318.2019.1610919

21. Moulos, V., et al.: A robust information life cycle management framework for securing and governing critical infrastructure systems. Inventions **3**(4), 71 (2018). https://doi.org/10.3390/inventions3040071

22. OpenAPI Specification. https://github.com/OAI/OpenAPI-Specification/blob/master/versions/3.0.3.md. Accessed 04 Mar 2020

23. OpenJS Foundation, Node-RED tool. https://nodered.org/. Accessed 04 Mar 2020

24. PortForward H2020 Project. https://www.portforward-project.eu/. Accessed 27 Feb 2020

25. SmartShip H2020 Project. https://www.smartship2020.eu/. Accessed 27 Feb 2020

26. The JSON Data Interchange Syntax, 2nd edn., December 2017. http://www.ecma-international.org/publications/files/ECMA-ST/ECMA-404.pdf

27. The Marketplace of the European Innovation Partnership on Smart Cities and Communities. https://eu-smartcities.eu/. Accessed 27 Feb 2020

28. The Worldwide Network of Port Cities. http://www.aivp.org/en/. Accessed 27 Feb 2020

29. Volman, Y.: Report on open data, July 2019. https://ec.europa.eu/digital-single-market/en/open-data. Accessed 27 Feb 2020

30. Yang, Y., Zhong, M., Yao, H., Yu, F., Fu, X., Postolache, O.: Internet of things for smart ports: technologies and challenges. IEEE Instrum. Meas. Mag. **21**(1), 34–43 (2018). https://doi.org/10.1109/mim.2018.8278808

9th Mining Humanistic Data Workshop (MHDW 2020)

A Graph-Based Extension for the Set-Based Model Implementing Algorithms Based on Important Nodes

Nikitas-Rigas Kalogeropoulos, Ioannis Doukas, Christos Makris,
and Andreas Kanavos[✉]

Computer Engineering and Informatics Department,
University of Patras, Patras, Greece
{kalogeropo,doukas,makri,kanavos}@ceid.upatras.gr

Abstract. The purpose of this paper is the expansion of the set-based model, namely an information retrieval model, with the use of graphs. The indexing process implements a graphical representation, while the querying and document representation are based on the classical set-based model. The root of the set-based model corresponds to the use of term sets to complete the querying process based on the terms of the query. However, in the weighting process, this paper presents a wholly different approach elaborating on algorithms that may clearly benefit the process based on the k-core decomposition of each single graph. The main focus will finally be the estimation and presentation of the most important nodes belonging to each graph. These intend to be regarded as keywords presenting the evaluation of their major influence.

Keywords: Information retrieval · Retrieval models · Set-based model · Important nodes · K-core decomposition · Graph degeneracy

1 Introduction

In Information Retrieval (IR), two of the main research subjects involve the creation of an effective and efficient retrieval model as well as the detection of keywords in textual data. In this study, following the work presented in [16], we make an effort to combine those subjects, thus creating a new model by implementing a graphical representation of texts using keywords as important nodes, which are boosted at the weighting process. The case of the study is focused on whether the keywords can actually improve the retrieval process or not. The main difference among the proposed methods lies in the algorithms of discovering important nodes.

The set-based model is responsible for the retrieval process whereas, it is considered a combination of a set-theoretic and algebraic model. The algebraic notion of the model is expressed by the similarity function, which resembles the vector space model. More to the point, given a query, the model creates clustered

© IFIP International Federation for Information Processing 2020
Published by Springer Nature Switzerland AG 2020
I. Maglogiannis et al. (Eds.): AIAI 2020 Workshops, IFIP AICT 585, pp. 143–154, 2020.
https://doi.org/10.1007/978-3-030-49190-1_13

sets of terms by utilizing the query terms. The termsets are then formed as the apriori algorithm proposes [1].

A well-structured graphical IR model is a rare subject of study. The main onus of the study is aimed at demonstrating either the graphical representation or the scoring functions. However, authors in [10] proposed a complete graphical model; their implementation consists of unweighted directed graphs for each text of the collection and thus, the flow of the text is captured. The nodes of the graph represent the unique terms of the text while the edges refer to the relationship of the corresponding nodes within a partition of the text, expressed by a fixed-sized sliding window. As scoring function for the model, their implementation was based on the TF-IDF and BM25 using successive normalizations. One main difference regarding their scoring function, was the hypothesis that the weight of a vertex (TW), which corresponds to a unique text term, contains more information than the term frequency. Therefore, their function can be summarized as $TW - IDF$, challenging the term independence assumption.

To further consolidate our point, we should mention that the above graph-of-words model was utilized in [16] on an attempt to estimate the keywords of a given text using algorithms based on graph degeneracy [14]. There, a method known as k-core decomposition, which creates subgraph having specific structural properties, was proposed in order to study the cohesion on social networks. The k-core decomposition of a graph G is considered as a maximal connected subgraph consisting of nodes with a degree at least equal to k. Following the above definition, a subgraph has core equal to k only when the entity of its nodes has a degree of k or more. The k-core, where k is maximal, is often called MainCore; it is used as the starting point of the keyword finding study, which afterwards is expanded on the remaining levels of decomposition. At lower levels, the cores tend to be large, and the core cohesion rises at higher levels of decomposition. A well known algorithm for the purpose of finding the cores of a graph at $O(m)$ complexity was optly introduced in [2].

The decomposition aspect of defining the important nodes of a graph can be considered as a novelty. Centrality measures such as degree, closeness, and betweenness centralities are constituted as the most common alternatives [3,4,9]. More specifically, the degree centrality is based on the node degree, thus it can not necessarily reflect the magnitude of its importance. On the other hand, the closeness and betweenness centralities depend on the calculation of geodesic paths, which are difficult to be computed in complex graphs, especially on complete ones. Authors in [6] have focused on keyword extraction using graphical representation on texts as they elaborated on supervised methods using node centrality as well as unsupervised methods exploiting the HITS algorithm [5].

The information retrieval models consist of set theoretic, algebraic and probabilistic models, where the main emphasis is given on the set-based model [7,8]. A model, based on set theory, implements algebraic notions on scoring functions and document-queries representation, which is derived from the vector space model [12]. The set-based model considers sets of terms; these terms in turn consist of a given query, known as termsets. The sets are mined using the apriori algorithm [1] that is responsible for supporting a minimum frequency boundary for each termset. There are however some cases where the set-based model uses a proximity measure to assure that terms are close enough, so as to have a rational relationship.

As mentioned above, the set-based model represents queries and documents in a similar concept as the vector space model. The same applies to the scoring function, which calculates the similarity between a given query and the collection documents. The gist of our proposal is based on the logical assumption that every text consists of words that carry great importance, known as keywords. Therefore, the corresponding text can be graphically represented by important nodes. If we can initially detect them and, in following amplify their importance, expressed by a boost on their weight, the retrieval process will be augmented.

2   Graphical Extension of Set-Based Model Using Important Nodes

Each document is represented as an undirected weighted complete graph. When node importance is considered, then this complete graph is in need of further processing aiming at edge pruning; this procedure is essential due to the fact that the core decomposition has only one level and therefore the whole graph is considered as important [14]. In following, a collection sized graph is created by the union of the respective text graphs. That is the point where, depending on the method, the important nodes are boosted by a value equal to their "importance". Finally, with the use of graph theory, a weight is produced for each term, which is considered at the retrieval process by the set-based model.

2.1   Rational Path Graph

Each document graph is created with the assumption that every term is related likewise to the other terms, as this particular word has been included in the text. Every term of a given document is represented by a node in the graph and the relationship between two nodes as a weighted edge with weight W_{out}. Moreover, each node has a self loop edge, that is an edge with an identical starting and ending node having weight W_{in}. The graph construction process is simplified by taking into consideration the two following theorems.

Theorem 1. *Given a node N_i in document D_j with term frequency of the corresponding term equal to tf_i, the in-weight of the self edge (N_i, N_i) is computed as*

$$W_{in} = \frac{tf_i \times (tf_i + 1)}{2} \tag{1}$$

Theorem 2. *Given the nodes N_i, N_j in document D_j with term frequency of the corresponding terms equal to tf_i and tf_j respectively, the out-weight of the edge (N_i, N_j) is computed as*

$$W_{out} = tf_i \times tf_j, \quad \text{WHEN} \quad N_i \neq N_j \tag{2}$$

With the use of these two theorems, we propose an alternative algorithm of the rational path graph that can be cost efficient as the time complexity is $O(n^2) + O(m^2)$, where n is the number of the text terms and m the number of unique terms encountered in the text, as presented in Algorithm 1. We have to take into account the fact that this algorithm depends also on the way the documents are stored and consists of two steps; the term counting process as well as the graph creation. If the counting process is eliminated by the pre-processing of the text then the time complexity is $O(m^2)$.

Algorithm 1. Proposed Graph Construction Algorithm

1: **input** Document D_j
2: **output** Graph G of Document D_j
3: Given array A, list L, term t, node n, neighbour ng
4: Insert each t in L
5: **for all** $t \in L$ **do**
6:     **if** $t \notin A$ **then**
7:         $tf = L.count(term)$
8:         $A = (term, tf)$
9:     **end if**
10: **end for**
11: **for** $t \in A$ **do**
12:     $n = A[0]$
13:     $tf_t = A[1]$
14:     **if** $n \notin G$ **then**
15:         Add n to G with $W_{in} = \frac{tf_t \times (tf_t + 1)}{2}$
16:     **end if**
17:     **for** $ng \in A$ **do**
18:         **if** $edge(n, ng[0]) \notin G$ **then**
19:             Initialize $edge(n, ng[0])$ with $W_{out}(n, ng[0]) = tf_t \times ng[1]$
20:         **end if**
21:     **end for**
22: **end for**

Initially, the algorithm creates a tuple of unique term and its respective term frequency by counting each and every individual word in the concrete text. In following, for each unique term, a node is created and the in-edge as well as the out-edge with every neighbour is initialized, if such an edge does not exist. Finally, the respective edge weight using the aforementioned theorems is calculated.

2.2   Edge Pruning

The proposed methods depend on the degree of each node. Concretely, due to the fact that the graph is complete, the degree of each node is equal to $N - 1$, where N stands for the number of nodes that the graph consists of. The in-edge is not taken into consideration and therefore, there is a need to delete edges with minimum information loss. At first glance, someone would propose methods related to the connectivity of the graph [17]. However, the completeness of the graphs does not allow to calculate paths between nodes in a realistic manner. The computational complexity of such an act is $O(n!)$ [13]. Thus, a more naive approach was decided to be used, where initially the average weight of all graph edges are calculated and in following, all edges, with less weight than the average edge multiplied by a percentage P, are removed. P value is experimentally defined and is different in each collection. After this process, the important node estimation can be implemented on each graph separately.

2.3 Important Nodes Detection

The proposed methods focus on discovering the important nodes of a graph while simultaneously based on this graph's k-core decomposition. The decomposition of a graph is used for detecting influential nodes, where, in their absence, the graph might lose its connectivity. Authors in [14] suggested that given a graph $G(V, E)$, a subgraph $S(V', E')$ is considered as the k-core decomposition of G if the degree of each node in V' is less than k, considering that $V' \supseteq V$ and $E' \supseteq E$. For example, the following Fig. 1 presents the decomposition of a random graph G; the respective cores start with light grey nodes moving on to darker and finally to red ones.

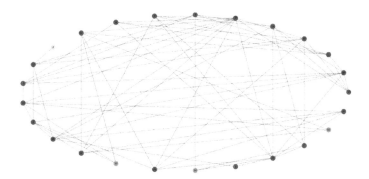

Fig. 1. K-core decomposition of a graph

It is important to note that the k core, where the $k+1$ level of decomposition does not exist, is called main core.

2.3.1 Main Core

Initially, we consider that the main core includes all the key nodes of the graph similarly to [11]. The edges regarding those nodes have their weight amplified in the union graph.

2.3.2   Density Method

Following the logical process of [16], i.e. the assumption of existence of all key nodes in the main core is too simplistic, we attempt to estimate the density of each core level of the text graph and consider as key nodes the nodes of the most dense subgraph. The densest subgraph was chosen by using the elbow method and the density of a subgraph $S(V', E')$ is computed as

$$density(S) = \frac{|E'|}{|V'| \times (|V'| - 1)} \tag{3}$$

2.3.3   CoreRank Method

Finally, the scoring method [16] is implemented into our model. CoreRank attempts to sort the nodes by the sum of the core number in which every neighbour exists. Thereafter, we assume that the important nodes should be chosen on document size basis and thus, the first 30% of the sorted node list are considered as important.

2.4   Union Graph and Graphs Weights

Ultimately, a collection size graph is created as the union of each text graph. Its nodes represent all the terms of the collection and the respective edges consist of the edges of each graph. The union graph edge weight is calculated as the sum of the weight in each graph, in which it exists.

The proposed union graph algorithm updates the current union graph U with the graph G as presented in Algorithm 2. Initially, the union graph U is an empty graph, while the proposed algorithm checks for each term whether it constitutes an important node and determines the value of importance h. At this point, in case the model does not consider the node importance, then the important node list will be empty and therefore the value h will be equal to 1. In following, it checks if the term exists or not in the union graph. In case the condition is true, the W_{in} weight of the term node in union graph is updated by the sum of the respective W_{in} in graph multiplied by h (line 11). Subsequently, the update of the value of the out-edge weight for each node of the union graph takes place (lines 13–14). In the absence of an edge between the term and the union graph node, one is initialized, whereas if the term does not exist in the union graph, the node is initialized and the update process begins.

When the union graph construction process is completed, a new weight NW for each node k emerges, derived from the union graph.

$$NW_k = \log \left(1 + a \times \frac{W_{out_k}}{(W_{in_k} + 1) \times (ng_k + 1)} \right) \times \log \left(1 + b \times \frac{1}{ng_k + 1} \right) \tag{4}$$

where W_{out_k} is the sum of out-edges and W_{in_k} stands for the weight sum of all in-edges terms for a node k. The number of neighbours that corresponds to that particular node is expressed as ng_k. Finally, a and b correspond to the gravity of the under review model against the set-based model.

Algorithm 2. Proposed Union Graph Construction Algorithm

1: **input** Graph G, Union Graph U
2: **output** Updated Union Graph including Graph UG
3: Given term t, node n, k-core list kc, value of importance h
4: **for all** $t \in G$ **do**
5:   **if** $t \in kc$ **then**
6:     Gain value of importance
7:   **else**
8:     $h = 1$
9:   **end if**
10:   **if** $t \in U$ **then**
11:     $W_{in}(t, U)+ = W_{in}(t, G) \times h$
12:     **for all** $n \in G$ where $n \neq t$ **do**
13:       **if** $edge(n, t) \in U$ **then**
14:         $W_{out}(n, t, U)+ = W_{out}(n, t, G) \times h$
15:       **else**
16:         Initialize $edge(n, t) \in U$ with $W_{out}(n, t, U) = W_{out}(n, t, G) \times h$
17:       **end if**
18:     **end for**
19:   **else**
20:     Add $t \in U$ with $W_{in}(n, t, U) = W_{in}(n, t, G) \times h$
21:     Repeat lines 12 to 18 for this case
22:   **end if**
23: **end for**

3   Documents and Query Representation

The retrieval process is handled by the set-based model. As mentioned, the introduced termset notion contributes to the reduction of computational complexity due to the fact that the volume of processed data is significantly lower [8]. Termsets are created with the use of association rule mining algorithms [1] and the gist of the process is that we combine two termsets, different in only one element of the set, in order to produce a new termset expanded by one new term. The sets should have elements greater than a lower frequency bound, thus decreasing the complexity even more.

3.1   Weighting Process

At this point, the need of combining the derived graph weight with the set-based model's weight appears. For each termset S_i, we calculate a new measure TN_{S_i} as the product of the graph weights of its terms.

$$TN_{S_i} = \prod_{k \in S_i} NW_k \qquad (5)$$

Thereafter, we include the new measure at the termset weight formula of a termset S_i in document D_j, where Sf_{ij} represents the termset frequency *(TF)* and $\frac{N}{dS_i}$ the inverse document frequency *(IDF)* of the corresponding termset

$$W_{S_{ij}} = (1 + \log Sf_{ij}) \times \log \left(1 + \frac{N}{dS_i}\right) \times tnw_{S_i} \qquad (6)$$

The query scoring function is more simplistic as it is expressed by the inverse document frequency of the termset S_i

$$W_{S_{iq}} = \log \left(1 + \frac{N}{dS_i}\right) \qquad (7)$$

3.2   Document Representation and Similarity

Finally, the document and query are represented as vectors in a similar manner with the vector space model. However, the vector space model uses TF/IDF as weight, instead of the above mentioned termset weighting process. Each vector d_j is associated with a text document and contains the weights of every termset in that document. Because the termset is based on the query terms, it is obvious that the size of the vector would be no more than 2^n, where n is the number of words that the query contains.

$$\vec{d_j} = (W_{S_{1j}}, W_{S_{2j}}, \cdots, W_{S_{2^n j}})$$
$$\vec{Q} = (W_{S_{1q}}, W_{S_{2q}}, \cdots, W_{S_{2^n q}}) \qquad (8)$$

As the set-based model dictates, the similarity between a document of the collection and the query is calculated using the cosine similarity. The result of this process is used for the ranking function of each model.

$$sim(Q, d_j) = \frac{\vec{d_j} \times \vec{Q}}{\|\vec{d_j}\| \times \|\vec{Q}\|} \qquad (9)$$

The issue at hand in this case is that the calculation of the $\|\vec{d_j}\|$ is extremely difficult due to the high number of frequent termsets generated by the model, aggravated especially in large documents. Therefore, following the approach of the original set-based model, we should only consider the sets, which contain only one element as an estimation of the above mentioned norm; however, in our case, due to the size of the collection, we were able to compute the norm in a reasonable time.

4   Results and Discussion

The Cystic Fibrosis (CF) Database [15] was used for the experimental evaluation, where all the included queries and documents were utilized. The number of queries and documents was 100 and 1238, respectively. We have initially examined whether the query size affected the retrieval process by using a subset of queries where the size of each one was less than 15. In following, all the proposed models as well as the set-based model were utilized as a basis of comparison. For each given query, the average precision of each model was calculated and afterwards, was compared with the average precision of the specific query of the set-based model. This specific comparison was expressed by the difference of the corresponding average precision values. In this way, we can determine if the under review model outperforms the set-based model.

Furthermore, the performance of each model against the set-based model in the set of queries can be quantified; this can be implemented by counting the number of queries where the model has greater average precision. It is important to note that a query is disregarded in case of equal results in that specific query between the models. Specifically, we have made evaluations with different values of importance variable h as well as pruning percentage value P in more than 84 experimental combinations.

For starters, the focus of study was to determine the performance of the important nodes amplification on the in-edges as well as out-edges of the main core model ($MainCore$) in comparison with the simple graphical extension of the set-based model (GSB). It seems necessary to amplify the weights of both type of edges since the results were better in that case as presented in Fig. 2.

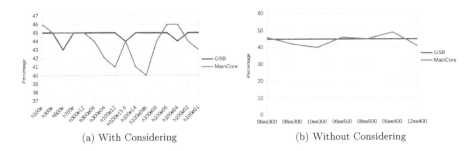

(a) With Considering   (b) Without Considering

Fig. 2. Amplification on important nodes-edges

In following, we examined the performance of all 4 models, namely the simple graphical extension of the set-based model (GSB), the graphical extension of the set-based model using main core's nodes as important nodes ($MainCore$), the graphical extension of the set-based model utilizing the most dense subgraph nodes as important nodes ($Density$) and the graphical extension of the set-based model employing CoreRank function ($CoreRank$) to determine the important nodes on 4 types of pre-processed textual data as depicted in Table 1. All the relevant information for each document has been initially included while this information was gradually pre-processed. Therefore 4 clusters of results are created, having different P values in each case. We can observe that in instances with low pre-process, the MainCore and the CoreRank models perform close to the set-based model, which is less affected by the noisy data.

Table 1. Proposed models evaluation for different pre-processed cases

Pre-processed case	Size of index	Result	Model
Low	48452	49	MainCore
None	58621	41.17	CoreRank
Slight	36988	47.42	MainCore
Full	11366	60.20	MainCore, GSB

Emphasizing on the full pre-processed case, which only consists of the document title and text, we can observe in Fig. 3 that our proposed models surpass the set-based model. At the best case, both GSB and $MainCore$ achieved a score of $60, 2\%$, having statistical significance p-value equal to $0, 02\%$. The $Density$ model tends to be similar to the $MainCore$ model due to the fact that the majority of graphs have low decomposition levels. However, they differentiate at cases, which the results are not so impressive.

In addition, we examined the impact of the significance variable h in Fig. 4. When the percentage of pruning is equal to 30%, the GSB, $MainCore$ and $Density$ models tend to present similar results. On the other hand, the $coreRank$ model comes last because of the need for higher pruning percentage value.

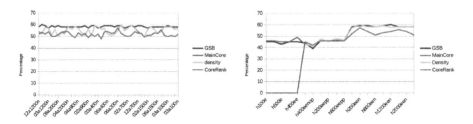

Fig. 3. Full pre-processed case   **Fig. 4.** Each significance variable case

Until this point, our aim was primarily focused on the number of queries that proposed models, which are actually superior to the set-based model disregarding the magnitude of that difference. In Fig. 5, all results are sorted in ascending order based on the set-based model, thus allowing to elaborate on the difference in average precision on each query. We choose to depict an average case and a case where $MainCore$, $Density$ and $CoreRank$ fall behind GSB.

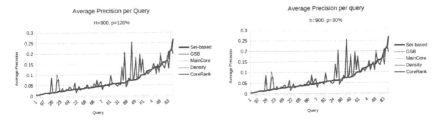

Fig. 5. Difference with set-based model

Finally, considering only the average precision on each query and ignoring the queries where those values occurred, we can introduce Fig. 6, which illustrates the course of average precision on each model in the above mentioned cases.

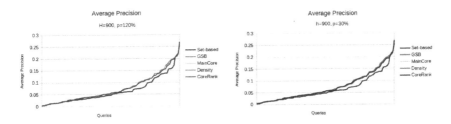

Fig. 6. Average precision of each model

5   Conclusions and Future Work

In this paper, we have proposed a number of methods for extending the set-based model with the use of graphs. These methods are improvements of the set-based model and are capable of handling noisy data in a fairly well manner. Experimental evaluation proves that the query size affects the retrieval results.

Nonetheless, the proposed methods perform similarly in some occurrences. Because of the fact that the graph is complete, as we assumed during the graph creation process, the pruned percentage variable seems to be more important than the significance variable; that precisely should be the motive for further research. One alternative is to relate each term of the document in sentence or paragraph level implemented by a moving window or alternatively utilize a proximity penalty at the edge weighting process.

Acknowledgement. Christos Makris and Andreas Kanavos have been co-financed by the European Union and Greek national funds through the Regional Operational Program "Western Greece 2014–2020", under the Call "Regional Research and Innovation Strategies for Smart Specialisation - RIS3 in Information and Communication Technologies" (project: 5038701 entitled "Reviews Manager: Hotel Reviews Intelligent Impact Assessment Platform").

References

1. Agrawal, R., Srikant, R.: Fast algorithms for mining association rules in large databases. In: 20th International Conference on Very Large Data Bases (VLDB), pp. 487–499 (1994)
2. Batagelj, V., Zaversnik, M.: An o(m) algorithm for cores decomposition of networks. CoRR cs.DS/0310049 (2003)
3. Freeman, L.C.: A set of measures of centrality based on betweenness. Sociometry **40**, 35–41 (1977)
4. Freeman, L.C.: The development of social network analysis: a study in the sociology of science. Soc. Netw. **27**, 377–384 (2004)
5. Kleinberg, J.M.: Authoritative sources in a hyperlinked environment. J. ACM **46**(5), 604–632 (1999)
6. Litvak, M., Last, M.: Graph-based keyword extraction for single-document summarization. In: Workshop on Multi-source Multilingual Information Extraction and Summarization (MMIES), pp. 17–24 (2008)
7. Pôssas, B., Ziviani, N., Meira Jr., W., Ribeiro-Neto, B.A.: Set-based model: a new approach for information retrieval. In: 25th International SIGIR Conference on Research and Development in Information Retrieval, pp. 230–237 (2002)
8. Pôssas, B., Ziviani, N., Meira Jr., W., Ribeiro-Neto, B.A.: Set-based vector model: an efficient approach for correlation-based ranking. ACM Trans. Inf. Syst. (TOIS) **23**(4), 397–429 (2005)
9. Prountzos, D., Pingali, K.: Betweenness centrality: algorithms and implementations. In: SIGPLAN Symposium on Principles and Practice of Parallel Programming (PPoPP), pp. 35–46 (2013)
10. Rousseau, F., Vazirgiannis, M.: Graph-of-word and TW-IDF: new approach to ad hoc IR. In: 22nd International Conference on Information and Knowledge Management (CIKM), pp. 59–68 (2013)
11. Rousseau, F., Vazirgiannis, M.: Main core retention on graph-of-words for single-document keyword extraction. In: Hanbury, A., Kazai, G., Rauber, A., Fuhr, N. (eds.) ECIR 2015. LNCS, vol. 9022, pp. 382–393. Springer, Cham (2015). https://doi.org/10.1007/978-3-319-16354-3_42
12. Salton, G., Wong, A., Yang, C.: A vector space model for automatic indexing. Commun. ACM (CACM) **18**(11), 613–620 (1975)
13. Sedgewick, R.: Algorithms in C, Part 5: Graph Algorithms, 3rd edn. Addison-Wesley-Longman, Boston (2002)
14. Seidman, S.B.: Network structure and minimum degree. Soc. Netw. **5**(3), 269–287 (1983)
15. Shaw, W.M., Wood, J.B., Wood, R.E., Tibbo, H.R.: The cystic fibrosis database: content and research opportunities. Libr. Inf. Sci. Res. **13**(4), 347–366 (1991)
16. Tixier, A.J., Malliaros, F.D., Vazirgiannis, M.: A graph degeneracy-based approach to keyword extraction. In: Conference on Empirical Methods in Natural Language Processing (EMNLP), pp. 1860–1870 (2016)
17. Zhou, F., Mahler, S., Toivonen, H.: Simplification of networks by edge pruning. In: Berthold, M.R. (ed.) Bisociative Knowledge Discovery. LNCS (LNAI), vol. 7250, pp. 179–198. Springer, Heidelberg (2012). https://doi.org/10.1007/978-3-642-31830-6_13

A Sentiment-Based Hotel Review Summarization Using Machine Learning Techniques

Agorakis Bompotas, Aristidis Ilias, Andreas Kanavos[(✉)], Christos Makris, Gerasimos Rompolas, and Alkiviadis Savvopoulos

Computer Engineering and Informatics Department,
University of Patras, Patras, Greece
{mpompotas,aristeid,kanavos,makri,robolas,asavv}@ceid.upatras.gr

Abstract. With the advent of social media, there is a data abundance so that analytics can be reliably designed for ultimately providing valuable information towards a given product or service. In this paper, we examine the problem of classifying hotel critiques using views expressed in users' reviews. There is a massive development of opinions and reviews on the web, which invariably include assessments of products and services, and beliefs about events and persons. In this study, we aim to face the problem of the forever increasing amount of opinionated data that is published in a variety of data sources. The intuition is the extraction of meaningful services despite the lack of sufficient existing architectures. Another important aspect that needs to be taken into consideration when dealing with brand monitoring, relates to the rapid heterogeneous data processing, which is vital to be implemented in real-time in order for the business to react in a more immediate way.

Keywords: Classification · Machine learning · Neural networks · Opinion mining · Sentiment analysis

1 Introduction

In the emergent field of Web 2.0, users' reviews, comments and reports have constituted a crucial area of interest for tourism businesses. As an escalating number of consumers are inclined to share as well as exchange their personal experiences in social networks, forums and websites, the tourism industry has radically altered the way of increasing and influencing customers' engagement with tourism brands [10]. In this new era of e-tourism, businesses, in order to keep up with the upsurging competition, have to develop innovative marketing strategies and techniques focused on customers' needs and satisfaction. Subsequently, in the last years, there has been a wide interest in extracting actionable insights on customers' behaviour and sentiment by leveraging user-generated content, that will enable businesses to identify and in following predict the usefulness of online reviews [4].

ⓒ IFIP International Federation for Information Processing 2020
Published by Springer Nature Switzerland AG 2020
I. Maglogiannis et al. (Eds.): AIAI 2020 Workshops, IFIP AICT 585, pp. 155–164, 2020.
https://doi.org/10.1007/978-3-030-49190-1_14

The widespread use of social media platforms has significantly contributed to the growth of the electronic word-of-mouth (eWOM) communication, which has notable impact on the tourism industry. This textual kind of communication is encapsulated in online reviews and has attracted researchers' interest in various domains. In particular, text and opinion mining systems have been proposed in the literature in order to analyse and classify customers' reviews, providing thus businesses with the capability of monitoring their online brand reputation [17, 20]. Moreover, due to the large volume of user-generated data, text summarization techniques have also been proposed in order to effectively and efficiently identify the top-k most informative sentences of hotel reviews [12].

In general, despite the textual information, reviews consist of a score rating mechanism, which can reflect the overall customer satisfaction in a very explicit way. Although customers' ratings have been found to be highly correlated with the sentiment polarity of the corresponding textual content of the reviews [5], there is still a strong interest in further examining and evaluating the textual content under specific technical attributes, which can influence customer ratings [22]. In any case, it is obvious that customers' reviews are a vital source of information for the tourism industry, as they enable businesses to have a clear view of the most important aspects deriving from them and thus they can better prioritize and optimize their marketing strategies.

The vast amount of user-generated content has led to the need of NoSQL databases in order to manipulate them in a scalable and productive way [21]. Therefore, in this paper, a NoSQL system with an automated tool that generates an intelligent mechanism for analysing data and exporting useful knowledge and insights to tourism traders, is proposed. As a result, businesses will be able to adjust their marketing strategies and adapt to the customer needs in time, and simultaneously reducing their human resource requirements.

The contribution of this work lies in the design of a new approach for analyzing hotel reviews using Latent Dirichlet Allocation (LDA) for aspect mining and Neural Networks (NN) for sentiment analysis. A dynamic architecture, which receives the data stream, on-line or off-line in order not to overload the systems of the participating hotels or their service providers, is proposed. It extracts the aspects along with the sentiment of the hotel reviewers by applying LDA and NN modules accordingly, then stores the data and finally, attempts to correlate the data with the reviewers. The process is not obvious, given the anonymity of the reviewers, but the attempt to correlate them can be implemented with extensive training of the NN. Our architecture proposes a novel platform utilizing the benefits of both algorithms, so that it can be used in an effective way in data forecasting.

The paper is organized as follows. Section 2 describes related work. The key design ideas and concepts of the architecture of the proposed Sentiment Analysis system are presented in Sect. 3. In Sect. 4 we present implementation details regarding the system infrastructure, while in Sect. 5 we provide our conclusions and thoughts relating to future work.

2   Related Work

Due to the growing available data that are generated on a daily basis from hotels worldwide, a turn of attention has been observed in academic literature in adopting new ways of managing the insightful hotel data, and extrapolate important and valuable information, which can later be used for sustainable economic growth. The nature of most of these data are mainly in the form of text, accompanied by a certain numerical grading. These two characteristics constitute a modern review regarding the user's accommodation. Such reviews contain in their main body the reviewer's opinion of the hotel as well as a grade that indicates the polarity or the sentiment towards the accommodation, and wholly characterizes the experience itself.

In [17], an overview of a review management tool is shown where a variety of hotel comments were collected, in order to hark the visitors' points and views of the hotel quality. At the same point, the work presented in [11] introduces a more general and non context-specific approach for opinion mining, based on customer reviews. More specifically, authors performed a summarizing of the numerous comments and reviews regarding particular products, and in following extracted a comprehensive polarity percentage that represents the sentiment of the buyers as a whole. Altogether, the sentiment of a review as well as the general sentiment that hotel reviews accumulate, can produce a meaningful abstraction and pinpoint either problems that the management can solve or aid potential customers in choosing their next hotel [18].

Social media compose platforms that welcome a vast amount of product and service reviews, which have an unbeatable advantage over classic comments under the designated product; more to the point, the graph representation and the links between reviews can provide deeper latent connections between sentiment and review. One such corresponding work has been implemented in [14], where authors demonstrated numerous academic researches that concentrate on consequential sentiment analysis through the scope of social media. Coauthoring an extension of their previous work, authors in [16] also showed the scalability of their methodologies, where massive collections of review data were processed with the aid of distributed computing frameworks, while maintaining robustness in terms of velocity of processing and accuracy of sentiment prediction.

However, the process of analyzing the sentiment in general and in retrospect, the sentiment polarity of reviews is not straightly performed into the raw collected data. A number of pre-processing layers must be beforehand executed so in the work presented in [9], this importance is greatly highlighted. Before advancing to the classification and performance evaluation steps, two important layers take place; data transformation and filtering. Data were cleaned and stripped of useless tags, and in following, stemming and lemmatization procedures occurred. During the filtering step, a statistical analysis to measure the dependency between word and category that the word is included, was performed with the aid of the Chi-square test. As shown in the performance evaluation step, all measurements were improved when considering the pre-processing procedure in comparison to completely avoiding that step, in terms of the three basic evaluation metrics, namely $F1$-measure, accuracy and recall.

As a result, the review management is immediately dependent on the afore-mentioned nature of the reviews, which is none other than a text collection. Thus, the branch of text mining as a tool to aid this process is deemed essential. There has been much academic literature throughout the latest decades regarding text mining and opinion mining techniques, either of probabilistic nature or not [1,3]. As a previous work on opinion clustering emerging in reviews, one can consider the setup presented in [6]. Other existing works that deal with customers' buying habits is presented in [13,15].

The machine learning algorithms have the advantage of dealing with high dimensional and nonlinear relationships, which is especially suitable for estab-lishing train dynamic model and train speed prediction on account of the dynamic and nonlinear nature [19]. One of the most classic text mining tech-niques that composed the foundation for modern opinion mining is the Latent Dirichlet Allocation (LDA) [2,7,8]. LDA is a probabilistic algorithm that can dis-cover the latent topics that may exist within the reviews of the collection. More specifically, LDA extracts the top N topics that are most common in a review, based on the representations of the most frequent words with the input being a term document matrix, whereas two distributions are considered as output; one for document-topic relations and the other for topic-word ones.

3   System Architecture

In this section, we will elaborate on the key design ideas and concepts regarding the architecture of the proposed Sentiment Analysis platform. As depicted in Fig. 1, our system consists of an Application Programming Interface (API) that serves as the gateway to an online hotel booking platform (or a channel manager), a NoSQL database and the Sentiment Analysis Infrastructure which in turn is divided into five different modules.

The flow of data within the system is relatively simple. Initially, hotel reviews are inserted in the database through the corresponding API, where they become available to the Sentiment Analysis Infrastructure. The Natural Language Pro-cessing module initially parses the stored reviews, transforms them into the appropriate form and eventually passes them to the Aspect Mining and Senti-ment Analysis modules. Subsequently, the intermediate results are given as input to the Results Combiner module, which produces the final outputs and stores them back to the database. Finally, both the initial reviews and the results of the analysis are easily accessible through the API.

3.1   Hotel Reviews Sentiment Analysis API

For exposing the Sentiment Analysis Infrastructure to the systems that will access it, a RESTful web service was implemented. Concretely, it supports both GET and POST requests and the data exchanged over the API are expected to be in the form of JavaScript Object Notation (JSON). The API allows the user

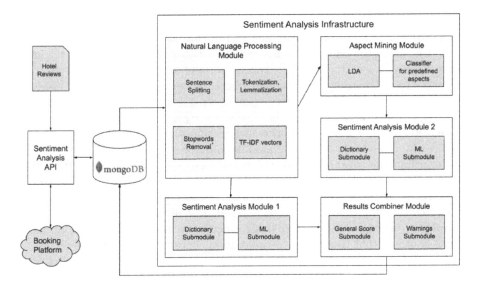

Fig. 1. Hotel reviews sentiment analysis' platform architecture

to insert new hotel reviews to the system and update or simply retrieve information about the old ones. The aforementioned functionality can be extended as well to the authors of the reviews. The access to the API is restricted and an authentication method is utilized for avoiding illwanted visiting. Regarding the API implementation, Python programming language in combination with the popular Flask microframework were selected, because of their lightweight and powerful properties.

3.2   Storage

For storing the hotel reviews along with the intermediate and final results produced by the Sentiment Analysis Infrastructure, a fast but flexible database system was required. Furthermore, the risk that the number of reviews can grow exponentially created the additional need for scale-out, which dictated us to swift away from the traditional RDBMs and to seek a NoSQL alternative. As no join operations were compulsory for our analysis, a document-based database was deemed as the best suited solution. More specifically, we opted to use the MongoDB, because of its maturity level along with the robustness it provides.

3.3   Sentiment Analysis Infrastructure

3.3.1   Natural Language Processing Module

The first module of the Sentiment Analyzer is responsible for processing the raw text of the hotel reviews with the aim of producing the vectors that will be used as input for the next modules. This process, which is also known as feature extraction, can be further analyzed into four separate stages: Sentence Splitting, Tokenization, Stopwords Removal and Tf/Idf Calculation.

In most cases, the importance of a review content is condensed within the first few sentences of a text. Therefore, tokenization of sentences is deemed as crucial, as well as extracting the sentences where the necessary information resides. Often, a simple split of the text string on every dot will suffice. However, there are many cases in the English language, where the period punctuation is used for reasons other than ending a sentence such as timestamp depiction (a.m., p.m.). That is why the sentence splitting module must be context-aware.

Regarding the tokenization of the text body, the first step is splitting the sentence into separate words by using the space string to perform the splitting. These words are generally referred to as tokens, which is no other than a sequence of characters grouped together to form a semantic unit. However, not all terms or units are useful for the final analysis, since there are words that are deemed trivial or others that contribute to the general context far more heavily.

A useful technique to apply to the extracted tokens is the stemming and lemmatization technique. Many words contained in the same document correlate, since they belong to similar derivational families and have similar meanings. Thus, it is deemed useful to extract a general lemma that applies to all words with similar prefixes, and remove the corresponding suffix. This procedure allows any Natural Processing Module to work faster, since it handles exceptionally less words in a smaller vocabulary, without sacrificing any percentage of context or meaningful information.

After the application of the above mentioned procedures, *Tf/Idf* weighting can be performed. There the term frequency definition is combined with the inverse document frequency, in order to produce a specific weight for every word that exists inside each document. This assigned weight takes higher values when the terms occur many times inside a few documents, and lower when the term occurs less times in a document or generally occurs in various documents. When the word exists in every document, it is deemed borderline meaningless.

Each stage is assigned to a sub-module designed and developed specifically for the corresponding task. In addition, these sub-modules are connected in order to form a pipeline that receives as input the collection of the reviews and produces the final vectors.

3.3.2   Aspect Mining Module

The Aspect Mining Module aims to detect the aspect where each sentence of the review refers to. In order to achieve this goal, both a supervised and an unsupervised learning approach are employed. Initially, each sentence is labeled by a Multiclass Classifier. The aspects are simply considered as the predefined labels, which are commonly found in hotel reviews (e.g., cleanliness, facilities, etc.) with the addition of an "undefined" class. However, some extra analysis is required in order to discover potential aspects that were omitted.

This analysis is performed by the second submodule of the Aspect Mining Module, which employs Latent Dirichlet Allocation (LDA). LDA is considered a generative probabilistic model of a collection of composites, made up of parts. It is designed based on the idea that each document in a collection can be described by a distribution of topics and simultaneously, each topic can be described by a distribution of words. In our scenario, where hotel reviews are in place of documents and the aim is to discover the aspects that characterize them, it is evident why LDA constitutes a perfect fit to our problem.

3.3.3 Sentiment Analysis Module

In the proposed system, there are two Sentiment Analysis Modules; the first one characterizes the whole review based on the polarity of the sentiment that expresses, while the second one attempts to do the same but for every aspect mentioned. The sentiments are both detected with the use of predefined rule-based sentiment annotators as well as machine learning models. The output of these modules constitutes a vector of sentiment scores that are then passed to the Results Combiner Module.

Regarding the training of the aforementioned models, a number of classifiers was employed and the Long Short Term Memory Neural Networks (LSTMs) emerged as the most efficient solution. Compared to the standard Neural Networks, which only allow information flowing forward from the input nodes to the output nodes, LSTMs are equipped with feedback connections. More to the point, based on this feature, LSTMs are able to effectively handle entire sequences of data and are best suited in fields such as speech recognition and text processing. Furthermore, LSTMs use "exploit" for regulating the flow of data within their cells in order to deal with the exploding and vanishing gradient problems that are the most common shortcomings of the traditional Recurrent Neural Networks (RNN).

3.3.4 Results Combiner Module

As derived from its name, the Results Combiner Module gathers the information about the extracted sentiment of reviews by the previous modules and attempts to produce an insight useful to the end user. It consists of two different submodules; the first one calculates a score of the review in order to quantify the overall customer satisfaction, whereas the second one issues warnings that might help the hoteliers to understand their shortcomings.

4 Implementation

The functionality of each aforementioned module is widely enhanced through the advancements of machine learning algorithms, whereas their efficiency, robustness and velocity of training have been proved throughout the scientific literature of the last decade. In this experimental work, the detection of the sentiment in each hotel review, as well as their polarity related to aspects that pertain them, is made feasible with the use of the following algorithms.

4.1 Long Short Term Memory (LSTM) Neural Networks

Neural Networks' capability has made possible the successful supervised training of classifiers on collections of data big enough; this training can ensure a wide captivation of patterns in the corresponding dataset. Given well structured data, the Long Short Term Memory Neural Networks (LSTM) can provide consequential classifications, especially when sequences must be managed. The case at hand can be directly associated with sequences since hotel review collections consist of text data, whilst their labels are the polarized sentiments of the document that need to be detected.

LSTMs' architecture is based on "*cell state*" and "*gates*" through which the input information is propagated. More accurately, there are three gates and two states in LSTMs: the *forget gate (f_t)* whose responsibility is to remove unnecessary information from the *cell state* taking as input the hidden state of the previous cell h_{t-1} and data record x_t. Next, the *input gate (i_t)* adds new information on the cell state by creating a vector of all possible values and multiplying them with the *tanh* function. In following, the *output gate (o_t)* transfers a percentage of information to the hidden state, so that the LSTM can maintain its robustness by preserving the long-term dependencies. Finally, regarding the two states, the *cell state (c_t)* represents the internal memory of the cell and the *hidden state (h_t)* decides the time frame of the recalled dependency. These characteristics are presented in the following Eq. 1.

$$f_t = \sigma(W_f(x_t + h_{t-1}) + b_f)$$
$$i_t = \sigma(W_i(x_t + h_{t-1}) + b_i)$$
$$o_t = \sigma(W_o(x_t + h_{t-1}) + b_o) \tag{1}$$
$$c_t = f_t c_{t-1} + i_t \sigma(W_c(x_t + h_{t-1}) + b_c)$$
$$h_t = o_t tanh(c_t)$$

4.2 Latent Dirichlet Allocation (LDA)

The fundamental functionality of Latent Dirichlet Allocation (LDA) resides in the idea that each document has a number of words (terms as a subset of the total word collection), which are partially involved in the said document as well as a number of topics, which are elaborated in this document. The detection of topics that the document consists of as well as the correlation of its words with those topics, can be considered as the utmost goal of LDA.

In this work, the hotel reviews can be seen as documents, whereas the aspects as topics, which the review is meant to analyze. LDA will parse each document and allocate each review word to a specific topic through a parameterized Dirichlet allocation, allowing thus a degree of initial randomness. Afterward, two calculations are performed: initially the number of words in the review that were assigned a specific topic divided by the number of words in any topic, as well as the percentage of allocations given a topic that were derived through a given word.

As a result, the probability of a word belonging to a topic is updated by the multiplication of the two aforementioned values. The re-assignment of documents to words and topics takes place until convergence and a stable mixture of topics are produced.

5   Conclusions and Future Work

The aim of the current study is the design of a new schema based on NoSQL databases for the manipulation of hotel reviewers' comments along with the appropriate modules based on LDA in terms of aspect mining as well as Neural Networks for hotel reviewers' sentiment. In this schema, the data stream is initially received, then the aspects along with the sentiment of the hotel reviewers are extracted and finally, the data with the reviewers are correlated. We proposed a novel architecture utilizing the benefits of Neural Networks along with LDA algorithm so that it can be used in an effective way in data forecasting.

For further work, we would like to compare the effectiveness of our architecture in larger sample. In addition, new classifiers can be considered in order to be compared with the current ones, such as Random Forest, Support Vector Machines, etc.

Acknowledgement. Agorakis Bompotas, Aristidis Ilias, Andreas Kanavos, Christos Makris, Gerasimos Rompolas and Alkiviadis Savvopoulos have been co-financed by the European Union and Greek national funds through the Regional Operational Program "Western Greece 2014-2020", under the Call "Regional Research and Innovation Strategies for Smart Specialisation - RIS3 in Information and Communication Technologies" (project: 5038701 entitled "Reviews Manager: Hotel Reviews Intelligent Impact Assessment Platform").

References

1. Blei, D.M.: Probabilistic topic models. Commun. ACM **55**(4), 77–84 (2012)
2. Blei, D.M., Ng, A.Y., Jordan, M.I.: Latent Dirichlet allocation. J. Mach. Learn. Res. **3**, 993–1022 (2003)
3. García, S., Luengo, J., Herrera, F.: Data Preprocessing in Data Mining. Intelligent Systems Reference Library, vol. 72. Springer, Heidelberg (2015). https://doi.org/10.1007/978-3-319-10247-4
4. Gavilan, D., Avello, M., Martinez-Navarro, G.: The influence of online ratings and reviews on hotel booking consideration. Tour. Manag. **66**, 53–61 (2018)
5. Geetha, M., Singha, P., Sinha, S.: Relationship between customer sentiment and online customer ratings for hotels - an empirical analysis. Tour. Manag. **61**, 43–54 (2017)
6. Gourgaris, P., Kanavos, A., Makris, C., Perrakis, G.: Review-based entity-ranking refinement. In: 11th International Conference on Web Information Systems and Technologies (WEBIST), pp. 402–410 (2015)
7. Griffiths, T.L.: Gibbs sampling in the generative model of latent Dirichlet allocation (2002)

8. Griffiths, T.L., Steyvers, M.: Finding scientific topics. Proc. Nat. Acad. Sci. **101**(suppl 1), 5228–5235 (2004)
9. Haddi, E., Liu, X., Shi, Y.: The role of text pre-processing in sentiment analysis. In: 1st International Conference on Information Technology and Quantitative Management (ITQM), pp. 26–32 (2013)
10. Harrigan, P., Evers, U., Miles, M., Daly, T.: Customer engagement with tourism social media brands. Tour. Manag. **59**, 597–609 (2017)
11. Hu, M., Liu, B.: Mining opinion features in customer reviews. In: Proceedings of the Nineteenth National Conference on Artificial Intelligence (AAAI), pp. 755–760 (2004)
12. Hu, Y., Chen, Y., Chou, H.: Opinion mining from online hotel reviews - a text summarization approach. Inf. Process. Manag. **53**(2), 436–449 (2017)
13. Iakovou, S.A., Kanavos, A., Tsakalidis, A.: Customer behaviour analysis for recommendation of supermarket ware. In: Iliadis, L., Maglogiannis, I. (eds.) AIAI 2016. IAICT, vol. 475, pp. 471–480. Springer, Cham (2016). https://doi.org/10.1007/978-3-319-44944-9_41
14. Kanavos, A., Perikos, I., Hatzilygeroudis, I., Tsakalidis, A.: Emotional community detection in social networks. Comput. Electr. Eng. **65**, 449–460 (2018)
15. Kanavos, A., Iakovou, S.A., Sioutas, S., Tampakas, V.: Large scale product recommendation of supermarket ware based on customer behaviour analysis. Big Data Cognit. Comput. **2**(2), 11 (2018)
16. Kanavos, A., Nodarakis, N., Sioutas, S., Tsakalidis, A., Tsolis, D., Tzimas, G.: Large scale implementations for twitter sentiment classification. Algorithms **10**(1), 33 (2017)
17. Kasper, W., Vela, M.: Sentiment analysis for hotel reviews. In: Computational Linguistics-Applications Conference, pp. 45–52 (2011)
18. Liu, B., Zhang, L.: A survey of opinion mining and sentiment analysis. In: Aggarwal, C., Zhai, C. (eds.) Mining Text Data, pp. 415–463. Springer, Heidelberg (2012). https://doi.org/10.1007/978-1-4614-3223-4_13
19. Savvopoulos, A., Kanavos, A., Mylonas, P., Sioutas, S.: LSTM accelerator for convolutional object identification. Algorithms **11**(10), 157 (2018)
20. Sun, Q., Niu, J., Yao, Z., Yan, H.: Exploring ewom in online customer reviews: sentiment analysis at a fine-grained level. Eng. Appl. Artif. Intell. **81**, 68–78 (2019)
21. Vonitsanos, G., Kanavos, A., Mylonas, P., Sioutas, S.: A NoSQL database approach for modeling heterogeneous and semi-structured information. In: 9th International Conference on Information, Intelligence, Systems and Applications (IISA), pp. 1–8 (2018)
22. Zhao, Y., Xu, X., Wang, M.: Predicting overall customer satisfaction: big data evidence from hotel online textual reviews. Int. J. Hosp. Manag. **76**, 111–121 (2019)

An Advanced Deep Learning Model for Short-Term Forecasting U.S. Natural Gas Price and Movement

Ioannis E. Livieris[1(✉)], Emmanuel Pintelas[1], Niki Kiriakidou[2], and Stavros Stavroyiannis[3]

[1] Department of Mathematics, University of Patras, Patras, Greece
livieris@upatras.gr, e.pintelas@math.upatras.gr
[2] Department of Statistics and Insurance Science,
University of Pireaus, Pireaus, Greece
kiriakidou@unipi.gr
[3] Department of Accounting and Finance, University of Peloponesse,
Antikalamos, Greece
computmath@gmail.com

Abstract. Natural gas constitutes one of the most actively traded energy commodity with a significant impact on many financial activities of the world. The accurate natural gas price prediction and the direction of price changes are considered essential since these forecasts are utilized in energy sustainability planning, commodity trading and decision making, covering both the supply and demand side of natural gas market. In this research, a new deep learning prediction model is proposed for short-term forecasting natural gas price and movement. The proposed forecasting model exploits the ability of convolutional layers for providing a deep insight in natural gas data and the efficiency of LSTM layers for learning short-term and long-term dependencies. Additionally, a significant advantage of the proposed model is its abilities to predict the price of natural gas on the following day (regression) and also to predict if the price on the next day will increase, decrease or stay stable (classification) with respect to today's price. The conducted series of experiments demonstrated that the proposed model considerably outperforms state-of-the-art deep learning and machine learning models.

Keywords: Deep learning · Convolutional layers · LSTM · Natural gas prediction · Time series

1 Introduction

Crude oil and natural gas play strategic roles in socio-economic development around the world and global demand for energy is continuously rising because developed countries consume large amounts of energy, while demand in developing countries is increasing. They constitute the major energy sources for the global economy and price forecasting is significant for a variety of reasons including energy investment, policy decisions, portfolio diversification and hedging

© IFIP International Federation for Information Processing 2020
Published by Springer Nature Switzerland AG 2020
I. Maglogiannis et al. (Eds.): AIAI 2020 Workshops, IFIP AICT 585, pp. 165–176, 2020.
https://doi.org/10.1007/978-3-030-49190-1_15

capabilities. Benchmarks for the crude oil include the Brent crude oil from four different fields in the North Sea, the Forties Blend, the Oseberg and Ekofisk, the Western Texas Intermediate extracted from U.S. wells and sent via pipeline to Oklahoma and the Dubai/Oman which consists a "basket" product from Middle East. Natural gas benchmark prices are the U.S. Henry hub natural gas, the Russian natural gas border price in Germany and the Indonesian Liquefied natural gas price in Japan.

Governments tighten up environmental regulations, seeking alternative energy sources to meet energy demand via reduction of the dependency on oil, with natural gas representing an economically viable alternative solution. While the three natural gas benchmarks exhibited a co-movement, there was a deviation (decoupling effect) of the U.S. natural gas [3,9,11], hereinafter referred as natural gas, after the Global Financial Crisis. The rapidly increasing demand for energy by emerging markets, along with the production decrease by the Organization of Petroleum Exporting Countries (OPEC) in Middle East, resulted in high oil and natural gas prices for three years. In U.S., the hydraulic fracturing (fracking) technique used to recover gas and oil from shale rocks reduced the overall production costs and therefore the natural gas price. This was reinforced by the locality of the market since unlike oil, natural gas is difficult to transport without a pipeline, unless it is liquefied which is costly. As a result, the prediction of natural gas price can potentially assist governments and financial investors for making their investment policies, gain significant profits and decrease their risks. Nevertheless, the accurate natural gas forecasting is generally considered, due to its chaotic nature, a complex and significantly challenging task.

During the last decade, significant deep learning techniques have been successfully applied in a variety of time-series forecasting problems [8,13,17]. These advanced techniques are probably the appropriate methods to extract knowledge from the noisy and chaotic nature of time-series data. Convolutional Neural Networks (CNNs) and LSTM networks constitute the most popular and widely utilized deep learning techniques. CNNs are based on convolutional layers which extract more valuable features by filtering out the noise of the input data while LSTM models are based on LSTM layers which capture sequence pattern information due to their distinct architecture. Nevertheless, classical CNNs are well suited to deal with spatial autocorrelation data, they are not usually adapted to correctly identify complex and temporal dependencies [1] while LSTM networks although they are dedicated to cope with temporal correlations, they manage only the features in the training set. Thus, a time-series prediction model which adopts the benefits of both techniques may significantly improve the forecasting performance.

In this work, we propose a new prediction model for short-term forecasting natural gas price which is based on the idea of exploiting the advantages of deep learning techniques. The proposed forecasting model exploits the capability of convolutional layers for learning the internal representation of the natural gas data and extracting useful patterns as well as the efficiency of LSTM layers for identifying short and long term dependencies. Additionally, the proposed prediction model has also ability of predicting the natural gas movement direction (increase, decrease or stay stable) of the next day with respect to today's price. Our conducted numerical experiments illustrate that the proposed model considerably outperforms state-of-the-art deep learning and machine learning models for the prediction of the natural gas daily price and movement.

The remainder of this paper is organized as follows: Sect. 2 presents a survey of recent studies, regarding the application of machine learning techniques in natural gas forecasting. Section 3 presents a detailed description of the proposed advanced deep learning model. Section 4 presents the data collection and Sect. 5 presentes a series of numerical experiments. Section 6 discusses the findings of this research and presents our conclusions.

2   Natural Gas Forecasting: State of the Art

The recent developments of data mining and deep learning drew the attention of scientific community, attempting to gain significant insights on forecasting principal resources prices such as natural gas. During the last years, the problem of predicting the next day's price of natural gas arises frequently, due to its significance as a profitable commodity. This led to the requirement and developement of new innovative forecasting models. In the sequel, we report the findings and outcomes from some rewarding studies regarding forecasting methodologies for natural gas price and movement.

Yu and Xu [16] proposed an improved back-propagation neural network model based on a combinational approach for short-term gas load forecasting. The proposed model was optimized by the real-coded genetic algorithm. They performed several modifications including an improved momentum factor and a self-adaptive learning rate as well as the determination of the initial weights and thresholds of the network by the genetic algorithm to avoid being trapped in local minimum. Such improvements exerted maximum performance of the neural network by accelerating the convergence speed and facilitating the forecasting efficiency. The data used in their research were recorded from Nov-2005 to Oct-2008 regarding natural gas load for Shanghai. Based on their preliminary numerical experiments, the authors stated that the proposed model was ideal for natural gas short-term load forecasting, presenting satisfactory prediction accuracy with a relatively small computation time.

Čeperić et al. [5] conducted a performance evaluation of traditional time-series models: Naive, AR and ARIMA as well as of the machine learning models: neural networks and strategic seasonality-adjusted support vector regression machines for short-term forecasting of Henry Hub spot natural gas prices. Additionally, they investigated the benefits of utilizing a feature selection technique as a pre-processing step. To evaluate the successfulness of the compated models in the short term forecasting of natural gas prices, they conducted a variety of numerical experiments ranging of different input variables and transformations, combinations of periods and window lengths. Their detailed experimental analysis illustrated the forecasting efficiency of machine learning models as well as the usefulness of feature selection techniques.

Merkel et al. [14] applied deep neural network methodologies for predicting natural gas short-term load. The authors utilized historical data from 62 operating areas from U.S. local distribution companies, covering a wide area of different geographical regions hence, represent a variety of climates. Their proposed model was evaluated against the traditional models: linear regression and artificial neural network. Their numerical experiments presented that the proposed deep learning model exhibited better short-term load forecasts on average. Moreover, they stated that even the much simpler linear regression model outperformed the proposed model, in some test cases. Finally, they concluded that although the deep learning techniques are a dominant option which usually outperforms simpler forecasting methods, it may not constitute the proper methodology for every operating area.

Nevertheless, none of the mentioned studies considered the adoption and combination of advanced deep learning techniques for natural gas price prediction and movement. Our contribution aims on imposing convolutional layers for learning the internal representation of the natural gas data and LSTM layers for efficiently identifying short-term and long-term dependencies. Moreover, in contrast to previous research studies, we provide performance evaluation of various deep learning and machine learning models for both regression and classification problems.

3   CNN-LSTM Model for Short-Term Forecasting Natural Gas

The main contribution of this research is the development of a forecasting model, named CNN-LSTM, utilizing advanced deep learning techniques for the short-term prediction of natural gas price and movement. The proposed model is based on of two main components.

The first component consists 2 convolutional layers of 32 and 64 filters of size $(2,)$, using same padding. Convolutional layers are specially designed data pre-processing layers which filter the input data for learning their internal representation. More specifically, the convolution kernel, called filter, can be considered as a tiny window which "slides" through each input instance and applies complex mathematical operations (convolutions) on each sub-region which this specified window "meets". The application of several convolution kernels on the input data, results in the development of new convolved features which are usually more useful than the original ones.

The second component consists of a LSTM layer of 70 units and a dense layer of 16 neurons. LSTM layers process the generated features in order to identify short-term and long-term dependencies in the times series and provide an accurate prediction. Memory blocks and adaptive gate units constitute the major novelty of a LSTM layer. The former contain memory cells with self-connections for memorizing the temporal state while the latter control the information flow in the memory block. With the treatment of the hidden layer as a memory unit, LSTM can cope the correlation within time-series in both short and long term.

An overview of the proposed CNN-LSTM forecasting model architecture is depicted in Fig. 1.

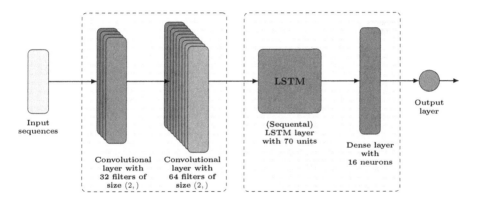

Fig. 1. CNN-LSTM forecasting model architecture

4   Data

The data utilized in this research concern the daily natural gas prices in USD from Jan-2015 to Dec-2019 which were obtained from U.S. Energy Information Administration (www.eia.gov). Table 1 summarizes the descriptive statistics including the measures: Minimum, Mean, Maximum, Median, Standard Deviation (Std. Dev.), Skewness and Kurtosis.

Table 1. Descriptive statistics for natural gas daily prices

Minimum	Mean	Maximum	Median	Std. Dev	Skewness	Kurtosis
1.49	2.75	6.24	2.78	0.37	0.98	5.25

The data were divided into training set and testing set. The training set consists of natural gas daily prices from 01-Jan-2015 to 31-Dec-2018 (1129 days) which ensures an adequate range of long and short-term trends. The testing set consists of daily prices from 01-Jan-2018 to 31-Dec-2019 (146 days) which ensures a substantial amount of unseen "*out-of-sample*" data for evaluating the compared forecasting models.

At this point, it is worth mentioning that in any attempt to increase the training dataset utilizing prices from past years, lead to the reduction of the performance of all evaluated forecasting models.

5   Experimental Methodology

In this section, we evaluate the performance of the proposed forecasting model against LSTM forecasting models and the state-of-the-art machine learning models: Support Vector Regression (SVR) [7], Artificial Neural Network (ANN) [6]

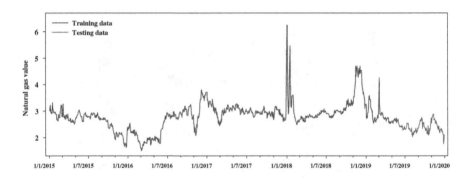

Fig. 2. Daily natural gas prices trend from January 2015 to December 2019

and Decision Tree Regression (DTR) [2]. For fairness and for performing an objective comparison, the hyper-parameters of all algorithms were selected in order to maximize their experimental performance. A brief description of the specification of each prediction model and its hyper-parameters is presented in Table 2.

The implementation code was written in Python 3.4 on a PC (Intel(R) Core(TM) i7-6700HQ CPU 2.6GHz, 16 Gbyte RAM) while the deep learning and machine learning models were implemented using Keras library [10] and Scikit-learn library [15], respectively. Notice that all LSTM models, the ANN as well as the proposed CNN-LSTM model were trained utilizing Adaptive Moment Estimation (ADAM) algorithm for 100 epochs with a batch size equal to 128 and a mean-squared loss function which reported the best overall results.

The regression performance of all forecasting models was measured using the performance metrics: Root Mean Square Error (RMSE) metric and the Mean Absolute Error (MAE). Furthermore, regarding the classification problem of predicting whether the natural gas price on the next day would increase (Up), decrease ($Down$) or stay stable ($-$) with respect to today's price, the performance of each model was evaluated using the performance metrics: Accuracy (Acc), Area Under Curve (AUC) and F_1-score (F_1). In this research, we utilized three different prices for the forecasting horizon, namely 4, 6 and 12. The forecasting horizon F stands for the number of natural gas daily prices which are taken into consideration by each model for predicting the daily price on the following day. Its price is critical for the efficiency of an intelligent forecasting model [12].

Tables 3, 4 and 5 present the performance of the proposed CNN-LSTM forecasting model against the state-of-the-art prediction models, relative to forecasting horizon 4, 6 and 12, respectively. It is worth mentioning that for each performance metric the best performance was highlighted in bold. Regarding the natural gas price prediction problem, CNN-LSTM and SVR highlighted the lowest RMSE and MAE score, followed by ANN and LSTM models which exhibited similar regression performance. Regarding the classification problem of predicting if the price will increase, decrease or stay stable on the following day, CNN-LSTM exhibited the best performance considerably outperforming all

Table 2. Parameter specification of state-of-art machine learning and deep learning forecasting models

Model	Description
SVR	Kernel = RBF, $C = 1.0$, gamma = 10^{-1}
ANN	1 hidden layer with 20 neurons and an output layer of 1 neuron
DTR	Criterion = 'mse', max depth = unlimited, min samples split = 2
$LSTM_1$	LSTM layer with 70 units
	Output layer with 1 neuron
$LSTM_2$	LSTM layer with 70 units
	Dense layer with 8 neurons
	Output layer with 1 neuron
$LSTM_3$	LSTM layer with 70 units
	LSTM layer with 30 units
	Output layer with 1 neuron
$LSTM_4$	LSTM layer with 50 units
	LSTM layer with 20 units
	Dense layer with 8 neurons
	Output layer with 1 neuron

other state-of-the-art models. More specifically, CNN-LSTM reported 55.25%, 55.03% and 53.97% accuracy for forecasting horizon equal to 4, 6 and 12, respectively, followed by $LSTM_2$ which reported 50.69%, 50.69% and 49.44%, in the same situations. Moreover, CNN-LSTM exhibited the best (highest) AUC for all prices of forecasting horizon and the best F_1-score for $F = 6$ and $F = 12$.

Next, we demonstrate a deeper insight about the classification efficiency of the proposed forecasting model CNN-LSTM by presenting the confusion matrix regarding all forecasting horizons and compare it with that of the $LSTM_2$ model which presented the best performance among state-of-the-art models. The confusion matrix can be considered as a complete evaluation methodology for describing and depicting in a compact way, valuable and useful information, regarding to a model's forecasting performance.

Tables 6 and 7 present the confusion matrices of $LSTM_2$ and CNN-LSTM, respectively. Notice that each row and each column of all confusion matrices represent the instances in an actual and in a predicted class, respectively. Firstly, based on the presented confusion matrices we can easily conclude that the exclusive prediction accuracy of the "*Stable*" class is very high for both compared prediction model. Additionally, the CNN-LSTM model managed to exhibit the best distribution of correctly identified instances per class for every forecasting horizon. This probably means that this model managed to keep a balance on learning the patterns which describe every class, consisting in total a more reliable and robust prediction model. In contrast, the $LSTM_2$ model seems to be significantly biased since it misclassified most "*Down*" instances as "*Up*".

This implies that it ignored most data patterns and information which describe and seperate "Up" and "Down" classes.

Table 3. Performance comparison of the CNN-LSTM model against traditional regression models for $F = 4$

Model	RMSE	MAE	Acc	AUC	F_1
ANN	0.113	0.087	51.53%	0.651	0.584
SVR	**0.093**	**0.067**	50.69%	0.638	0.565
DTR	0.125	0.100	47.22%	0.578	0.473
LSTM$_1$	0.109	0.083	49.44%	0.632	0.557
LSTM$_2$	0.112	0.086	50.69%	0.656	**0.638**
LSTM$_3$	0.110	0.084	49.44%	0.618	0.532
LSTM$_4$	0.111	0.084	50.07%	0.605	0.508
CNN-LSTM	**0.093**	**0.067**	**55.25%**	**0.680**	0.571

Table 4. Performance comparison of the CNN-LSTM model against traditional regression models for $F = 6$

Model	RMSE	MAE	Acc	AUC	F_1
ANN	0.106	0.081	50.14%	0.651	0.579
SVR	**0.092**	**0.067**	48.61%	0.633	0.566
DTR	0.125	0.099	47.64%	0.578	0.472
LSTM$_1$	0.107	0.082	51.36%	0.643	0.566
LSTM$_2$	0.102	0.077	50.69%	0.631	0.553
LSTM$_3$	0.106	0.080	49.86%	0.634	0.561
LSTM$_4$	0.114	0.087	50.83%	0.618	0.527
CNN-LSTM	0.093	**0.067**	**55.03%**	**0.674**	**0.589**

Table 5. Performance comparison of the CNN-LSTM model against traditional regression models for $F = 12$

Model	RMSE	MAE	Acc	AUC	F_1
ANN	0.119	0.092	49.86%	0.629	0.550
SVR	**0.094**	**0.069**	48.39%	0.635	0.558
DTR	0.128	0.099	50.97%	0.592	0.482
LSTM$_1$	0.111	0.086	48.33%	0.632	0.563
LSTM$_2$	0.109	0.084	49.44%	0.628	0.551
LSTM$_3$	0.104	0.079	51.67%	0.649	0.579
LSTM$_4$	0.127	0.100	49.31%	0.624	0.545
CNN-LSTM	0.104	0.078	**53.97%**	**0.670**	**0.620**

Table 6. Confusion matrices of LSTM$_2$ model for forecasting horizon 4, 6 and 12

	Down	–	Up		Down	–	Up		Down	–	Up
Down	14	0	55	Down	22	0	47	Down	40	0	29
–	2	15	0	–	5	12	0	–	10	7	0
Up	9	0	49	Up	16	0	42	Up	31	0	27
		$F = 4$				$F = 6$				$F = 12$	

Table 7. Confusion matrices of CNN-LSTM model for forecasting horizon 4, 6 and 12

	Down	–	Up		Down	–	Up		Down	–	Up
Down	28	0	41	Down	31	0	28	Down	35	0	34
–	5	12	0	–	5	12	0	–	9	8	0
Up	20	0	38	Up	20	0	38	Up	27	0	31
		$F = 4$				$F = 6$				$F = 12$	

Summarizing, it is worth mentioning that the interpretation of Tables 3, 4, 5, 6 and 7 highlight that CNN-LSTM model is generally preferable for forecasting natural gas price and movement, considerably outperforming traditional state-of-the-art models in both regression and classification tasks.

In the sequel, we evaluate the forecasting reliability of the proposed model CNN-LSTM, by performing a test of autocorrelation in the residuals [4]. This test examines the presence of autocorrelation between the residuals (differences between predicted and actual prices) which in case it exists, implies that the forecasting model may be inefficient, since it did not manage to capture all the possible information contained in the training set. Two significant tools for testing the autocorrelation of the residuals are the Auto-Correlation Function (ACF) plot and the Ljung-Box Q-test. The ACF [4] is obtained from the linear correlation of each residual to the others in different lags and illustrates the intensity of the temporal auto-correlation. The *portmanteau* Ljung-Box Q-test [4] assesses the null hypothesis (H_0) that "a series of residuals exhibits no autocorrelation for a fixed number of lags".

Figures 3, 4 and 5 present the Auto-Correlation Function (ACF) plot of LSTM$_2$ and CNN-LSTM, for forecasting horizon equal to 4, 6 and 12, respectively. Notice that the confident limits (blue line) are constructed assuming that the residuals follow a Gaussian probability distribution. The ACF plot of CNN-LSTM are within 95% percent confidence interval for all lags regarding $F = 6$, which verifies that the residuals have no auto-correlation while for $F = 4$ and $F = 12$ the ACF plots present a small spike at lag 5, which reveal that there exists some negligibly autocorrelation in the residuals. In contrast, the ACF plots of LSTM$_2$ indicated that the assumption of no auto-correlation in the errors is violated which suggests that the model's forecasts may be inefficient, relative to all utilized prices of the forecasting horizon.

Table 8 reports the statistical analysis, performed by Ljung-Box Q-test for 10 lags with significance level $\alpha = 5\%$. The portmanteau test suggests that the CNN-LSTM model does not violate the assumption of no autocorrelation in the errors for $F = 4$ and $F = 6$ which implies that its forecasts may be efficient; while for the $LSTM_2$ model, it suggests that there exists significant autocorrelation in the residuals at the 5% level.

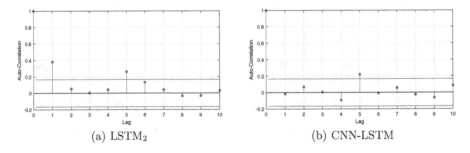

(a) $LSTM_2$ (b) CNN-LSTM

Fig. 3. ACF plots on the residuals of $LSTM_2$ and CNN-LSTM for $F = 4$

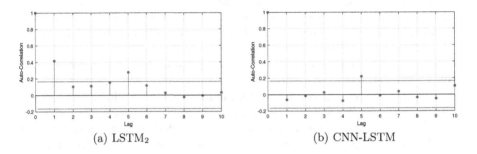

(a) $LSTM_2$ (b) CNN-LSTM

Fig. 4. ACF plots on the residuals of $LSTM_2$ and CNN-LSTM for $F = 6$

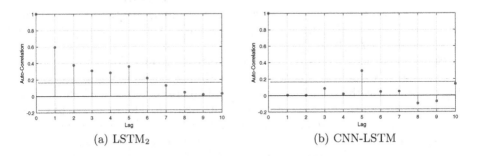

(a) $LSTM_2$ (b) CNN-LSTM

Fig. 5. ACF plots on the residuals of $LSTM_2$ and CNN-LSTM for $F = 12$

6   Discussion and Conclusions

In this section, we perform a discussion regarding the numerical performance of our proposed CNN-LSTM model for forecasting natural gas price and movement as well as the main findings and the limitations of this research.

Table 8. Ljung-Box Q-test for 10 lags with significance level $\alpha = 5\%$

Model	$F = 4$		$F = 6$		$F = 12$	
	p-value	H_0	p-value	H_0	p-value	H_0
LSTM$_2$	0.0001	Rejected	0.0270	Rejected	0	Rejected
CNN-LSTM	0.0974	Accepted	0.1072	Accepted	0.0207	Rejected

The main contribution of this work is the development of a new forecasting model for the short-term prediction of natural gas price and movement. The proposed forecasting model exploits the capability of convolutional layers for learning the internal representation of the natural gas data and the efficiency of LSTM layers for identifying short-term and long-term dependencies. A significant advantage of the model is that it has the ability to predict the price of natural gas on the next day (regression) and also predicts if the price on the next day will increase, decrease or stay stable (classification) with respect to today's price. The presented numerical experiments highlighted that although LSTM models constitute a wide and efficient choice for addressing time-series problems, their use along with convolutional layers could provide a significant boost in increasing the forecasting performance.

The problem of forecasting natural gas price and movement can be considered to belong on chaotic time series problems. This means that accurate and reliable predictions are almost impossible since these problems are close to random walk processes, while the identification of possible existing patters and their proper distinguishment among a large pool of noisy instances, seems to be a significantly challenging task.

The proposed forecasting model managed to achieve a noticeable performance increase in terms of accuracy, compared to traditional state-of-the-art prediction models, although the RMSE and MAE scores were slightly better. One possible reason is that the feature preprocessing stage, provided by the convolutional layers, managed to restrict the noise of each input sequence instance, extracting valuable and meaningful feature maps which assisted the LSTM model on its final prediction task.

It is worth mentioning that in real world applications such as the decision support for investment tasks regarding to natural gas stocks, a prediction model which achieves high classification accuracy would be considered much more efficient and valuable, compared to a model with better regression performance but lower accuracy score, since these investment decisions follow a *"buy, hold, sell"* strategy based on the price movement predictions *"Up, Stable, Down"*. Therefore, the proposed model has a potential to assist trading and investment decisions forming up a reliable natural gas price movement predictor.

Finally, a limitation of the prediction model that it is unable to efficiently identify and report possible input sequences which can actually lead to more accurate predictions. This ability could be crucial and significant in real world applications, since investment and trading decisions would be performed just only when the model identified reliable and accurate patterns, while noisy and uncertain input signals would be totally ignored, leading to safer decisions and probably higher returns. This constitutes an interesting and promising idea, which we intend to pursue in our future research.

References

1. Bengio, Y., Courville, A., Vincent, P.: Representation learning: a review and new perspectives. IEEE Trans. Pattern Anal. Mach. Intell. **35**(8), 1798–1828 (2013)
2. Breiman, L.: Classification and Regression Trees. Routledge, Abingdon (2017)
3. Brigida, M.: The switching relationship between natural gas and crude oil prices. Energy Econ. **43**, 48–55 (2014)
4. Brockwell, P.J., Davis, R.A.: Introduction to Time Series and Forecasting. Springer, Heidelberg (2016). https://doi.org/10.1007/978-3-319-29854-2
5. Čeperić, E., Žiković, S., Čeperić, V.: Short-term forecasting of natural gas prices using machine learning and feature selection algorithms. Energy **140**, 893–900 (2017)
6. Lopes, N., Ribeiro, B.: Neural networks. Machine Learning for Adaptive Many-Core Machines - A Practical Approach. SBD, vol. 7, pp. 39–69. Springer, Cham (2015). https://doi.org/10.1007/978-3-319-06938-8_3
7. Deng, N., Tian, Y., Zhang, C.: Support Vector Machines: Optimization Based Theory, Algorithms, and Extensions. Chapman and Hall/CRC, Boca Raton (2012)
8. Fawaz, H., Forestier, G., Weber, J., Idoumghar, L., Muller, P.: Deep learning for time series classification: a review. Data Min. Knowl. Disc. **33**(4), 917–963 (2019). https://doi.org/10.1007/s10618-019-00619-1
9. Gatfaoui, H.: Linking the gas and oil markets with the stock market: investigating the US relationship. Energy Econ. **53**, 5–16 (2016)
10. Gulli, A., Pal, S.: Deep Learning with Keras. Packt Publishing Ltd., Birmingham (2017)
11. Lin, B., Li, J.: The spillover effects across natural gas and oil markets: based on the VEC-MGARCH framework. Appl. Energy **155**, 229–241 (2015)
12. Livieris, I.E., Pintelas, E., Kotsilieris, T., Stavroyiannis, S., Pintelas, P.: Weight-constrained neural networks in forecasting tourist volumes: a case study. Electronics **8**(9), 1005 (2019)
13. Livieris, I.E., Pintelas, E., Pintelas, P.: A CNN-LSTM model for gold price time series forecasting. Neural Comput. Appl. (2020, to appear)
14. Merkel, G.D., Povinelli, R.J., Brown, R.H.: Short-term load forecasting of natural gas with deep neural network regression. Energies **11**(8), 2008 (2018)
15. Pedregosa, F., et al.: Scikit-learn: machine learning in python. J. Mach. Learn. Res. **12**, 2825–2830 (2011)
16. Yu, F., Xu, X.: A short-term load forecasting model of natural gas based on optimized genetic algorithm and improved BP neural network. Appl. Energy **134**, 102–113 (2014)
17. Zhao, B., Lu, H., Chen, S., Liu, J., Wu, D.: Convolutional neural networks for time series classification. J. Syst. Eng. Electron. **28**(1), 162–169 (2017)

Fake News Detection Regarding the Hong Kong Events from Tweets

Maria Nefeli Nikiforos[1]([✉])(iD), Spiridon Vergis[1](iD), Andreana Stylidou[1](iD),
Nikolaos Augoustis[1](iD), Katia Lida Kermanidis[1](iD),
and Manolis Maragoudakis[2](iD)

[1] Department of Informatics, Ionian University, Corfu, Greece
{c19niki,c19verg,c19styl,c19avgo,kerman}@ionio.gr
[2] Department of Information and Communication Systems Engineering,
University of the Aegean, Samos, Greece
mmarag@aegean.gr

Abstract. The rapid development of network services has led to the exponential growth of online information and the increasing number of social media users. These services are exploited by malicious accounts that spread fake news and propaganda in vast user networks. Consequently, an automated solution for fake news and deception detection is required. This paper introduces a new data set consisting of 2,366 tweets written in English, regarding the Hong Kong events (August, 2019), and a well-defined method for fake news detection that uses both linguistic and network features. Our approach is tested with experiments using 2 machine learning models, achieving high performance compared to previous research.

Keywords: Deception detection · Fake news detection · Linguistic analysis · Twitter · Text analysis

1 Introduction

Due to the rapid development of network services and with the number of social media users constantly increasing, the size of information uploaded daily on the internet grows aggressively. This, combined with the ever growing number of malicious accounts created on social media, facilitates the spreading of fake news and propaganda in vast user networks [25]. Therefore, it is practically impossible for people to fact-check manually every piece of online information, and thus an automated solution based on modern technology is required.

Unlike previous work (to the authors' best knowledge), the approach proposed in this paper: a. uses both linguistic and network features to detect deceptive language in tweets for fake news detection, b. creates a new original data set which contains 2,366 tweets in English, regarding the Hong Kong events from August 2019, and c. identifies several attributes as determinant for fake news

© IFIP International Federation for Information Processing 2020
Published by Springer Nature Switzerland AG 2020
I. Maglogiannis et al. (Eds.): AIAI 2020 Workshops, IFIP AICT 585, pp. 177–186, 2020.
https://doi.org/10.1007/978-3-030-49190-1_16

detection. Experiments with 2 machine learning models are conducted. The performance of each model is presented extensively in Sect. 6. The data set is available for research purposes at this address: https://hilab.di.ionio.gr/wp-content/uploads/2020/02/HILab-Fake_News_Detection_For_Hong_Kong_Tweets.xlsx.

This paper is organized as follows: in Sect. 2 the past related work is discussed. In Sect. 3 the data set used for the fake news detection is analyzed. In Sect. 4 the linguistic and network features of the data set are presented. In Sect. 5 our methodology regarding SMOTE over-sampling and feature selection is outlined. In Sect. 6 the machine learning experiments and their results regarding the proposed approach are discussed. Finally, in Sect. 7 the paper is concluded and guidelines for future work are discussed.

2 Related Work

Due to the exponential growth of information created and uploaded on the internet daily, many researchers have focused on finding alternative ways of fact-checking that information. One of the first tools based on text analysis is the one presented by Houvardas and Stamatatos [12] for automatic authorship identification. Their tool can be considered a preliminary deception detector.

Along with the development of such tools, many researchers and journalists also started creating data sets with false and true news, in order to check the accuracy of these tools. Politifact [5], for example, is a website which offers short phrases and sentences, fact-checked by journalists. Another popular data set is FEVER [1] which consists of 185,000 short claims, created from Wikipedia sentences. Similar to FEVER, the LIAR [29] data set contains 13,000 short statements drawn from Politifact and categorised into 6 different classes (pants-fire, false, barely-true, half-true, mostly-true, true).

Recent papers regarding the automated fact-checking have created data sets using information from the social media. BUZZFEEDNEWS [11] contains 2,282 posts from 9 Facebook accounts of news agencies. Another data set containing posts from Facebook is Some-Like-It-Hoax [28], which consists of 15,500 posts from 32 Facebook pages. These posts are labeled based on the author, and not on the information contained within the post. Similar data sets based on Twitter are PHEME [9], which contains a collection of rumours and non-rumours, and CREDBank [17], which consists of 60 million Tweets labeled by human annotators.

Other data sets contain whole articles instead of short sentences and posts from social media. FakeNewsNet [24] contains whole false articles connected with Twitter posts. Another similar data set is "Bluff The Listener and The Onion" [21], which consists of whole false articles, which are intended to be false by the authors (e.g. to express humor). BS Detector is also a data set that contains a list of unreliable news websites, and it labels automatically an article based on its information sources.

Another crucial factor for the accuracy of a fact-checking tool is the model used for the machine learning procedure. In Shojaee's et al. [23] work, Support

Vector Machines and Naive Bayes classification algorithms are used for deception detection in reviews, using lexical and syntactic features, with accuracy 84% and 74%, respectively. Alowibdi et al. [6] conclude that a Naive Bayes-Decision Tree hybrid is the most effective classifier when it comes to deception detection using network features (accuracy 85%). Songram et al. [26] use k-nearest neighbour and Support Vector Machine, to detect messages leading to deception. The most accurate classifier was the Support Vector Machine with 99.21% accuracy.

More recent works suggest the use of neural networks to detect fake news, such as the model presented in Ruchansky's et al. [22] paper. Their model was tested with 2 data sets, and manages to surpass every other conventional classifier. Linguistic approaches have also been proposed in recent literature. Other research is that of Péerez-Rosas and Mihalcea [19], who present results from LIWC word class analysis used for deceptive text, and Hai et al. [10], who use logistic regression (semi-supervised learning) to detect fake news.

3 Data Set

The data collected for the fake news detection consist of a set of 2,366 tweets written in English, regarding the Hong Kong events, and posted in August 2019 [2]. Our approach uses both linguistic and network features (Sect. 4). Certain network features, which are available for these tweets, are also collected. Additionally, certain linguistic features are extracted from the text of each tweet. A label feature is also added for each tweet, with value either "fake", or "real".

3.1 Fake News

In August 2019, Twitter disclosed 936 accounts originated from People's Republic of China, which were deliberately attempting to sow political discord in Hong Kong, including undermining the legitimacy and political positions of the protest movement on the ground. These accounts were suspended on violations of Twitter's manipulation policies; spam, coordinated activity, fake accounts, featured activity, and ban evasion [2].

For the purposes of our research, tweets posted from these accounts were collected, in order to create a data set which contains false information, and are from now on referred to as "fake news". This data set originally consisted of 1,703,470 tweets. It is preprocessed, in order to extract tweets that actually: a. contain text, b. are written in English, and c. are about the Hong Kong political events (August, 2019). After preprocessing, the final fake news data set consists of 272 tweets in total.

3.2 Real News

For the purposes of our research, tweets posted from 9 Twitter accounts of renowned news agencies from August, 2019 to December, 2019 were collected, in order to create a data set which contains true and valid information, and are from now on referred to as "real news". The news agencies are BBC Asia, BBC News (World), CCTV, China Daily, China Xinhua News, China.org.cn, Global Times, People's Daily (China) and SHINE.

This data set originally consisted of 2,133 tweets. It is preprocessed, in order to extract tweets that actually: a. contain text, b. are written in English, and c. are about the Hong Kong political events (August, 2019). After preprocessing, the final real news data set consists of 2,094 tweets in total.

4 Features

The data set created in this research contains a plethora of features, both linguistic- and network-oriented. The final data set contains 23 features in total. The linguistic features are shown in Table 1 and the network features in Table 2.

Table 1. Linguistic features.

Feature	Tweet example
Tweet text	Hong Kong Open: Wade Ormsby wins first European Tour title
Num syllables	33
Avg syllables	3
Avg Words in Sentence	10
Flesh-Kincaid	21.01
Num big Words	2
Num long sentences	0
Num short sentences	2
Num sentences	1
Num words	11
Rate adverbs adjectives	0.2727

Table 2. Network features.

Feature	Tweet example
User id	363345298
User display name	dalotbaba
User screen name	D3ZwcCm1Q1WNkKWaakHKQw=
Follower count	12033
Following count	10186
Account creation date	12/3/10 12:00 AM
Tweet time	12/11/17 12:00 AM
In reply to user id	2147483647
Like count	42
Retweet count	2
Num URLs	3

4.1 Linguistic Features

A plethora of linguistic features is used in our research. (These features are selected and extracted according to [15] and [7]). The features selected in this work are based on Burgoon et al. [15], and Li et. al. [7]. Both of these works use linguistic analysis for deception detection and attitude identification. From these works, the features best suited deception detection are used. The final set of features for each tweet of the data set includes: a. the tweet text, b. the number of syllables, c. the number of words, d. the number of sentences, e. the number of big words, f. number of syllables per word, g. number of short sentences, h. the number of long sentences, i. the Flesh-Kincaid level, j. the average number of words per sentence, and k. the rate of adjectives and adverbs (Table 1).

A feature that is widely used for fake news detection is the average number of syllables per word in the tweet text. The extraction of this feature is performed with the Loughran Master Dictionary [3,16], which is used to determine which tokens are classified as proper English words, and their syllable count. In order to match the tweet text tokens with the words of the dictionary, tweet text is appropriately prepared; all punctuation marks, hashtags, at-mentions, and links are ignored. Due to the nature of tweets, tweet text may contain tokens that are either misspelled, or represent an assemblage of words, e.g. #behindthechair. To cover such cases, their respective syllable count value was replaced with the average syllable count of English words.

A python script is used to extract the rest of linguistic features. Twitter text has idioyncrasies that render its linguistic processing quite interesting and that have been tackled in various contexts, the TraMOOC system being one of them [27]. The Natural Language Toolkit (NLTK) library [4] is used to tag the text (PartOfSpeech-tagging) in order to identify the adjectives and adverbs. As for the long and short sentences, their threshold is set according to the research paper of Pennebaker et al. [18]. More specifically, sentences with less than 8 words are considered "short", while sentences with more than 25 words are "long". Similarly, words with more than 6 letters are considered "big".

A particularly unique and useful feature is the Flesh-Kincaid level [30]. It indicates how difficult it is to comprehend a particular piece of text; a high FK level means highly understandable text, and vice versa.

4.2 Network Features

The network features which are used in our research are collected directly from Twitter, and they are selected according to [13] and [14]. The first work presents a fake news data repository which consists of data collected from Twitter. The second work is a survey which reviews fake news detection approaches on social media. The final set of features for each tweet of the data set, which contains the features best suited for the proposed approach from both of the aforementioned works, includes: a. user id, b. user display name, c. user screen name, d. follower count, e. following count, f. account creation date, g. tweet time, h. in reply to user id (reply to specific user), i. like count, j. retweet count, and k. number of URLs (Table 2).

These features show how users form networks and interact within them on social media, based on their interests, topics and relations, which serve as the fundamental paths for information diffusion. Fake news dissemination processes tend to form an echo chamber cycle, highlighting the value of using network-based features to represent these types of network patterns for fake news detection.

5   Methodology

Following the preprocessing of the data set, as well as the collection and extraction of its network and linguistic features, comes the preparation of the data set for the machine learning experiments. Due to the imbalance between the number of fake news and real news learning examples (272 to 2,094, respectively), SMOTE over-sampling is performed, as defined in [8], and thereby "synthetic" fake news training examples are created. This imbalance has a bad effect on the performance of the minority class prediction, and therefore, over-sampling of the minority examples has been considered necessary. In real conditions, fake news is expected to be proportionally much less than real news. Consequently, imbalance of data will also exist in future research. Therefore, it is very likely that smoothing techniques, such as SMOTE, will be necessary. A feature selection is also performed, in order to identify the features which are more suitable and useful for fake news detection. The tool used for these tasks is the RapidMiner Studio (https://bit.ly/2OaBX1N).

5.1   SMOTE Over-Sampling

The classification categories (labels), fake and real, of the data set are not equally represented (272 to 2,094 learning examples, respectively). Consequently, "synthetic" fake news training examples are created using SMOTE over-sampling.

According to Chawla et al. [8], the test set for the machine learning experiments must not include any "synthetic" examples. Therefore, prior to SMOTE over-sampling, the data set is split in 80% training set and 20% test set, with stratified sampling; it ensures that the label distribution in the subsets is the same proportionally as in the whole data set. The training set consisted of 1,893 examples: 1,675 with value "real" and 218 with value "fake" for the label feature. The test set to be used for the machine learning experiments consists of 473 examples: 419 with value "real" and 54 with value "fake" for the label feature.

The final step is "SMOTING" the minority label ("fake") of the training set. As a result, the final training set to be used for the machine learning experiments consists of 3,350 examples: 1,675 with value "real" and 1,675 (including 1,457 "synthetic" examples) with value "fake" for the label feature.

5.2   Feature Selection

In order to identify the features which are more suitable and useful for fake news detection, feature selection is performed. It is observed that certain network features are determinant for the fake news detection. These features, sorted from the most to the least determinant, are: a. user id, b. account creation date, c. following count, d. user display name, and e. user screen name. More specifically, it is observed that the machine learning algorithms take into consideration only one of these features (from most to least determinant), while completely ignoring the other features (linguistic and network). Therefore, to ensure that the models actually "learn", and thus obtain reliable results from the machine learning experiments, these features are removed from the training and test sets.

Consequently, the machine learning experiments (Sect. 6) are conducted with the training and test sets that were designed as described above, and without the aforementioned features, finally resulting in 18 remaining features.

6   Experiments and Results

The tool used to conduct the experiments with machine learning algorithms, the collection of results, the comparison of the models, and the identification of wrong predictions is the RapidMiner Studio. All models were trained with the SMOTE over-sampled training set and tested with the original test set, as described in Sect. 5.

An initial set of experiments were run using the Naive Bayes classifier, since it is commonly used in previous works [6,23] and can be used to compare the trained model's accuracy. Laplace correction is used in order to smooth the conditional probabilities. The produced model achieves 99.79% accuracy, which is high, compared to related work (Sect. 2). Precision and recall for each label are also high (Table 3). More specifically, the following are observed: a. all examples labelled as "real" are classified correctly, with a class recall of 100% and a class precision of 99.76%, and b. all examples labelled as "fake" are classified correctly except 1, with a class recall of 98.15% and a class precision of 100%. The wrong prediction concerning the only misclassified example occurs because, unlike the majority of the examples originally labelled as "fake", it does not contain long sentences or big words (linguistic features), while containing 2 URLs (network feature).

Table 3. Naive Bayes confusion matrix.

	True real	True fake	Class precision
Predicted real	419	1	99.76%
Predicted fake	0	53	100.00%
Class recall	100.00%	98.15%	

A second set of experiments using the Random Forest algorithm were implemented and applied. The Random Forest algorithm tries to minimize the overall error rate, so, in an unbalance data set, the larger class will get a low error rate while the smaller class will have a larger error rate [20]. Certain parameters need to be defined: a. the gain ratio is defined as the split criterion (no pruning), with maximal depth defined to 50, b. the number of trees to generate is set to 100, c. the subset ratio of randomly chosen features to test is set to 2, and d. the majority vote is defined as the voting strategy; it selects the label that is predicted by the majority of tree models. The produced model achieves 99.37% accuracy, which is high, compared to related work (Sect. 2). Precision and recall for each label are also high (Table 4). More specifically, the following are observed: a. all examples labelled as "real" are classified correctly, with a class recall of 100% and a class precision of 99.29%, b. all examples labelled as "fake" are classified correctly except 3, with a class recall of 94.44% and a class precision of 100%. The wrong predictions concerning the 3 misclassified examples occur because, unlike the majority of the examples originally labelled as "fake", they contain more than 7 words (linguistic feature) and 2 URLs (network feature).

Table 4. Random forest confusion matrix.

	True real	True fake	Class precision
Predicted real	419	3	99.29%
Predicted fake	0	51	100.00%
Class recall	100.00%	94.44%	

7   Conclusions and Future Work

Unlike previous work (to the authors' best knowledge) the approach proposed in this paper: a. uses both linguistic and network features to detect deceptive language in tweets for fake news detection, b. creates a new original data set which contains 2,366 tweets in English, regarding the Hong Kong events from August 2019, and c. identifies several attributes as determinant for fake news detection.

To conclude, this paper described an innovative and well-defined method for detecting fake news in social media, by using both linguistic and network features to detect deceptive language, and identifying several attributes as determinant for fake news detection. The proposed method is tested on a new original data set consisting of 2,366 tweets in English, regarding the Hong Kong events (August 2019). During the experiment phase, 2 machine learning models are used. Both models managed to predict the examples labelled "real" and "fake" with high accuracy when compared with previous works. More specifically, the Naive Bayes model achieves an accuracy of 99.79% and the Random Forest model achieves an accuracy of 99.37%. This work draws guidelines for future work where more non-"synthetic" fake news will be utilized to train and test the machine learning models. Additionally, more models could be tested in order to improve the overall performance in such tasks. Finally, the features that turned out to be determinant could be further examined, to identify what makes them so.

Acknowledgements. This project has received funding from the GSRT for the European Union's Horizon 2020 research and innovation programme under grant agreement No. 644333.

References

1. Fact extraction and verification. http://fever.ai/
2. Information operations directed at Hong Kong. https://blog.twitter.com/en_us/topics/company/2019/information_operations_directed_at_Hong_Kong.html
3. Loughran-McDonald dictionary. https://sraf.nd.edu/textual-analysis/resources/
4. Natural language toolkit. https://www.nltk.org/
5. Fact-checking U.S. politics (2007). https://www.politifact.com/truth-o-meter/
6. Alowibdi, J.S., Buy, U.A., Philip, S.Y., Stenneth, L.: Detecting deception in online social networks. In: 2014 IEEE/ACM International Conference on Advances in Social Networks Analysis and Mining (ASONAM 2014), pp. 383–390. IEEE (2014)
7. Burgoon, J.K., Blair, J.P., Qin, T., Nunamaker, J.F.: Detecting deception through linguistic analysis. In: Chen, H., Miranda, R., Zeng, D.D., Demchak, C., Schroeder, J., Madhusudan, T. (eds.) ISI 2003. LNCS, vol. 2665, pp. 91–101. Springer, Heidelberg (2003). https://doi.org/10.1007/3-540-44853-5_7
8. Chawla, N.V., Bowyer, K.W., Hall, L.O., Kegelmeyer, W.P.: SMOTE: synthetic minority over-sampling technique. J. Artif. Intell. Res. **16**, 321–357 (2002)
9. Derczynski, L., Bontcheva, K.: PHEME: veracity in digital social networks. In: UMAP Workshops (2014)
10. Hai, Z., Zhao, P., Cheng, P., Yang, P., Li, X.L., Li, G.: Deceptive review spam detection via exploiting task relatedness and unlabeled data. In: Proceedings of the 2016 Conference on Empirical Methods in Natural Language Processing, pp. 1817–1826 (2016)
11. Hamza, S., Craig, S., Lauren, S., Ellie, H., Jeremy, S.V.: Hyperpartisan Facebook pages are publishing false and misleading information at an alarming rate. Buzzfeed News (2016)
12. Houvardas, J., Stamatatos, E.: N-gram feature selection for authorship identification. In: Euzenat, J., Domingue, J. (eds.) AIMSA 2006. LNCS (LNAI), vol. 4183, pp. 77–86. Springer, Heidelberg (2006). https://doi.org/10.1007/11861461_10

13. Shu, K., Mahudeswaran, D., Wang, S., Lee, D., Liu, H.: FakeNewsNet: a data repository with news content, social context and dynamic information for studying fake news on social media (2018)
14. Shu, K., Sliva, A., Wang, S., Tang, J., Liu, H.: Fake news detection on social media: a data mining perspective (2017)
15. Li, C., Guo, X., Mei, Q.: Deep memory networks for attitude identification. In: Proceedings of the Tenth ACM International Conference on Web Search and Data Mining, pp. 671–680. ACM (2017)
16. Loughran, T., McDonald, B.: When is a liability not a liability? Textual analysis, dictionaries, and 10-Ks. J. Finance **66**(1), 35–65 (2011)
17. Mitra, T., Gilbert, E.: CREDBANK: a large-scale social media corpus with associated credibility annotations. In: Ninth International AAAI Conference on Web and Social Media (2015)
18. Pennebaker, J.W., Boyd, R.L., Jordan, K., Blackburn, K.: The development and psychometric properties of LIWC2015. Technical report (2015)
19. Pérez-Rosas, V., Mihalcea, R.: Experiments in open domain deception detection. In: Proceedings of the 2015 Conference on Empirical Methods in Natural Language Processing, pp. 1120–1125 (2015)
20. Rodriguez-Galiano, V.F., Ghimire, B., Rogan, J., Chica-Olmo, M., Rigol-Sanchez, J.P.: An assessment of the effectiveness of a random forest classifier for land-cover classification. ISPRS J. Photogram. Remote Sens. **67**, 93–104 (2012)
21. Rubin, V.L., Conroy, N.J., Chen, Y.: Towards news verification: deception detection methods for news discourse. In: Hawaii International Conference on System Sciences (2015)
22. Ruchansky, N., Seo, S., Liu, Y.: CSI: a hybrid deep model for fake news detection. In: Proceedings of the 2017 ACM on Conference on Information and Knowledge Management, pp. 797–806 (2017)
23. Shojaee, S., Murad, M.A.A., Azman, A.B., Sharef, N.M., Nadali, S.: Detecting deceptive reviews using lexical and syntactic features. In: 2013 13th International Conference on Intelligent Systems Design and Applications, pp. 53–58. IEEE (2013)
24. Shu, K., Mahudeswaran, D., Wang, S., Lee, D., Liu, H.: FakeNewsNet: a data repository with news content, social context and dynamic information for studying fake news on social media. arXiv preprint arXiv:1809.01286 (2018)
25. Shu, K., Sliva, A., Wang, S., Tang, J., Liu, H.: Fake news detection on social media: a data mining perspective. ACM SIGKDD Explor. Newslett. **19**(1), 22–36 (2017)
26. Songram, P., Choompol, A., Thipsanthia, P., Boonjing, V.: Detecting Thai messages leading to deception on Facebook. In: Huynh, V.-N., Inuiguchi, M., Le, B., Le, B.N., Denoeux, T. (eds.) IUKM 2016. LNCS (LNAI), vol. 9978, pp. 293–304. Springer, Cham (2016). https://doi.org/10.1007/978-3-319-49046-5_25
27. Sosoni, V., et al.: Translation crowdsourcing: creating a multilingual corpus of online educational content. In: Proceedings of the Eleventh International Conference on Language Resources and Evaluation (LREC 2018) (2018)
28. Tacchini, E., Ballarin, G., Della Vedova, M.L., Moret, S., de Alfaro, L.: Some like it hoax: Automated fake news detection in social networks. arXiv preprint arXiv:1704.07506 (2017)
29. Wang, W.Y.: "liar, liar pants on fire": A new benchmark dataset for fake news detection. arXiv preprint arXiv:1705.00648 (2017)
30. Wikipedia contributors: Flesch-kincaid readability tests Wikipedia, the free encyclopedia (2019). https://en.wikipedia.org/w/index.php?title=Flesch%E2%80%93Kincaid_readability_tests&oldid=931233970. Accessed 21 Jan 2020

Improving Movie Recommendation Systems Filtering by Exploiting User-Based Reviews and Movie Synopses

Konstantina Iliopoulou, Andreas Kanavos[⊠], Aristidis Ilias, Christos Makris, and Gerasimos Vonitsanos

Computer Engineering and Informatics Department,
University of Patras, Patras, Greece
k.iliopoulou1@gmail.com,
{kanavos,aristeid,makri,mvonitsanos}@ceid.upatras.gr

Abstract. This paper addresses the subject of Movie Recommendation Systems, focusing on two of the most well-known filtering techniques, Collaborative Filtering and Content-based Filtering. The first approach proposes a supervised probabilistic Bayesian model that forms recommendations based on the previous evaluations of other movies the user has watched. The second approach composes an unsupervised learning technique that forms clusters of users, using the K-Means algorithm, based on their preference of different movie genres, as it is expressed through their ratings. Both of the above approaches are compared to each other as well as to a basic method known as Weighted Sum, which makes predictions based on the cosine similarity and the euclidean distance between users and movies. In addition, Content-based Filtering is implemented through K-Means clustering techniques that focus on identifying the resemblance between movie plots. The first approach clusters movies according to the Tf/Idf weighting scheme, applying weights to the terms of movie plots. The latter identifies the likeness between movie plots, utilizing the BM25 algorithm. The efficiency of the above methods is calculated through the Accuracy metric.

Keywords: Recommendation systems · Movie Recommendation Systems · Collaborative Filtering · Content-based Filtering · Text analysis

1 Introduction

Rapid Internet growth continually creates an immense amount of data, as well as the need to find more productive ways to handle it. Users daily have to face the process of choosing between overwhelming varieties of different products during their interaction with any digital platform, a pursuit often tiring and disorienting.

© IFIP International Federation for Information Processing 2020
Published by Springer Nature Switzerland AG 2020
I. Maglogiannis et al. (Eds.): AIAI 2020 Workshops, IFIP AICT 585, pp. 187–199, 2020.
https://doi.org/10.1007/978-3-030-49190-1_17

As one of the most popular research issues, one can consider the subject of improving the quality of ranking in Information Retrieval results. To this extent, information need is expressed through the form of queries submitted to a search engine or platform with the intention of receiving any available fact regarding the inquiry [1,11]. Effective retrieval techniques and methodologies have been mostly derived from the class of probabilistic models, and several approaches have been successfully implemented in this direction [1,3].

Recommendation Systems provide a sound solution for the information flood each user has to face daily during their interaction with online platforms. Aiming to provide users with the ability to find products that may be of their interest, make up the target of these systems in an automatic, fast and efficient way. Their recommendations are based on the analysis of previous user behavior, with respect to the evaluation of products as well as the recognition of the similarity between different users and products. This occurs, in order to derive a prediction of which products a user will consider interesting. Due to their wide-ranging scope of application, the research community takes an active interest in the field.

This paper addresses the subject of Movie Recommendation Systems, focusing on two of the most well-known filtering techniques, Collaborative Filtering, and Content-based Filtering. Specifically, Collaborative Filtering is implemented through two different approaches. The first approach proposes a supervised probabilistic Bayesian model that forms recommendations based on the estimation of the probability a user gives a specific rating to some movie, by examining either the rating given to that movie by the rest of the users or the rating the user gave to other movies he/she has watched. The second approach is an unsupervised learning technique that forms clusters of users using the K-Means algorithm, based on their preference of different movie genres, as it is expressed through their ratings. Both of the above approaches are compared to each other and also to a basic method known as Weighted Sum that makes predictions based on the cosine similarity and the euclidean distance between users and movies. Content-based Filtering is implemented through K-Means clustering techniques that focus on identifying the similarity between movie plots. The first approach clusters movies according to the Tf/Idf weighting scheme, applying weights to the terms of movie plots. The second approach identifies the similarity between movie plots utilizing the BM25 algorithm.

The rest of the paper is organized as follows. Section 2 presents the related work. Section 3 overviews the basic concepts and algorithms used in this paper. Sections 4 and 5 detail the implementation and evaluation respectively. Finally, in Sect. 6, our concluding remarks and future work are presented.

2   Related Work

In [4], authors depict the setup for an opinion-based entity ranking system. The intuition behind their work is that each entity can be represented by all the review texts and that the users of such a system can determine their preferences on several attributes during the evaluation process. Thus, we can expect that a user's query would consist of preferences on multiple attributes. Authors in [10] further improved the setup by developing schemes, which take into account sentiment and clustering information about the opinions expressed in reviews; also authors propose the naive consumer model as an unsupervised schema that utilizes information from the web to yield a weight of importance to each of the features used for evaluating the entities.

In addition, in [8], the authors propose a novel probabilistic network scheme that employs a topic identification method, in order to modify the ranking of results as the users select documents. Also, a novel framework aiming to provide the necessary tools for the refinement of search results, taking into account feedback provided by the user, is introduced in [7]. More specifically, the corresponding approach examines query-independent document processing and representation resulting in a lexical based inter-document similarity, that allows clusters to be formed.

Bayesian networks are known to perform well in the recommendation problem, as shown in the studies of [6,13,15]. The main difference between what we propose and the research in [13] is that we aim to predict the actual rating given by a user on a scale of 1–5, and not simply predict whether users will like or dislike an item. We can clearly observe that the authors of this work propose a hierarchical, Bayesian, content-based approach that aims to improve the current recommendation systems by incorporating context-related information when building the user profiles. Similar is the work presented in [15], where a collaborative filtering technique based on a simple Bayesian classifier as a solution to the recommendation problem, is introduced. Related to the above contributions is [6], as authors propose a Bayesian model that incorporates user preference information expressed in their reviews; the research uses collaborative techniques and topic modeling to solve the recommendation problem.

Furthermore, K-Means algorithm, being one of the most applicable clustering algorithms, often fits in the recommendation scheme. The research presented in [16] aims to improve the scalability of collaborative filtering recommendation systems by exploiting the bisecting K-Means clustering algorithm. The key idea is to apply the clustering algorithm in the user-item matrix and utilize the formed clusters as user neighborhoods. In order to form predictions for a specific user, the system implements the collaborative filtering algorithm by examining only the users' neighborhood. The approach in [2] exploits K-Means clustering, in order to form user clusters based on their ratings and a softmax regression classifier to predict the cluster each user belongs to. What is aimed here, is for the system to recommend the highest-rated movies from that cluster. In addition, the study in [9] discusses the clustering of similar documents by using the K-Means clustering algorithm and the Tf/Idf representation of the documents.

The research conducted in [12] centers on rating-based collaborative filtering. Its onus is to build user profiles and predict all missing values by developing a generative latent variable model, which extends already existing models such as the multinomial mixture model and LDA and is called the User Rating Profile model (URP). As a previous work on opinion clustering emerging in reviews, one can consider the setup presented in [5]. Authors propose a probabilistic network scheme, e.g., inference network, which consists of four component levels, in following takes as input the belief of the user for each query (initially, all entities are equivalent) and produces a new ranking for the entities as output.

The work presented in [14] proposes a scheme for user clustering so as to identify similar tastes in movies; also, the clustering techniques are prone to discovering relationships between movie plots and movie genres. Our work however differentiates from this study since we focus on capturing similarities between movie plots regardless of the genre they ultimately belong to.

3   Preliminaries

The representation of a text in a comprehensible form for data mining and text pre-processing is the first important and critical task, considering tokenization, stop-words removal, punctuation and number removal, POS tagging, lower case as well as stemming. Text representation is based on the assumption that any text is described through its constituent words and is essential about replacing words with a numerical value, making the text editable by standard methods of analysis.

3.1   Text Representation

There are two main categories of text representation:

- Tuples, where the text is represented by a plurality of fields. The number of fields is equal to the size of the vocabulary and each field corresponds to a different word.
- Vector, where the text is represented by a vector. Each different word in the vocabulary corresponds to a component of the vector and defines one of the dimensions of the vector space. Representing a text document using vectors, is the most common approach, as it allows for more efficient calculations.

3.2   Tf/Idf

Tf/Idf constitutes one of the most popular algorithms to weigh a keyword in any content, assigning the importance to that keyword based on the combination of term frequency (Tf) and inverted document frequency (Idf) weights. It developed for Information Retrieval, however it is also widely used in Data Mining in combination with classification and clustering algorithms.

Specifically, given a term k_i of the document d_j, the weight w_{ij} defined by the Tf/Idf, is denoted as $Tf/Idf_{i,j}$ so as to apply:

$$Tf/Idf_{i,j} = Tf_{i,j} \times Idf_i \tag{1}$$

3.3 BM25

The word retrieval function BM25 is known due to ranking sets of documents based on query terms appearing in the documents of interest, regardless of their proximity within the document. Specifically, BM is a family of scoring functions with slightly different components and parameters, while various variants of the basic equation of the BM25 are encountered. In our work, a variant of the basic equation of BM25 was used, in which Idf is normalized to avoid negative values of the ranking function.

3.4 Principal Component Analysis

Principal Component Analysis (PCA) is one of the most commonly used methods for dimensionality reduction and feature extraction. It creates uncorrelated linear combinations of the original possibly correlated variables, and by utilizing the eigenvalues and eigenvectors of the variance/covariance matrix, it projects the data on a space of different dimensions transforming them in a way they can be adequately described by fewer dimensions.

3.5 Similarity Metrics

In this paper, vectors represent users or movies, and the similarity is expressed by the distance of these vectors. The two metrics used in the movie recommendation system are Cosine Similarity, which measures the similarities between two vectors, calculating its cosine of the angle between them, and Euclidean Distance, which expresses the similarity of two vectors, estimating the Euclidean distance between them. The similarity between all users or movies in the dataset can be represented by an array whose rows and columns correspond to users or movies. The value of each cell is the similarity between the elements in the corresponding row and column.

3.6 User Based Collaborative Filtering

User-based collaborative filtering makes predictions and suggestions based on the similarities among users. The movies suggested to the user are similar to those users have found interesting, that is, they have rated them highly. For example, assuming two users (U_A and U_B) who have seen the same movies and have both scored them with high ratings, as well as a new movie that U_A is watching and enjoying, the question will be: will this movie be suggested to U_B? A positive response occurs; judging by the past behavior of the two users, it is concluded that they have similar preferences.

3.7 Item Based Collaborative Filtering

Item-based collaborative filtering implements predictions and suggestions based on similarity among movies. The movies suggested to the user are similar to the ones they have found interesting in the past. The similarity among movies arises by examining the scores received by other users of the system. For example, let us assume three users U_A, U_B and U_C who have seen two movies M_1 and M_2 and have rated them with roughly the same ratings, which makes these movies quite alike. If a fourth user U_D watches the first movie M_1 and scores it high the system will also propose the second movie M_2 to this viewer.

3.8 Weighted Sum

The simplest way of predicting user ratings is known as Weighted Sum and results from the inner product of the user-movie matrix along with the similarity matrix. User preferences can be modeled by a MxN matrix, known as user-item matrix, where M is the total number of users and N is the total number of items available in the system. In this paper, movies are considered items, each cell contains the rating of a specific user for a concrete movie (or is empty in case that they have not provided with an evaluation). Therefore, each user is represented by a vector, whose components are the ratings of the movies they evaluated. Similarly, movies are represented by vectors containing the ratings assigned to them by the users. The aim is to fill the missing values of the matrix with the predicted ratings.

4 Implementation

4.1 Dataset

The dataset used in this study is called ml-latest-small and is available on the MovieLens research site run by GroupLens Research at the University of Minnesota[1]. It consists of 9742 movies and 610 users, and describes the rating given to the movies by the users on a scale of 1 to 5. Each user has rated at least 20 movies, and each movie is rated by at least one user.

The dataset was extended in order to include also the movie plots by using the identifiers available in the dataset for gaining access to the content of the imdb and tmdb web pages. For each movie, the plots from these two sites were concatenated, and text pre-processing techniques were used with the NLTK Python tool, namely tokenization, lowercase conversion, numbers, and punctuation removal as well as stemming.

The ratings and number of users before and after the removal of low ratings, are presented in Table 1. It is worth noticing that after the removal of ratings with values lower than 3, 5, the mean rating per genre is greater than 4, 5; before the removal, this rating was in the range of 3, 5 to 3, 8. In addition, concerning the number of users per genre, it is shown that the same genres are considered as popular before and after the removal of low ratings (Fig. 1).

---

[1] https://grouplens.org/datasets/movielens/.

Table 1. Ratings and number of users before and after removal of low ratings

Genres	Number of movies	Rating before	Rating after	Number of users before	Number of users after
Adventure	1263	3,61	4,24	606	588
Animation	611	3,63	4,21	527	458
Children	664	3,48	4,2	559	482
Comedy	3756	3,56	4,24	609	603
Fantasy	779	3,57	4,26	583	528
Romance	1596	3,63	4,24	606	588
Drama	4361	3,75	4,3	610	606
Action	1828	3,55	4,23	608	596
Crime	1199	3,75	4,31	603	581
Thriller	1894	3,62	4,25	609	599
Horror	978	3,45	4,24	535	472
Mystery	573	3,75	4,29	580	542
Sci-Fi	980	3,53	4,23	605	570
War	382	3,87	4,33	551	513
Musical	334	3,58	4,21	470	397
Documentary	440	3,77	4,21	223	191
IMAX	158	3,8	4,25	458	415
Western	167	3,64	4,23	420	357
Film-Noir	87	3,84	4,26	239	209
no genres listed	34	3,61	4,22	26	20

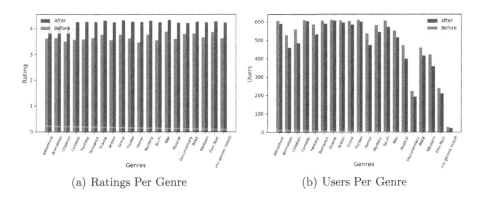

(a) Ratings Per Genre   (b) Users Per Genre

Fig. 1. Ratings and number of users before and after removal of low ratings

4.2 Input Data for the Clustering Algorithm

In following, the construction of the matrices given as input to the clustering algorithm for the cases of user clustering and movie clustering, was implemented. Concretely, BM25, Tf/Idf and User Preference scores are taken into consideration for our proposed implementations.

4.2.1 Scores Matrices

BM25 scores can be utilized in a 1863×1863 matrix, where its rows and columns correspond to the different movies of the dataset. Each cell holds the BM25 ranking score for the plot of the movie as the column defines the query, and the row defines the plot of the movie.

On the other hand, Tf/Idf scores can be utilized in a 1863×5432 matrix. Specifically, each row corresponds to a different movie, and the columns correspond to the stemmed terms of all the movie plots. Each cell holds the Tf/Idf weight of the column term for the movie plot in the corresponding row.

4.2.2 User Preference Matrix

The user preference matrix represents the users' preferences for the different genres of movies. Since our goal is to provide the user with movie recommendations, the first step was to remove all ratings less than $3, 5$. If a user has not rated any movies with a rating greater or equal to $3, 5$, the user is excluded from the procedure. For every user, the total number of movies being watched, belonging to a particular genre, was counted. In following, this count was divided by the total number of movies the user has watched. Specifically, each matrix row represents a different user, each column corresponds to a different movie genre, and each cell defines the percentage of preference of that user towards that particular genre.

4.2.3 Clustering

Our approach regarding the implementation of a recommendation system utilizing the K-Means clustering algorithm is two-fold, namely, user clustering and movie clustering.

Regarding the user clustering approach, the examination of users' ratings, the percentage calculation of their different genres preference, as well as the clustering based on these percentages, are implemented. The movie clustering approach is utilized in two different cases, namely focusing on the plot of each movie and implementing content-based filtering. In the first case, each movie is represented by a vector containing the Tf/Idf weights of the terms of the movie plots, while in the second case, by a vector containing the corresponding BM25 scores. In both implementations, each user is assigned to the cluster containing the highest number of movies being watched by this user. In order for the proposed method to recommend a movie to a user, the movies being watched by other users of the same cluster are initially examined. In following, the mean rating of those movies, by considering only the ratings given by the users of the cluster, is calculated and finally, the movies with the highest ratings are recommended.

The data is given as input in the form of the matrices, as mentioned above. Dimensionality reduction is considered to be an essential step before executing the K-Means clustering, and the technique utilized for this purpose is Principal Component Analysis (PCA).

4.2.4   Classification

The aim of recommendation systems is to calculate the probability of the movie rating given to a movie by a user while taking into consideration the ratings given by other users. Thus, a user-based and item-based collaborative filtering, as well as a combination of these two methods, are implemented. In the user-based case, each movie is represented by a vector containing all users' ratings given to that movie. Similarly, in the item-based case, users are considered as observations, and the movies form the observation features. The combinatorial filtering results from the mean of the predicted ratings, are derived from the user-based as well as the item-based filtering.

A user id, representing the user to whom movies will be recommended, and the user-movie matrix are given as input. Moreover, the missing values of each row of the user-movie matrix were filled by the mean rating of the user corresponding to that row. For the probability calculation, the multinomial Naive Bayes algorithm is utilized where we have set $a = 1$ for Laplace Smoothing. The specific algorithm is chosen because the possible ratings are on a scale of 1 to 5, meaning they are not binary values and their distribution is not known.

Regarding the data splitting, in the case of user-based filtering, 70% was randomly used for training and 30% for testing. On the other hand, when considering the item-based filtering, the users to whom recommendations will be made are defined as test set whereas training set includes the rest of the users.

5   Evaluation

For the evaluation of our proposed methods, we have used Accuracy, which is one of the most commonly used metrics for the evaluation of a system prediction. Since our goal is to compare the different approaches presented in our work, we have converted the ratings to binary values using a unified manner, in a way that high ratings ($>= 3, 5$) are replaced by the value 1 and the lower ratings ($< 3, 5$) are replaced by the value 0. In the case of Bayesian classifier, high ratings are considered the ones with value equal to or greater than 3.

For our experiments, 10 users were randomly chosen, with the only requirement having watched and rated at least 100 movies. The accuracy was calculated for each user by examining their actual ratings in relation to the predicted ratings for the movies they have watched. In following, the mean of the predictions accuracy for the different methods is calculated.

The first two principal components were the ones carrying the largest amount of information, as depicted in Table 2. In the case of movie clustering, even though the first two components held a small percentage of the total variance, our experiments showed that using more components in the clustering phase did not significantly improve the clustering results.

Table 2. Principal component variance

PCA features	User preference matrix	Tf/Idf matrix	BM25 matrix
0	0,34391	0,00394	0,06221
1	0,24211	0,00370	0,01613
2	0,09896	0,00334	0,01260
3	0,06825	0,00313	0,01207
4	0,05264	0,00303	0,01166
5	0,04318	0,00284	0,01114
6	0,02570	0,00279	0,00972
7	0,02316	0,00262	0,00931
8	0,02169	0,00261	0,00856
9	0,01582	0,00248	0,00769
10	0,01369	0,00245	0,00731
11	0,01183	0,00238	0,00724
12	0,00943	0,00236	0,00693
13	0,00888	0,00232	0,00664
14	0,00794	0,00227	0,00630

In order to determine the optimal number of clusters to be formed, the elbow curve method has been used. The optimal number of clusters k, in the user clustering is set as 5, and in the case of movie is set as 4. Even for the case of movie clustering, the elbow curve method provided ambiguous results, and after testing the algorithm numerous times, it was observed that high values of k lead to uneven distribution of points inside the clusters, as presented in Table 3. Furthermore, by examining the most frequent words of the movie plots in each cluster, it was found that for values bigger than 4, the formed clusters had in common the most frequent words, indicating that there was no clear separation regarding the content of the movie plots.

Furthermore, Tables 4, 5 and 6 introduce the experimental results in terms of Clustering, Classification using Bayesian model and Weighted Sum, respectively. Regarding clustering, the Tf/Idf movie method yields the best accuracy results. It is worth mentioning that the accuracy of the user clustering method is equal to 66.17%, and even though it is lower than the movie clustering method accuracy, it outperforms the basic Weighted Sum approaches.

Table 3. Sum of squared errors

Number of clusters	User clustering	Tf/Idf movie clustering	BM25 movie clustering
1	130.5	1840.6	72655490
2	101.3	1835.8	69883117
3	86.9	1831.6	68966348
4	79.1	1827.7	68471660
5	73.8	1825.3	68207625
6	69.9	1822.2	67713490
7	66.5	1820.1	67586018
8	63.3	1816.8	67131015
9	61.4	1817.3	66882121
10	59.4	1811.1	66828590
11	57.6	1810.3	66513930
12	56.3	1809.5	66236101
13	54.7	1808.3	66236317
14	53.7	1805.7	66045114
15	52.3	1804.9	65882937
16	50.6	1802.1	65557487
17	49.6	1801	65666520
18	49.2	1801.2	65355018
19	48.1	1797	65455797

Table 4. Clustering

User clustering	66,17%
Tf/Idf movie clustering	67,96%
BM25 movie	63,86%

Table 5. Classification (Bayes)

User based	80,96%
Movie based	83,64%
User and movie based	30,45%

In addition, regarding the classification experimental evaluation, the best result was derived from the movie based probabilistic Bayesian approach. Specifically, the Bayesian model outperforms the basic Weighted Sum model with a difference approximately 24% for the user-based case and about 20% for the movie-based case. The low accuracy score of the combinational Bayesian approach is due to the fact that the system examined only the first 1000 movies for the movie-based method.

Finally, the high similarity of the Weighted Sum results can be considered because of the low dimensionality of the user vectors utilized in our experiments.

Table 6. Weighted sum for cosine similarity and euclidean distance

Cosine similarity			Euclidean distance		
User based	Movie based	User and movie based	User based	Movie based	User and movie based
56,21%	64,14%	60,45%	56,21%	64,14%	60,21%

6 Conclusions and Future Work

This paper offers an extensive analysis of different approaches for the implementation of Movie Recommendation Systems, providing an integrated solution to the recommendation problem. On one hand, it proposes the Bayesian Collaborative filtering approach that renders the best results, outweighing the other models discussed in this paper. On the other hand, it proposes a Content-based technique based on movie clustering according to their plots through the Tf/Idf weighting scheme, which yields a solution to the movie recommendation problem when user preference information is not available. Furthermore, the three different implementations are introduced, namely, K-Means for users and movies clustering, Naive Bayes classification and Weighted Sum for user-based, item-based and both in combination collaborative filtering.

Future work is bound to include the construction of a hybrid model combining the Bayesian and clustering techniques. The user clustering approach, despite not being the most accurate one, provides an adequate way of detecting similarities between users concerning their preferences towards the different genre of movies. It could serve as a base for the probabilistic approach, i.e., only the users belonging to the same cluster would be considered for the calculation of the probabilities of each prediction. Furthermore, it is deemed appropriate to test different techniques for dimensionality reduction, other than the PCA method. Finally, an interesting approach would be to give, as query, one term at time in the BM25 plot clustering.

Acknowledgement. Andreas Kanavos, Aristidis Ilias and Christos Makris have been co-financed by the European Union and Greek national funds through the Regional Operational Program "Western Greece 2014–2020", under the Call "Regional Research and Innovation Strategies for Smart Specialisation - RIS3 in Information and Communication Technologies" (project: 5038701 entitled "Reviews Manager: Hotel Reviews Intelligent Impact Assessment Platform").

References

1. Baeza-Yates, R.A., Ribeiro-Neto, B.A.: Modern Information Retrieval: The Concepts and Technology Behind Search, 2nd edn. Pearson Education Ltd., Harlow (2011)
2. Byström, H.: Movie Recommendations from User Ratings. Stanford University (2013)

3. Croft, W.B., Metzler, D., Strohman, T.: Search Engines: Information Retrieval in Practice. Pearson Education, London (2009)
4. Ganesan, K., Zhai, C.: Opinion-based entity ranking. Inf. Retrieval **15**(2), 116–150 (2012)
5. Gourgaris, P., Kanavos, A., Makris, C., Perrakis, G.: Review-based entity-ranking refinement. In: 11th International Conference on Web Information Systems and Technologies (WEBIST), pp. 402–410 (2015)
6. Jiang, M., Song, D., Liao, L., Zhu, F.: A Bayesian recommender model for user rating and review profiling. Tsinghua Sci. Technol. **20**(6), 634–643 (2015)
7. Kanavos, A., Kotoula, P., Makris, C., Iliadis, L.: Employing query disambiguation using clustering techniques. Evol. Syst. 1–11 (2019)
8. Kanavos, A., Makris, C., Plegas, Y., Theodoridis, E.: Ranking web search results exploiting wikipedia. Int. J. Artif. Intell. Tools (IJAIT) **25**(3), 1–26 (2016)
9. Lydia, E.L., Govindaswamy, P., Lakshmanaprabu, S., Ramya, D.: Document clustering based on text mining K-means algorithm using euclidean distance similarity. J. Adv. Res. Dyn. Control Syst. (JARDCS) **10**(2), 208–214 (2018)
10. Makris, C., Panagopoulos, P.: Improving opinion-based entity ranking. In: 10th International Conference on Web Information Systems and Technologies (WEBIST), pp. 223–230 (2014)
11. Manning, C.D., Raghavan, P., Schütze, H.: Introduction to Information Retrieval. Cambridge University Press, Cambridge (2008)
12. Marlin, B.: Modeling user rating profiles for collaborative filtering. In: 16th International Conference on Neural Information Processing Systems, pp. 627–634 (2004)
13. Miyahara, K., Pazzani, M.J.: Improvement of collaborative filtering with the simple Bayesian classifier. Inf. Process. Soc. Japan **43**(11) (2002)
14. Phorasim, P., Yu, L.: Movies recommendation system using collaborative filtering and K-means. Int. J. Adv. Comput. Res. (IJACR) **7**(29), 52 (2017)
15. Pomerantz, D., Dudek, G.: Context dependent movie recommendations using a hierarchical Bayesian model. In: Gao, Y., Japkowicz, N. (eds.) AI 2009. LNCS (LNAI), vol. 5549, pp. 98–109. Springer, Heidelberg (2009). https://doi.org/10.1007/978-3-642-01818-3_12
16. Sarwar, B.M., Karypis, G., Konstan, J., Riedl, J.: Recommender systems for large-scale e-commerce: scalable neighborhood formation using clustering. In: 5th International Conference on Computer and Information Technology (ICCIT), pp. 291–324 (2002)

The Converging Triangle of Cultural Content, Cognitive Science, and Behavioral Economics

Georgios Drakopoulos[1]([✉]) [iD], Ioanna Giannoukou[3] [iD], Phivos Mylonas[1] [iD], and Spyros Sioutas[2]

[1] Department of Informatics, Ionian University, Kerkyra, Hellas
{c16drak,fmylonas}@ionio.gr
[2] CEID, University of Patras, Patras, Achaia, Hellas
sioutas@ceid.upatras.gr
[3] Department of Management Science and Technology,
University of Patras, Achaia, Hellas
igian@upatras.gr

Abstract. How online cultural content is chosen based on conscious or subconscious criteria is an central question across a broad spectrum of sciences and for the entertainment industry, including content providers and distributors. To this end, a number of tailored analytics forming the backbone of recommendation engines specialized for retrieving cultural content are proposed. Their strength derives directly from well-established principles of cognitive science and behavioral economics, both scientific fields exploring aspects of human decision making. Another novel contribution of this conference paper is that these analytics are implemented in Neo4j expressed as Cypher queries. Various aspects of the cultural content and digital consumers can be naturally represented by appropriately configured vertices, whereas edges represent various connections indicating content delivery preferences. Early experiments conducted over a synthetic dataset mimicking the distributions of preferences and ratings of well-known movie datasets are encouraging as the proposed analytics outperformed the baseline of a multilayer feedforward neural network of various configurations. The synthetic dataset contains enriched preferences of mobile digital consumers of cultural content regarding literature of the Greek region of Ionian Islands.

Keywords: Cognitive science · Behavioral economics · Cultural content · Content delivery · Graph recommendation · Graph databases · Graph analytics · Neo4j · Cypher · Humanistic data

1 Introduction

Interpreting and predicting, within a reasonable degree of error, the selection of online cultural content or even a sequence of such selections, has been a central topic in various scientific fields ranging from economics and social science to

© IFIP International Federation for Information Processing 2020
Published by Springer Nature Switzerland AG 2020
I. Maglogiannis et al. (Eds.): AIAI 2020 Workshops, IFIP AICT 585, pp. 200–212, 2020.
https://doi.org/10.1007/978-3-030-49190-1_18

artificial intelligence (AI) and machine learning (ML) as well as to interested parties such as platform managers and content providers.

During the current decade the creation cultural content has reached unprecedented levels in terms of number of generators, languages, modalities, and topics. Given the ease of access to equipment ranging from an off the shelf smartphone to a digital camera as well as the prevalent culture encouraging creativity and originality, a considerable number of independent content contributors has been added to established entities such as cultural foundations, academic institutions, government agencies, and private organizations.

The primary research objective of this conference paper is to lay the groundwork for graph analytics based on sound principles of both behavioral economics and cognitive science and tailored for the recommendation of personalized delivery of cultural content. Recommendations not only assist in navigating among the plethora of available digital cultural content, but also help the digital consumer discover new and potentially interesting material. The contribution of this work is that augments the few cultural analytics, especially those implemented over a graph database, whereas giving new directions to them.

The principal motivation besides this work is that the delivery of cultural content requires specific conditions which differentiate it from ordinary digital entertainment. Specifically, cultural, educational, and location parameters must be taken into consideration.

The remaining of this work is structured as follows. Section 2 briefly reviews scientific literature regarding recommendation engines, behavioral economics, and cognitive science. The architecture and the queries of the proposed recommendation system as well as the intuition behind them are given in Sect. 3. The results of the experiments conducted so far with the proposed analytics and the baseline neural networks (NNs) are presented in Sect. 4. Finally, the conclusions and the directions for future work are given in Sect. 5. Tensors are represented with capital calligraphic letters, whereas capital and small boldface are reserved for matrices and vectors respectively. Table 1 summarizes the notation of this work.

Table 1. Notation of this conference paper

Symbol	Meaning
$\triangleq$	Definition or equality by definition
$\{s_1, \ldots, s_n\}$	Set with elements $s_1, \ldots, s_n$
$|S|$	Set cardinality
$\tau(S_1, S_2)$	Tanimoto similarity coefficient for sets S_1 and S_2
$c(\mathbf{d_1}, \mathbf{d_2})$	Cosine similarity coefficient for vectors $\mathbf{d_1}$ and $\mathbf{d_2}$
$\mathbf{O}_{n_1, n_2}$	Zero matrix of dimensions $n_1 \times n_2$

2   Previous Work

Scientific literature abounds with works regarding general- and special purpose recommendation systems for various tasks relying on diverse technologies. Then, a shift towards adaptive and content-based recommendation systems was made as is made clear from works like [26] and [21]. Initializing a recommendation system and associate issues are explored in [20]. Recently, with the advent of Semantic Web, incorporating trust into recommender systems has been also added to the line of research [1]. Applications of recommendation systems include software engineering as discussed in [28].

Cultural analytics are the offshoot of social sciences and data science aiming at providing deeper insight into the individual and collective cultural background [23] and [24]. Possible transitions to data-driven cultural analytics are discussed among others in [14], whereas applications include tracing social patterns in social media [29] such as Instagram [15] and flickr [32].

Behavioral economics is a field studying human behavior from a decision-making point of view [5]. Recurring major topics include conflict and compliance [30], corporate management [19], public policy [7], rewards and gamification [2], and learning to evaluate rational choices with a multitude of criteria [9]. The psychological grounds of the field are given in [16], while a recent overview of the field is given in [36].

Cognitive science covers the study of human mental activity at various levels [31]. Sources include high level psychological and sociological observations, education, as well as low level data about brain physiology and connectivity [8]. A framework for evaluating decision making is presented in [13] and mental decision models in [37]. A thorough revision of human decision making from a cognitive science perspective is given in [4]. The relationships between brain functionality and the structure of the human nervous system are explored in [33], while the connections between cognitive sciences and language are investigated in [3].

Tensor algebra is the generalization of matrix algebra to three or more dimensions [17]. Traditionally, tensors were widely applied to singal processing applications such as brain MRIs [35], MIMO radars [25], multispectral imaging [27], and face recognition [34]. However, recently tensor analytics have been implemented over Neo4j in order to combine structural and functional higher order analytics in [11]. Moreover, a genetic algorithm for approximately clustering a tensor with spatiosocial data has been implemented in [12].

3   Analytics

3.1   Implementation

Figure 1 depicts the overview of analytics architecture. In essence, the architecture is a long feedback loop where digital consumers are given suggestions as to which piece of cultural content to select based on their past decisions. Neo4j is a graph database where graphs are natural, namely they are physically represented as a graph [10]. From an implementation perspective, a data structure which is efficient and versatile enough to store an implementation of the property graph, the conceptual model of Neo4j, is described in [18]. The Neo4j instance was interfacing with a Python client running the py2neo module, which allows both the formulation of dynamic Cypher queries and the delcarative manipulation of the database.

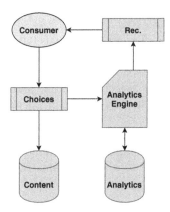

Fig. 1. Proposed analytics architecture.

3.2   Ties to Behavioral Economics and Cognitive Science

The recommendation architecture is explicitly or implicitly based on findings from behavioral economics and cognitive science. Also, it should be noted that the names of these findings are not unique as various studies may give them different names. The first finding establishes that a digital consumer is very likely to follow the recommendations. This is part justifies the frequent selections.

Proposition 1 (Default options). *A digital consumer is more likely to follow certain default options rather than change them.*

The second finding establishes that properly designed recommendations are likely to be relevant.

Proposition 2 (Sliding window). *There is a limited selection window where the preferences of the digital consumer remain constant.*

The third finding justifies the inclusion of past selections to the recommedations list as well as suggestions which are similar to past selections.

Proposition 3 (Cognitive bias). *A consumer will tend to select content she/he agrees with.*

3.3 Analytics

The first task is to define the entities, which in the graph database world are usually but not exclusively modeled as vertices, as well as the possible connections between them, which frequently form the edges. Here it should be noted that representing connections as vertices may sound counterintuitive, but within a graph database design context may well make sense.

For the purposes of this work, the following entities are considered:

- Digital consumers, which often are individuals but may well represent institution accounts, company accounts, or intelligent agents. Currently, they have the following properties: *name*, which is the unique vertex name, *hist*, which contains the last n content selections of the particular consumer, and *kw*, which is an array of at least three of the prespecified keywords of the right column of Table 2.
- Cultural content, which may well assume any form such as text, video, or music. Currently, they are composed of the following properties: *id*, which is the unique vertex id, and *kw*, which contains the keywords related to that verex.

How content simialrity can be quantified? A first approach is to compute the Tanimoto similarity coefficient between two content vertices and to insert a unique edge labeled SIMILAR with the actual coefficient value being a single edge property. Recall that said coefficient is defined as:

$$\tau\left(S_1, S_2\right) \triangleq \frac{|S_1 \cap S_2|}{|S_1 \cup S_2|} = \frac{|S_1 \cap S_2|}{|S_1| + |S_2| - |S_1 \cap S_2|} \tag{1}$$

An alternative approch relies on semantics and mapping sets to distributions. Specifically, each aspect keyword in the list of a content vertex is connected to a fundamental content type, as shown in Table 2. Consider, for instance, the following (fictional) keyword list:

$$['lyrics', 'music', 'opera', 'director', 'singer', 'actor', 'author'] \tag{2}$$

Given the entries of Table 2, then the corresponding distribution is:

$$\mathbf{d} \triangleq \left[\frac{4}{7}, \frac{1}{7}, \frac{2}{7}\right] \tag{3}$$

The above distribution was derived by dividing the number of keywords from each category of Table 2 (in the order they are shown) to the total number of keywords in the list. Also, observe that each keyword has been selected on purpose to represent a specific aspect of the content type. Thus, aspect-specific analytics can be constructed as well. Moreover, each keyword has been assigned to only one category in order to avoid ambiguity. Once two distributions are given, their proximity can be computed using the cosine similarity:

$$c\left(\mathbf{d_1}, \mathbf{d_2}\right) \triangleq \frac{\sum_{i=1}^{p} \mathbf{d_1}\left[i\right] \mathbf{d_2}\left[i\right]}{\left(\sum_{i=1}^{p} \mathbf{d_1}\left[i\right]\right)^{\frac{1}{2}} \left(\sum_{i=1}^{p} \mathbf{d_2}\left[i\right]\right)^{\frac{1}{2}}} \tag{4}$$

Table 2. Keyword map to fundamental types.

Type	Keywords
Music	lyrics, opera, singer, instruments, soprano, music
Literature	author, structure, ending, plot, twist, literature
Theater	actor, director, lighting, performance, script, theater

In order to create a digital consumer vertex the following Cypher query should be used. Notice that every Cypher query must return a result, in this case the newly created vertex. Also, the **merge** clause ensures that at most one unique vertex is create, as if for some reason a duplicate vertex is attempted to be inserted, then no new vertex will be added to the graph. On the other hand, in such a scenario the **create** clause would have created a duplicate vertex.

```
merge (dc:consumer, {name: '<name>' ,
     hist: ['<ccid_1>', ... , '<ccid_n>'] ,
     kw: ['<kw_1>', ... , '<kw_n>']})
return dc
```

The following Cypher constraint ensures that the property *name* of a vertex of a type *consumer* is unique:

```
create constraint on (dc:consumer)
assert dc.name is unique
```

Having ensured the uniqueness of each consumer, the next query returns a list of all consumers in the system:

```
match (dc:consumer)
return dc.name as name order by name
```

Moreover, when a digital consumer accesses a certain piece of cultural content, then an ACCESS relationship is additionally created to indicate a generic access type with the *hits* property set to one. The **merge** clause is used as a safeguard against inserting multiple access relationships between the same pair of vertices.

```
match (dc:consumer {name: 'name'}),(cc:content {id:'id'})
merge (dc)-[r:ACCESS {hits: 1}]->(cc)
return r as edge
```

On the contrary, when this is not the first time the consumer asks for this content, then the *hits* property can be updated like this:

```
match (dc:consumer)-[r:ACCESS]->(cc:content)
where dc.name='name' and cc.id='id'
set r.hits = r.hits + 1
return r.hits as hits
```

To access all the distinct cultural content a specific consumer with a given name has ever accessed it suffices that the following query is issued:

```
match ( dc : consumer ) − [:ACCESS]−>( cc : content )
where dc . name = 'name '
return distinct ( cc . id )
```

In this case the label ACCESS is used as it is not important whether the consumer was interested on the content as a whole or focused on specific aspects thereof.

Likewise, to find the top consumers having accessed the most unique cultural content, it suffices to run this Cypher query:

```
match ( dc : consumer ) − [:ACCESS]−>( cc : content )
return dc as account , count( distinct ( cc )) as amount
limit p
```

Counting all the hits a consumer has ever done up to this point can be performed in the following way:

```
match ( dc : consumer )−[ r :ACCESS]−>( cc : content )
where dc . name = 'name '
with distinct ( r ) as rel
return sum( rel . hits )
```

The second group of graph cultural analytics dels with aspects of cultural vertrices. For instance, in a vertex about opera, one consumer may be particularly interested in the composer, one in the lyrics, and a third one in the year it was composed. Assuming that these aspects have been appropriately codified as a keyword in the *kw* property array of the respective vertex, then in addition the following relationship is created when the specific aspect is accessed for the first time:

```
match ( dc : consumer ) − [:ACCESS]−>( cc : content )
where dc . name = 'name ' and cc . id = 'id '
merge ( dc )−[ r :ASPECT:: '<aspect>' { hits : 1}]−>( cc )
return r
```

The above query raises the following three major architectural questions:

- When should a ASPECT::<aspect> be added or updated? We believe that the safest point to do is right after the corresponding ACCESS relationship has been added or updated. Even then an aspect is explicitly requested, again the ACCESS should be processed first.
- Should there be a distinct ASPECT::<aspect> relationship or just the generic ACCESS enriched with independent counting for each aspect request? We believe that separating the ACCESS relationship will provide for faster analytics, since separate counting process can collect in parallel the ACCESS and the relationship is additionally ASPECT::<relationship> relationships for all consumers. Moreover, seeking an aspect is semantically a different search from that of asking for the entire content.

- Along a similar line of reasoning, should there be a separate and dedicated ASPECT::<aspect> for each aspect or an array property in a generic ASPECT property along with a two-dimensional key-value array containing the aspects accessed so far and their respective hits? Extending our previous argument, we believe that Neo4j is primarily about handling relationships. Thus, respecting this fundamental design decision, our analytics will be more efficient, especially when computing values dependent on multiple aspects for all consumers. Additionally, the analytics can be written more naturally requiring less maintenance by taking advantage of the dynamic query formulation offered by py2neo.

The third and arguably more significant group of analytis deals with predicting the next cultural content request from a given digital consumer. Notice that the analytics themselves cannot be directly computed with Cypher queries, but they rely heavily on data collected by them. The one standing out is compiling a short personalized recommendation list for all digital consumers.

Here is presented an adaptive recommendation system combining past choices of the same consumer and similar content. The recommendations are updated after every decision, which in the long term yields statistically sound results. The list consists of $q_0 \equiv 0 \pmod 2$ suggestions, which was six in our senarios

- Out of them half were the most frequently accessed vertices in the t_0 decision past the current one, which in our case was three decisions ago. This small number not only saves memory space but it also consistent with the fact that a consumer will look for similar material over a short time window. These constitute sublist Q_p.
- The other half consists of the most similar vertices based on the vertices the consumer has seen so far excluding vertices already seen. These constitute sublist Q_n, which represents the novelty factor of the system.

The top half is selected adaptively based on the decisions the consumer has made in the recent past: If more options were from past options, then Q_p is the top of the list followed by Q_n, otherwise it is *vice versa*.

The Cypher queries for the verices representing cultural content are the same *mutatis mutandis*. For instance, along a similar line of reasoning, a cultural content vertex is created using this Cypher query:

```
merge ( cc : content , { id :   '<id>' ,  kw :  [ '<kw_1>' ,  ...] } )
return  cc
```

Finally, to clear the entire dataset the following Cypher query can be issued:

```
match ( v ) detach delete v
```

Note that the above query is inefficient for large datasets, practically when the order of vertices exceeds a few thousands.

3.4   Implicit Adjacency Tensor Format

Since each edge of the analytics graph, namely the graph stored at the database, is mandatorily labeled and there are multiple possible labels, it follows that said graph is by definition a multilayer graph as defined in [11]. This type of graphs can be represented with adjacency tensors, which are direct generalizations of the adjacency matrices for simple graphs. Such a tensor $\mathcal{T}$ is defined as in Eq. (5) where n is the total number of vertices and e is the total number of edges:

$$\mathcal{T} \in \{0,1\}^{n \times n \times e} \tag{5}$$

Specifically, the element $\mathcal{T}[v_i, v_k, l_j]$ where $1 \leq i,j \leq n$ and $1 \leq k \leq e$ equals one if and only if there is an edge with label l_k from v_i to v_j. Otherwise, it equals zero.

Notice that within the context of this work the adjacency tensor $\mathcal{T}$ is never explicitly constructed as it is never required, thus saving computational time. Nonetheless, the partitions of $\mathcal{T}$ are of great interest, since they reveal underlying connectivity patterns. A tensor layer can be obtained by fixing one of the three indexing integers. By focusing on the last integer, each resulting layer corresponds to an adjacency matrix formed by considering only a specific edge label. This yields two seprate cases.

Assuming there are n_d consumer and n_c content vertices with $n = n_d + n_c$ and also that the consumer vertices are all placed in $\mathcal{T}$ before the content ones, then a layer with consumer-to-content analytics has the form:

$$\mathcal{T}[:,:,k] = \left[\begin{array}{c|c} \mathbf{O}_{n_d,n_d} & \mathbf{A}_k \\ \hline \mathbf{O}_{n_c,n_d} & \mathbf{O}_{n_c,n_c} \end{array}\right], \quad \mathbf{A}_k \in \{0,1\}^{n_d \times n_c} \tag{6}$$

This layer, which is an adjacency matrix on its own right, corresponds to a special case of directed bipartite graph where the edge tails belong only to the consumer vertex set, denoted by V_d, and the edge heads belong only to the content vertext set, denoted by V_c. This is expected as only form of communication is that of a vertex $v_d \in V_d$ reaching one or more vertices of V_c. In this case, the maximum possible layer density happens when $\mathbf{A}_k$ has non-zero entries and equals:

$$\rho_0 \leq \frac{n_d n_c}{n^2} = \frac{n_d(n-n_d)}{n^2} = \frac{n_d}{n} - \left(\frac{n_d}{n}\right)^2 = \frac{n_d}{n}\left(1 - \frac{n_d}{n}\right) \tag{7}$$

On the other hand, when the analytics are content-to-content, then the respective layer has the form:

$$\mathcal{T}[:,:,k] = \left[\begin{array}{c|c} \mathbf{O}_{n_d,n_d} & \mathbf{O}_{n_d,n_c} \\ \hline \mathbf{O}_{n_c,n_d} & \mathbf{B}_k \end{array}\right], \quad \mathbf{B}_k \in \{0,1\}^{n_c \times n_c} \tag{8}$$

In these layers, matrices $\mathbf{B}_k$ represent the dynamic arising from connectivity patterns only between vertex pairs of V_c. In this case, the density ρ_0 of each layer is at most:

$$\rho_0 \leq \frac{n_c^2}{n^2} = \left(\frac{n_c}{n}\right)^2 \tag{9}$$

4   Results

4.1   Dataset

In order to evaluate in the *proof of concept* stage the proposed cultural analytics, a synthetic dataset has been created based on the preferences and features of real-world datasets about literature, opera, and theater. There are ten thousand requests in total from two thousand cultural consumers about nine hundred cultual vertices, with the three types of content being equally represented. Each request is a tuple of the form, where there may be up to three optional features:

$$(\text{consumer}, \text{vertex}[, \text{aspect}_1, \text{aspect}_2, \text{aspect}_3]) \tag{10}$$

The request distribution for each of three content types was Zipf with exponents in the rage of $[2, 3]$ in order to ensure that the distributions were converging both in the mean value and in variance. The Zipf distribution models many human-derived activities such as the letter frequency of words in natural languages, voting [6], and synthetic music generation [22].

As a baseline, four feedforward neural networks (FFNNs) have been chosen whose respective configurations are shown in Table 3. In this table each tuple entry corresponds to the total number of neurons of that given layer, whereas the number of entries is the number of layers. Always the first and the last layers are the input and output ones respectively, whereas any intermediate layers are hidden ones places in the order they are written. Layers are fully connected with each other, whereas the biases and the synaptic weights are randomly initialized.

Table 3. Configurations of the FFNN.

Name	FFNN1	FFNN2	FFNN3	FFNN4
Structure	8:8:1	8:4:1	8:8:1	8:4:1

Each such network is fed a sequence of content vertex ids and the final output of an FFNN is alao such an id. In each hidden layer the activation function is the parametric SoftPlus function $\varphi_f(\cdot)$, which is a smooth approximation to the ubiquitous ReLU function and additionally has the desired leaky property which avoids synaptic weight saturation. It is defined as:

$$\varphi_f(u; \alpha_0, \beta_0) \triangleq \ln(1 + \exp(\alpha_0 u + \beta_0)) \tag{11}$$

The activation function at the output layer neuron for the configurations FFNN1 and FFNN2 is the parametric sigmoid function $\varphi_s(\cdot)$:

$$\varphi_s(u; \alpha_0, \beta_0) \triangleq \frac{1}{1 + \exp(-\alpha_0 u + \beta_0)} \tag{12}$$

For the configurations FFNN3 and FFNN4 the activation function is the hyperbolic tangent function $\varphi_t(\cdot)$:

$$\varphi_t(u; \alpha_0, \beta_0) \triangleq \alpha_0 \tanh(\beta_0 u) \tag{13}$$

4.2   Accuracy

Table 4 lists the accuracy of the proposed methodology with either the Tanimoto similarity coefficient (P1) or the cosine similarity coefficient (P2). From the results it can be seen that P2 achieves slightly better accuracy than P1. This can be attributed, partly at least, to the fact that P2 is based on a semantically aware method, even an indirect one. On the other hand, P1 is semantically oblivious, reducing the real semantic question to a set similarity problem and in turn to a mere matching problem.

Table 4. Accuracy for the next content selection.

Method	P1	P2	FFNN1	FFNN2	FFNN3	FFNN4
Accuracy (%)	87.33	89.15	79.94	81.48	82.41	84.72

5   Conclusions and Future Work

This conference paper presented a batch of fundamental graph analytics for cultural content recommendation expressed in the form of Neo4j Cypher queries. The latter are based not only on the past decisions of a specific digital consumer, as frequent selections within a certain window, but also on content similarity metrics. The latter rely on a set of keywords describing the aspects of other main properties of the specific piece of cultural content. On that set either a semantically oblivious or a semantically aware similarity metric can be applied in order to yield the final list of recommendations. Early results from a synthetic dataset indicate that the semantically aware similarity metric yields better results in terms of the prediction accuracy. Moreover, both methods outperform a baseline consisting of four configurations of a basic feedforward neural network. Thus, the proposed methodology can offer both better accuracy and interpretability, something neural networks typically lack.

Currently the proposed methodology considers a number of consumer-to-content or content-to-content analytics only. Therefore, the addition of consumer-to-consumer analytics would be a significant addition, since various clusterings of the digital consumer set may yield improved recommedations based on the preferences of similar consumers. Moreover, time is going only forward and as a consequence no rollback methods are available to face possible system anomalies. Finaly, another direction worth exploring is incorporating semantics into possible consumer set similarity metrics, provided such a move has a meaning.

Acknowledgment. This conference paper is funded by Interreg V-A Greece-Italy Programme 2014–2020 "Fostering capacities and networking of industrial liaison offices, exploitation of research results, and business support" (ILONET), co-funded by the European Union, European Regional Development Funds (ERDF), and by national funds of Greece and Italy.

References

1. Andersen, R., et al.: Trust-based recommendation systems: an axiomatic approach. In: Conference on World Wide Web, pp. 199–208 (2008)
2. Bernheim, B.D., DellaVigna, S., Laibson, D.: Handbook of Behavioral Economics: Foundations and Applications, vol. 2. Elsevier (2019)
3. Bloch, M.: Language, anthropology, and cognitive science. Man **26**, 183–198 (1991)
4. Busemeyer, J.R.: Cognitive science contributions to decision science. Cognition **135**, 43–46 (2015)
5. Camerer, C.F., Loewenstein, G.: Behavioral Economics: Past, Present Future. Princeton University Press, Princeton (2003)
6. Chatterjee, A., Mitrović, M., Fortunato, S.: Universality in voting behavior: an empirical analysis. Sci. Rep. **3**, 1049 (2013)
7. Chetty, R.: Behavioral economics and public policy: a pragmatic perspective. Am. Econ. Rev. **105**(5), 1–33 (2015)
8. Clark, A.: Mindware: An Introduction to the Philosophy of Cognitive Science. Oxford University Press, Oxford (2000)
9. Diamond, P., Vartiainen, H., et al.: Introduction to Behavioral Economics and Its Applications. Introductory Chapters (2007)
10. Drakopoulos, G.: Tensor fusion of social structural and functional analytics over Neo4j. In: IISA. IEEE (2016). https://doi.org/10.1109/IISA.2016.7785365
11. Drakopoulos, G., Kanavos, A., Mylonas, P., Sioutas, S.: Defining and evaluating Twitter influence metrics: a higher-order approach in Neo4j. Soc. Netw. Anal. Min. **7**(1), 1–14 (2017). https://doi.org/10.1007/s13278-017-0467-9
12. Drakopoulos, G., et al.: A genetic algorithm for spatiosocial tensorclustering: exploiting TensorFlow potential. Evol. Syst. (2019). https://doi.org/10.1007/s12530-019-09274-9
13. Fellows, L.K.: The cognitive neuroscience of human decision making: a review and conceptual framework. Behav. Cogn. Neurosci. Rev. **3**(3), 159–172 (2004)
14. Hall, G.: Toward a postdigital humanities: cultural analytics and the computational turn to data-driven scholarship. Am. Lit. **85**(4), 781–809 (2013)
15. Hochman, N., Schwartz, R.: Visualizing Instagram: tracing cultural visual rhythms. In: AAAI Conference on Weblogs and Social Media (2012)
16. Kahneman, D.: Maps of bounded rationality: psychology for behavioral economics. Am. Econ. Rev. **93**(5), 1449–1475 (2003)
17. Kolda, T.G., Bader, B.W.: Tensor decompositions and applications. SIAM Rev. **51**(3), 455–500 (2009)
18. Kontopoulos, S., Drakopoulos, G.: A space efficient scheme for graph representation. In: ICTAI, pp. 299–303. IEEE, November 2014
19. Kremer, M., Rao, G., Schilbach, F.: Behavioral development economics. In: Handbook of Behavioral Economics: Applications and Foundations 1, vol. 2, pp. 345–458. Elsevier (2019)
20. Lam, X.N., Vu, T., Le, T.D., Duong, A.D.: Addressing cold-start problem in recommendation systems. In: Ubiquitous Information Management and Communication, pp. 208–211 (2008)
21. Lops, P., de Gemmis, M., Semeraro, G.: Content-based recommender systems: state of the art and trends. In: Ricci, F., Rokach, L., Shapira, B., Kantor, P.B. (eds.) Recommender Systems Handbook, pp. 73–105. Springer, Boston, MA (2011). https://doi.org/10.1007/978-0-387-85820-3_3

22. Manaris, B., Vaughan, D., Wagner, C., Romero, J., Davis, R.B.: Evolutionary music and the Zipf-Mandelbrot Law: developing fitness functions for pleasant music. In: Cagnoni, S., et al. (eds.) EvoWorkshops 2003. LNCS, vol. 2611, pp. 522–534. Springer, Heidelberg (2003). https://doi.org/10.1007/3-540-36605-9_48

23. Manovich, L.: Cultural analytics: visualising cultural patterns in the era of "more media". Domus, March 2009

24. Manovich, L.: How to follow global digital cultures, or cultural analytics for beginners. In: Deep Search: They politics of search beyond Google (2009)

25. Nion, D., Sidiropoulos, N.D.: Tensor algebra and multidimensional harmonic retrieval in signal processing for MIMO radar. IEEE Trans. Signal Process. **58**(11), 5693–5705 (2010)

26. Pazzani, M.J., Billsus, D.: Content-based recommendation systems. In: Brusilovsky, P., Kobsa, A., Nejdl, W. (eds.) The Adaptive Web. LNCS, vol. 4321, pp. 325–341. Springer, Heidelberg (2007). https://doi.org/10.1007/978-3-540-72079-9_10

27. Peng, Y., Meng, D., Xu, Z., Gao, C., Yang, Y., Zhang, B.: Decomposable nonlocal tensor dictionary learning for multispectral image denoising. In: CVPR, pp. 2949–2956 (2014)

28. Robillard, M., Walker, R., Zimmermann, T.: Recommendation systems for software engineering. IEEE Softw. **27**(4), 80–86 (2009)

29. Salah, A.A., Manovich, L., Salah, A.A., Chow, J.: Combining cultural analytics and networks analysis: studying a social network site with user-generated content. J. Broadcast. Electron. Media **57**(3), 409–426 (2013)

30. Schmid, A.A.: Conflict and Cooperation: Institutional and Behavioral Economics. Wiley, Hoboken (2008)

31. Stillings, N.A., Chase, C.H., Feinstein, M.H., Garfield, J.L.: Cognitive Science: An Introduction. MIT Press, Cambridge (1995)

32. Ushizima, D., Manovich, L., Margolis, T., Douglas, J.: Cultural analytics of large datasets from flickr. In: AAAI Conference on Weblogs and Social Media (2012)

33. Varela, F.J., Thompson, E., Rosch, E.: The Embodied Mind: Cognitive Science and Human Experience. MIT Press, Cambridge (2016)

34. Vasilescu, M.A.O., Terzopoulos, D.: Multilinear analysis of image ensembles: TensorFaces. In: Heyden, A., Sparr, G., Nielsen, M., Johansen, P. (eds.) ECCV 2002. LNCS, vol. 2350, pp. 447–460. Springer, Heidelberg (2002). https://doi.org/10.1007/3-540-47969-4_30

35. Westin, C.F., Maier, S.E., Mamata, H., Nabavi, A., Jolesz, F.A., Kikinis, R.: Processing and visualization for diffusion tensor MRI. Med. Image Anal. **6**(2), 93–108 (2002)

36. Wilkinson, N., Klaes, M.: An Introduction to Behavioral Economics. Macmillan International Higher Education (2017)

37. Yechiam, E., Busemeyer, J.R., Stout, J.C., Bechara, A.: Using cognitive models to map relations between neuropsychological disorders and human decision-making deficits. Psychol. Sci. **16**(12), 973–978 (2005)

Application and Algorithm: Maximal Motif Discovery for Biological Data in a Sliding Window

Miznah H. Alshammary$^{(\boxtimes)}$, Costas S. Iliopoulos, Manal Mohamed, and Fatima Vayani

Department of Informatics, King's College London, London, UK
{miznah.alshammary,c.iliopoulos,manal.mohamed, fatima.vayani}@kcl.ac.uk

Abstract. Since the discovery of motifs in molecular sequences for real genomic data, research into this phenomenon has attracted increased attention. Motifs are relatively short sequences that are biologically significant. This paper utilises the bioinformatics application of the algorithm outlined in [5], testing it using real genomic data from large sequences. It intends to implement bioinformatics application for real genomic data, in order to discover interesting regions for all maximal motifs, in a sliding window of length ℓ, on a sequence x of length n.

Keywords: Motif discovery · Sequence motifs · Bioinformatics application

1 Introduction

Alongside the advancement of next-generation sequencing technology, there has been an increase in the production of genomic data requiring de novo assembly and analyses, one such analysis is motif discovery [1, 8–12]. Motifs, whilst biologically significant, are relatively short sequences. Examples of motifs include protein-binding sites, such as transcription factor recognition sites [4]. This paper captures the bioinformatics application of the maximal motif discovery to solve real genomic data problems. Using the algorithms in [5], which differ significantly from the well-established (ℓ, d)-motif search problem, this paper seeks to find all ℓ length motifs from a given collection of sequences that occur in at least k sequences, where each occurrence of the motif can contain up to d mismatches [13].

The restricted length of the motif is one limitation of (ℓ, d)-motif search approaches. in fact, a longer or shorter motif could be more significant. Thus, this paper focuses on the more general problem of maximal motif discovery. As a maximal motif m˜ d, k is not determined by a given length, its significance is based on its number of occurrences compared to its substrings. A motif is considered maximal, as it cannot be extended to the left or right without its number of occurrences being reduced.

As importance is placed on the number of occurrences, the first parameter k sets a minimum threshold for the number of occurrences of a reported maximal motif. A motif m˜ d, k, occurs in the ℓ-length window ending at position i in a given string X,

I. Maglogiannis et al. (Eds.): AIAI 2020 Workshops, IFIP AICT 585, pp. 213–224, 2020.
https://doi.org/10.1007/978-3-030-49190-1_19

each of which must occur at least k times in the window and contain at most d 'don't care symbols'.

The first parameter k sets a minimum threshold for occurrences of maximal motifs. The second parameter d is more restrictive: mismatches occur in up to d specific positions in the motif, known as 'don't care letters' and denoted by $\Diamond$. Therefore, a motif is also maximal, as its 'don't care letters' cannot be specialised without reducing its number of occurrences. For example, given the sequence ACGTTATGTT and d = 1, it should be concluded that the significant motif is A$\Diamond$GTT rather than, for instance, GTT, both of which have the same number of occurrences.

However, this important observation would be missed if the restriction of $\ell = 3$. Notably, a purely de novo approach is used, with only one sequence needed as input.

Furthermore, Grossi et al. [3] proposed that the most current combinatorial solution for maximal motif discovery is a data structure termed a motif trie. A motif trie [3] represents all prefixes, suffixes and occurrence positions of each maximal motif m˜ d, k in the set Md, k of maximal motifs.

This research presents an output-sensitive algorithm with a time complexity of $O(nd + d3 \cdot \sum m˜ d, k \in Md, k |occ(m˜ d, k)|)$, where occ(m˜ d, k) is the set of occurrences of m˜ d, k, assuming the input sequence of length n is built on a constant-sized alphabet. Through further research, Iliopoulos et al. [5] proposed the first online algorithm to find occurrences of all maximal motifs in a sliding window in time, where w is the size of the machine word $O(ndl + d\lceil\frac{l}{w}\rceil \cdot \sum_{i=l}^{n-1} |DIFF_i^i 1|)$ and DIFFii−1 is the symmetric difference of the set of occurrences of maximal motifs at x [i−ℓ..i−1] and at x [i−ℓ+1..i]. The space complexity of the algorithm presented in this paper is $O(\ell 2)$. This results suggests an improvement in the time required to solve the same problem using the motif trie [2]; this would instead be $O(ndl + d^3 \cdot \sum_{i=l, m̃_{d,k} \in M_{i,d,k}}^{n-1} |occ(m̃ d, k)|)$. This presents a significant improvement, as a single occurrence of a maximal motif would be reported $O(\ell 2)$. times when using the latter approach. Therefore, the proposed algorithm results in an acceleration of $O(d2w)$ per occurrence of a maximal motif.

Implementing bioinformatics applications was the main motivation for creating a dynamic structure, in order to facilitate a sliding window on the input sequence. Specifically, this endows the additional ability to discover interesting ℓ-length regions of the sequence. This is particularly useful in various forms of bioinformatics, including the prediction of the origin of chromosomal replication (OriC) [6]. The length of OriC in model bacterial species ranges from 120 to 300 bp; for example, in E. coli, it is 240 bp E. coli [7].

Additionally, motifs that occur within OriC, such as DnaA boxes, show that d and k are small constants (for example, d = 2 and k = 4) in practice [2]. Before presenting the results of this paper, the following parameters need to be defined: m˜ d, k occurs in the

ℓ-length window ending at position i in a given string X, each of which must occur at least k times in the window and contain at most d 'don't care symbols'. These definitions are used throughout the rest of the paper. The organisation of the rest of this paper is as follows. In Sect. 2, we present preliminaries in detail. This is followed by Sect. 3 where we summarise our contribution and the experimental result to this problem. Finally, we briefly conclude and state the future work in Sect. 4.

2 Preliminaries

The proposed existing algorithm works online; to use this effectively, one must add a string of letters $(/\in \Sigma)$ to the start of x, whilst also appending a unique letter $(/\in x)$ to the end of x to ensure that the motif graph (augmented suffix tree Tx) of the final window is clear.

2.1 Maximal Motif Discovery Algorithm

In order to redefine and extend the original definition of the motif graph, each internal node V of the suffix tree ST is outlined with the following:

- For an internal node V, an integer variable $|occ(V)|$, which holds the number of occurrences of V in the window of ℓ-length on X and is Seed(V), is now defined relative to the window, not the whole string, Seed(V) is a Boolean variable, which is TRUE if node V is a seed in the window, and FALSE otherwise.
- Each node V where Seed(V) = TRUE is further augmented with the following:
- The Boolean variable Motif (V) is TRUE if node V represents a singleton motif in the window, and FALSE otherwise.
- A bit-vector B(V) of total size bits shows the occurrence positions of V in the window. In order to maintain B(V) efficaciously, an integer variable pivot(V) is introduced, which represents an anchor so that B(V) is only updated when an occurrence of V is added or deleted, rather than in every step i of the algorithm.

Example 1. Given the string x = **AGCTAGTTCTAGCTAGCTAG$**, the set of seeds is {V1 = AG, V2 = AGCTAG, V3 = CTAG, V4 = CTAGCTAG, V7 = T}. For d=1 and k=2, we find the following set M1, 2 of motifs from the motif graph shown in Fig. 1.

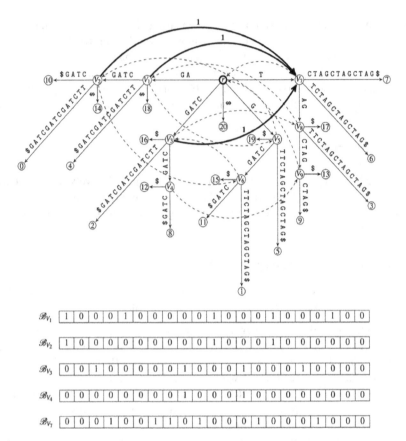

Fig. 1. The motif graph for the suffix tree of the string x = **AGCTAGTTCTAGCTAGCTAG$**, given d = 1 and k = 2. Each leaf node has been labelled with the index i of the suffix X[i..n−1] that it represents, where i ∈ [0, n). Suffix links are shown as dashed directed edges. The set of all internal nodes,{v1,...,v9}, represents the right-maximal repeated factors of x. As |occ(v5)| = 5 = |occ(v1)|, v5 is not a seed; as |occ(v1)| = 5≠ |occ(v8)| = 4, v1 is a seed, and so on. Thus, the set of all seed nodes is {v1, v2, v3, v4, v7}. Motif edges and their labels are bold, All other explicit nodes are labelled V and root node r is outlined in bold. Suffix links are shown as dashed directed edges.

$\tilde{M}_{1,2}$	AG	AG◊T	AGCTAG	AGCTAG◊T	CTAG	CTAG◊T	CTAGCTAG
$|occ(\tilde{M}_{1,2})|$	5	4	3	2	4	3	2

2.2   Adding a Letter from the Right

When a letter x[i]=α has been added to the right of the window, the following cases are checked in order, only in the case of |occ(α)| ≥ k in the window.

If α now extends at least k occurrences of some motif $M^{\sim} \in Mi, d, k$, it becomes the suffix of a new motif $M^{\sim\prime} = M\Diamond d', \alpha$, which happens in the window at least k times, where $d' \in [0, d]$. In this case, the new motif $M^{\sim\prime}$ is added to Mi, d, k. If the number of occurrences of $M^{\sim}$ is equal to $M^{\sim\prime}$, $M^{\sim}$ is deleted from Mi, d, k as it is no longer maximal. The letter α can be added to Mi, d, k as a singleton motif if and only if it is not already in Mi, d, k and one of the following is true:

- No motifs have been added to M*i, d, k*
- One motif $M^{\sim\prime}$ has been added to M*i, d, k* and $|occ(\alpha)| > |occ(M^{\sim\prime})|$;
- Two or more motifs have been added to M*i, d, k*

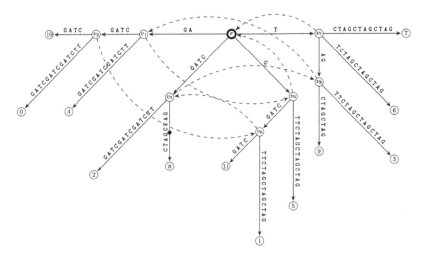

Fig. 2. The implicit suffix tree of the string x = AGCTAGTTCTAGCTAGCTAG. Each leaf node has been labelled with the index of the suffix j that it represents, for all suffixes j ∈ [0, 12). Observe that, the most recent leaf to be added is suffix j−1 = 11. The active point, A = ⟨v3, 4, 15⟩, The active point is a black dot on the path between nodesV3 and node 8. The longest repeated suffix x[12..19] = CTAGCTAG is the path from r to A. and root node r is outlined in bold. Suffix links are shown as dashed directed edges.

Example 2. Observe that, for example, suffixes 10 and 11 were added as leaf nodes when letter X[16] = C was added.

2.3   Deleting a Letter from the Left

When the leftmost letter α of the window has been deleted, every motif $M^{\sim\prime} = \alpha M^\sim i, d, k$ must be deleted if now $occ|M^\sim\prime| < k$ in the window. After this possible deletion, the following cases might be considered:

- If $M^\sim = \Sigma$, and thus $M^\sim\prime = \alpha$, then nothing more is done.
- If $M^\sim \neq \Sigma$, then $M^\sim$ is added to Mi, d, k, if and only if $M^\sim (/\in Mi, d, k)$ and it is not a prefix of a motif $M^{\sim\prime\prime} \in Mi, d, k$ such that $|occ|M^{\sim\prime\prime}| = |occ|M^\sim|$. Finally, the results are printed Sx, where $Sx[i]=|Mi, d, k|$ and $\ell \leq i < n$.

Example 3. Considering Fig. 2, the deletion of the leftmost letter (A) would result in the deletion of leaf node 0 which represents the longest suffix. This would cause the subsequent deletion of node V2 as it would have one remaining child, the edges from V1 to V2 and V2 to leaf node 10 would be merged.

3   Experimental Results and Contribution

3.1   Contribution

The patterns that are the focus of this paper are commonly found in molecular structures and, therefore, are biologically important.

A traditional desktop-based programming environment was used to display the coding program of the bioinformatics application using Java programming language. The experiment required an Intel Pentium CPU4415U@ 2.30 GHz processor, 4.00 GB of RAM, a 64-bit Operating System, Windows 10 and MS.Net Framework 4.5.

This experiment sought to find interesting regions within genomes by finding the maximal motif [5] in the proposed algorithm that works in an online manner. Firstly, the main computational challenge in reporting motifs in a sliding window is the maintaining of the left- and rightmost seeds, which is twofold: verifying their maximality (nodes) and updating their relationship with neighbouring seeds (edges). Such changes to the motif graph identify and, therefore, efficiently update only the subset of motifs occurring at both ends of the window. The following describes the effect on Mi, d, k and the motif graph when adding a letter to the right of the window, and deleting a letter from the left, which simulates the sliding window on x.

This paper has sought to further discover interesting regions in large genomic sequences, by implementing program codes of the algorithm in [5], and testing it using real genomic data to discover all maximal motifs in a sliding window of ℓ-length = 200, on a sequence x of length n.

The application requires the following input parameters. The values for all the parameters are provided by the end user:

- The length n of the string X.
- The length ℓ of the window on X.
- The maximum number d of allowed don't care symbols.
- The minimum number k of occurrences of maximal motifs (Fig. 3).

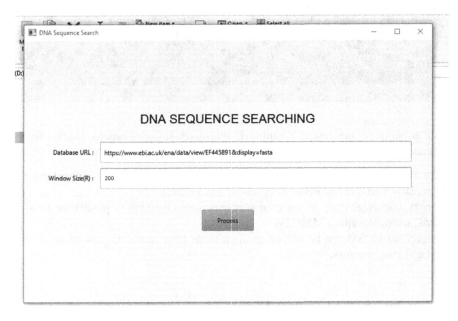

Fig. 3. The application Layout Panel, For the input dataset of the string x, real sequences from the European Nucleotide Archive (ENA) were used. The ENA maintains an extensive record of the world's nucleotide sequencing information, covering raw sequencing data, sequence assembly information and functional annotation. In addition, a database of nucleotide sequences EF445891.1, Escherichia coli strain ATCC 11775 tna operon, was also used [https://www.ebi.ac. uk/ena/data/view/EF445891]. It is important to note that the application utilised could accept any URL of any real genomic dataset input for testing, in order to discover all maximal motifs in a sliding window of ℓ-length = 200.

3.2 Implementation

The outline of maximal motif discovery for biological data in a sliding window can be found in the Appendix.

3.3   Results

In addition to the research outlined, bioinformatic applications similar to the application of the algorithms presented in this paper are outlined below:

- An experimental study of all UniProt protein sequences to discover novel pairs of circularly permuted proteins using algorithm saCSCr.
- An experimental study of bacterial genomes from GenBank to predict the locus of OriC using algorithm MMDSW.
- Algorithm EDSM can be utilised to align reads from newly-sequenced genomesto related pan-genomes.

4   Conclusions and Future Work

In summary, this paper has implemented a bioinformatic application of the motif discovery algorithm, with the purpose of finding biologically significant regions in genomic sequences. In addition, this paper has verified previous theoretical findings by implementing the algorithm in and testing it with real genomic data, in order to discover all maximal motifs in a sliding window of ℓ-length = 200 on a sequence x of length.

With regard to future work, one interesting avenue could be finding maximal motifs that occur a minimum number of times in each sequence, given a set of multiple sequences, somewhat resembling the (ℓ, d)-motif search problem. Furthermore, this paper's implementation of maximal motifs could be extended to gapped maximal motifs. Refinement of these results could take place by restricting the minimum length of a maximal motif or adding a probabilistic post-processing step.

Appendix

```java
package Business_Objects;
    import java.io.PrintStream;
    import java.util.ArrayList;
    import java.util.List;
    import java.lang.*;
    public class Suffix {
        private List<Node> nodes = new ArrayList();
        public Suffix(String str) {
          this.nodes.add(new Node());
          for(int i = 0; i < str.length(); ++i) {
            this.addSuffix(str.substring(i));
          }
        }
        public static String fromUnicode(String unicode) {
          String str = unicode.replace("\\", "");
          String[] arr = str.split("u");
          StringBuffer text = new StringBuffer();
          for (int i = 1; i < arr.length; i++) {
            int hexVal = Integer.parseInt(arr[i], 16);
            text.append(Character.toChars(hexVal));
          }
          return text.toString();
        }
        public static String toUnicode(String text) {
          StringBuffer sb = new StringBuffer();
          for (int i = 0; i < text.length(); i++) {
            int codePoint = text.codePointAt(i);
            if (codePoint > 0xffff) {
              i++;
            }
            String hex = Integer.toHexString(codePoint);
            sb.append("\\u");
            for (int j = 0; j < 4 - hex.length(); j++) {
              sb.append("0");
            }
            sb.append(hex);
          }
          return sb.toString();
        }
    private void addSuffix(String suf) {
        int n = 0;
        int n2;
```

```
      label37:
      for(int i = 0; i < suf.length(); n = n2) {
        char b = suf.charAt(i);
        List<Integer> children = ((Node)this.nodes.get(n)).ch;
        for(int x2 = 0; x2 != children.size(); ++x2) {
          n2 = (Integer)children.get(x2);
          if (((Node)this.nodes.get(n2)).sub.charAt(0) == b) {
String sub2 = ((Node)this.nodes.get(n2)).sub;
            int j;
              for(j = 0; j < sub2.length(); ++j) {
            if (suf.charAt(i + j) != sub2.charAt(j)) {
                  int n3 = n2;
                  n2 = this.nodes.size();
                  Node temp = new Node();
                  temp.sub = sub2.substring(0, j);
                  temp.ch.add(n3);
                  this.nodes.add(temp);
                  ((Node)this.nodes.get(n3)).sub  =  sub2.substring
(j);
                  ((Node)this.nodes.get(n)).ch.set(x2, n2);
                  break;
                }
              }
              i += j;
              continue label37;
            }
          }
          n2 = this.nodes.size();
          Node temp = new Node();
          temp.sub = suf.substring(i);
          this.nodes.add(temp);
          children.add(n2);
          return;
        }
      }
      public void visualize() {
        if (this.nodes.isEmpty()) {
          System.out.println("<empty>");
        } else {
        this.visualize_f(0, "");
        }
      }
      private void visualize_f(int n, String pre) {
      List<Integer> children = ((Node)this.nodes.get(n)).ch;
      PrintStream var10000;
          Object var10001;
```

```
            if (children.isEmpty()) {
            var10000 = System.out;
            var10001 = this.nodes.get(n);
            System.out.println("\u002d" + ((Node)var10001).sub);
            } else {
            var10000 = System.out;
            var10001 = this.nodes.get(n);
            System.out.println( fromUnicode("\\u2510")   +   ((Node)-
var10001).sub);
        for(int i = 0; i < children.size() - 1; ++i) {
            Integer c = (Integer)children.get(i);
            System.out.print(pre + fromUnicode("\\u251c\\u2500"));
            this.visualize_f(c, pre + " ");
            }
            System.out.print(pre + fromUnicode("\\u2514\\u2500"));
            this.visualize_f((Integer)children.get(children.size()   -
1), pre + " ");
            }
        }
    }
```

References

1. Carvalho, A.M., Freitas, A.T., Oliveira, A.L., Sagot, M.: Arm efficient algorithm for the identification of structured motifs in DNA promoter sequences. IEEE/ACM Trans. Comput.-Biol. Bioinform. **3**(2), 126–140 (2006)
2. Fuller, R.S., Funnell, B.E., Kornberg, A.: The dnaA protein complex with the E. coli chrornosomal replication origin (oriC) and other DNA sites. Cell **38**(3), 889–900 (1984)
3. Grossi, R., Mermcorri, G., Pisanti, N., Trani, R., Vinc, S.: Motif trie: efficient text index for pattern discovery with don't cares. Theor. Comput. Sci. **710**, 74–87 (2018)
4. van Helden, J., Andre, B., Collado-Vides, J.: Extracting regulatory sites from the upstream region of yeast genes by computational analysis of oligonucleotide frequencies. J. Mol. Biol. **281**(5), 827–842 (1998)
5. Iliopoulos, C.S., Mohamed, M., Pissis, Solon P., Vayani, F.: Maximal motif discovery in a sliding window. In: Gagie, T., Moffat, A., Navarro, G., Cuadros-Vargas, E. (eds.) SPIRE 2018. LNCS, vol. 11147, pp. 191–205. Springer, Cham (2018). https://doi.org/10.1007/978-3-030-00479-8_16
6. Leonard, A.-C., Méchali, M.: DNA replication origins. Cold Spring Harb. Perspect. Biol. **5**(10), a010116 (2013)
7. Meijer, M., et al.: Nucleotide sequence of the origin of replication of the Escherichia coli K-12 chromosome. Proc. Nat. Acad. Sci. **76**(2), 580–584 (1979)
8. Pavesi, G., Mercghetti, P., Mauri, G., Pesole, G.: Weeder Web: discovery of transcription factor binding sites in a set of sequences from co-regulated genes. Nucleic Acids Res. **32**(Web-Server-Issue), 199–203 (2004)
9. Pisanti, N., Carvalho, A.M., Marsan, L., Sagot, M.-F.: RISOTTO: fast extraction of motifs with mismatches. In: Correa, J.R., Hevia, A., Kiwi, M. (eds.) LATIN 2006. LNCS, vol. 3887, pp. 757–768. Springer, Heidelberg (2006). https://doi.org/10.1007/11682462_69

10. Pissis, S.P.: MoTeX-ll; structured MoTif eXtraction from large-scale datasets. BMC Bioinf. **15**, 235 (2014)
11. Pissis, S.P., Stamatakis, A., Pavlidis, P.: MoTeX: a word-based HPC tool for MoTif eXtraction. In: Gao, J. (ed.) ACM Conference on Bioinformatics, Computational Biology and Biomedical Informatics. ACM-BCB 2013, Washington, 22–25 September 2013, p. 13. ACM (2013)
12. Sinha, S., Tompa, M.: YMF: a program for discovery of novel transcription factor binding sites by statistical overrepresentation. Nucleic Acids Res. **31**(13), 3586–3588 (2003)
13. Waterman, M.S.: General methods of sequence comparison. Bull. Math. Biol. **46**(4), 473–500 (1984)

Fingerprints Recognition System-Based on Mobile Device Identification Using Circular String Pattern Matching Techniques

Miznah H. Alshammary[(⊠)], Costas S. Iliopoulos,
and Mujibur R. Khan

Department of Informatics, King's College London, London, UK
{miznah.alshammary,c.iliopoulos,md.khan}@kcl.ac.uk

Abstract. As fingerprint recognition systems have become increasingly adopted within a range of technology applications over the last decade, so too has their attention within emerging research. However, although this increased attention has led to an enhancement of the software and algorithms behind this recognition process, the majority of research has still not addressed the issues of incorrect rotation or proximity between the finger and the device. Current systems assume that the direction of the imprinted finger will align with that of the target fingerprint image; this decreases the accuracy of fingerprint recognition across a variety of finger orientations and scenarios.

In response to this use-case dilemma, this paper proposes a new technique of pattern matching that can account for this natural range of fingerprint orientations. This is achieved first through a preliminary stage of orientation identification, whereby the fingerprint image can be stored under multiple permutations by using approximate circular string-matching algorithms.

This enables the database of images for each approximate permutation of orientation to be stored in advance. It can then be matched against the strong information of the fingerprint at its exact relative rotation of input. The improved accuracy of recognition demonstrated through the results of this study may enable the functionality of fingerprint recognition to adapt to challenging device form-factors and provide the accuracy needed for military and medical applications.

Keywords: Mobile device fingerprinting · Fingerprint recognition · Rotation · Circular string matching

1 Introduction

With modern devices becoming increasingly configured for the high-speed transmission and sharing of data across mobile networks [6], this in turn has led the volume of information shared with unknown entities to rise. This has made the sharing of personal data through recognition systems a fundamental concern and is consequently pressuring manufacturers to increase recognition accuracy.

With precursors to fingerprint recognition dating back to the 19th century, the conceptual functionality of this technology has long since become attractive for

© IFIP International Federation for Information Processing 2020
Published by Springer Nature Switzerland AG 2020
I. Maglogiannis et al. (Eds.): AIAI 2020 Workshops, IFIP AICT 585, pp. 225–231, 2020.
https://doi.org/10.1007/978-3-030-49190-1_20

tracking and managing criminal records. However, as demonstrated by the case of criminal records in Argentina [5], it also improves forensics and the effectiveness of local police. Furthermore, the unique profile of minutiae and ridge patterns that vary in fingerprints from one individual to the other have long made fingerprint recognition a highly accurate method of confirming and tracking identity. Moreover, past analogue methods – and even contemporary methods in the algorithm format – have refined the capacity to target this static structure, and then compare the imprint against past image records [4].

However, as this functionality has emerged as an authentication method for a range of computing devices whereby the rotation and direction of imprints has varied dramatically to match the mobile form-factor, this removes the traditional security advantage of fixed devices. In turn, this compromises the accuracy of fingerprint recognition in devices that require flexible finger orientation, many of which are used today for crucial functions such as communication and financial transactions.

Building on this dilemma, this study will explore past algorithms that have in part addressed this issue of relative proximity. It will then highlight contributions from the results which may constitute a recognition system that is prepared for these modern scenarios.

2 Literature Review

With traditional systems primarily focused on comparing the topographical similarity between an imprint and past stored images from the same user, past research has developed increasingly accurate systems of modelling the static structure of fingerprint minutiae. More recent models adopt a 3D structure that can account for pressure and depth [7–10].

However, although the contemporary recognition systems for minutiae-based matching enable more flexible user scenarios by predicting how the minutiae structure may morph in response to varying levels of pressure [11], this approach to matching still assumes that the finger is placed vertically. It is thus less accurate for devices held in a variety of orientations. Furthermore, in addition to lacking this flexibility for fingerprints other than in the vertical orientation, past methods also appear to experience reduced accuracy in a number of applications. These include comparing biological systems; the recovery of information and correlation of data from different files; and signal processing. The most significant algorithms explored in this study are the Landauand-Vishkin and the Needleman-Wunsch algorithms [3], both of which are incorporated into our proposed solution.

3 Our Contribution

Building on the lack of methods for accounting for orientation in previous studies, this paper proposes a pattern-matching process for mobile fingerprint authentication that uses classification to match fingerprint profiles. This is achieved by deriving the information of the minutiae by intercepting the fingerprint with a series of scan circles. This information is then translated into a string.

Following this initial stage, the string information of the fingerprint is then matched in a local image database. This matching process is conducted by a pattern-matching algorithm that is tolerant to topographical error and it thus enables the identification process of the minutiae to be done in linear time, according to the combined length of all the searched strings.

Furthermore, as this finger identification method leverages the efficiency of circular string matching, the accuracy of our identification method could be separated from the topographical similarity of the placed fingerprint relative to the vertical orientation. In addition, as our method utilised approximation rather than exact matching of the minutiae features, the distortion of the input image was significantly decreased.

However, in addition to the advantage of targeting circular strings rather than static features of the minutiae bound to a vertical orientation, our process also incorporated minutiae extraction, whereby the speed of the overall recognition process would be significantly impacted by this extraction speed. Moreover, in order to maximise the speed of extraction, we have aimed to improve the performance of minutiae extraction so that the overall execution time of the process is reduced.

Our developed alternative of Fast Minutiae Extraction saw a significant speed increase over Novel Minutiae Extraction-2 presented in [2] and Novel Minutiae Extraction presented in [1].

In addition, the series of scan circles, precise location and rotation of the input fingerprint captured by our method can be translated into a string. This information can then be stored as images within the fingerprint database for later matching. Moreover, this was achieved by using rapid circular string-matching algorithms, which enabled the total lengths of the strings to be searched in linear time, accelerating and enhancing the accuracy of the recognition process.

In this paper, our proposed algorithm not only aims to enhance minutiae extraction to improve the accuracy and flexibility of the fingerprint recognition process. It also reduces the overall time of execution. In order to outline our process, the following sub-sections detail the proposed algorithm in its two underlying components: Fast Novel Minutiae Extraction and our algorithm outline.

3.1 Fast Novel Minutiae Extraction

As our process repeatedly introduced minutiae extractions, this meant that the speed of this extraction process would significantly impact the overall time required for successful fingerprint recognition. Consequently, this project developed an alternative extraction method we refer to as Fast Novel Minutiae Extraction.

This alternative saw a significant speed increase over Novel Minutiae Extraction-2 presented in [2] and Novel Minutiae Extraction presented in [1].

The outline of Fast Novel Minutiae Extraction is presented below:

```
ALGORITHM Fast_Minutae_Extraction(char[][] img, int r, int cx, int cy)
// INPUT: "img", a 2d char array representing a fingerprint
// INPUT: "r", the radius of the circular string to be extracted
// INPUT: (cx, cy), the centre of the circular string to be extracted
// OUTPUT: "pattern", a circular binary string
{
        string topLeft;
        string topRight;
        string bottomRight;
        string bottomLeft;

        for(int i = (cx -r); i < cx; i++)
        {
                double dJ = Math.Sqrt(Math.Pow(r,2)  - Math.Pow((i-cx), 2));
                if(dJ == (int)dJ)
                {
                        int xOffset = cx -i;
                        int yOffset = (int)dJ;

                        if(pixel at img[cx - xOffset][cy + yOffset] < 125) {
                                Append "0" to the end of topLeft;
                        } else {
                                Append "1" to the end of topLeft;
                        }

                        if(pixel at img[cx + yOffset][cy + xOffset] < 125) {
                                Append "0" to the end of topRight;
                        } else {
                                Append "1" to the end of topRight;
                        }

                        if(pixel at img[cx + xOffset][cy - yOffset] < 125) {
                                Append "0" to the end of bottomRight;
                        } else {
                                Append "1" to the end of bottomRight;
                        }

                        if(pixel at img[cx - yOffset][cy - xOffset] < 125) {
                                Append "0" to the end of bottomLeft;
                        } else {
                                Append "1" to the end of bottomLeft;
                        }
                }
        }
        return topLeft + topRigt + bottomRight + bottomLeft;
}
```

3.2 Outline of the Algorithm

Our algorithm was structured to identify the circular strings from the saved fingerprint and input at the longest length: asmf/acdm was used to check that the relative rotation of the circular string of the input matched that of the saved fingerprint image. Furthermôre, the Needleman-Wunsch approximation algorithm was used to check the exactness of the alignment.

The main component that dominates the speed of execution is the extraction of minutiae from the image and constructing the circular string, which is repeatedly invoked throughout the whole process.

We have outlined the complete process of Fingerprint matching as below:

1. **Database Formation:** A database of circular strings was constructed, with the centre of the image classed as the effective centre.
2. **Concentric Circle-to-Strings Formation:** Concentric circles were drawn, and then (using Fast Novel Minutiae Extraction) converted into strings comprising of 0's and 1's. For example, assuming that Cir is the circular string of the ith image with a radius of r, all rotations of each of the circular strings are saved to the database. By letting DbRir be the collection of rotated strings from Cir; a Cir = "0111" would mean that DRir would hold values of "0111", "1011", "1101", "1110". Conversely, by letting DbRir be the collection of rotated strings from Cir; Cir = "0111" would mean that DRir would hold values of be "0111", "1011", "1101", "1110".
3. **Binary String Formation:** After the previous phase, Fast Novel Minutiae Extraction was repeated in order to construct circular binary strings for each circle.
4. **CsR List Formation:** After binary string formation, the process then proceeded to create a sorted CsR list of radius pairs and circular strings (<CStr, Radius>) in a descending order of the CStr length.
5. **Rotation Comparison:** Following list formation, the asmf/acdmf method was then applied along with the Needleman-Wunsch algorithm. This enabled the rotations to be compared, whereby a percentage of matched strings recorded as higher than a certain threshold (tS) would result in the sum of the match percentage being saved. The ith image was marked as the 'candidate image' and then the (i + 1) th image was selected until all images within the databased had been utilised. Following this process, this stage could be repeated after choosing a different centre point.
6. **Image Matching:** After the previous stages, the process finally returns to the match images for verification.

4   Experimental Results

We coded the program in C# using an Intel Pentium processor (CPU 4415U) with 2.30 GHz, the random-access memory was 4.00 GB, the Operating System was 64-bit Windows 10, and the platform was MS.Net Framework 4.5.

We aimed to improve the performance of minutiae extraction so that the overall execution time of the process is reduced.

Comparing the time required in milliseconds for each method, it is clear that our solution algorithm provides better results for the overall execution time of extracting minutiae from the image and constructing the circular string, which is repeatedly invoked throughout the whole process. This is presented in Table 1 and Fig. 1.

Table 1. Summary of findings

Database size	Time required for novel methods (Milliseconds)	Time required for fast methods (Milliseconds)
50	881300	67765
100	3276930	1290428

Table 1 shows that there are two main factors that ensure the accuracy and performance of the proposed algorithm. These are the size of the database and the time required for extracting minute details from an image and creating a circular chain that is invoked repeatedly throughout the entire process.

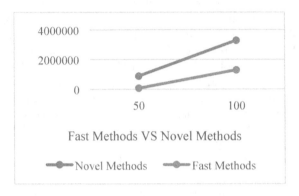

Fig. 1. Fast methods vs novel methods

Table 1 shows the results for two different database sizes. For all inputs, we captured the time required for each method and the results are compared in Fig. 1.

It is clear that our solution algorithm provides better results in terms of overall execution time and as the database size increases, it decreases the time required for extracting minutiae from the image and constructing the circular string, which is repeatedly invoked throughout the whole process.

5   Conclusion

With an increasing volume of devices adopting fingerprint recognition, this will pressurise manufacturers to re-evaluate existing minutiae-matching techniques and to explore enhanced models that are better adapted to the non-vertical orientations of input that are becoming prevalent among mobile devices.

Consequently, in response to the recent increase in algorithms and string-matching techniques, this paper explored this barrier of orientation flexibility, and how our proposed solution may lead to faster mobile user scenarios. As demonstrated by the results, our proposed solution offers an enhanced version of previous algorithms used for extracting topographical features of minutiae from the input image. This increases the overall efficiency of the identification process.

Overall, this study stands as an example of how mathematical algorithms can be used to enhance the functionality of a computing-based function in order to more accurately model a device's surrounding environment. Furthermore, in addition to accounting for a more realistic variety of user orientations in fingerprint recognition, this proposed system may also be able to enhance models beyond bioinformatics, which face a similar rise in device mobility and range of handheld orientation.

References

1. Ajala, O., Aljamea, M., Alzamel, M., Iliopoulos, C.S., Strigini, Y.: Fast fingerprint recognition using circular string pattern matching techniques. In: PATTERNS 2016: The Eighth International Conferences on Pervasive Patterns and Applications (2016)
2. Ajala, O.I., Iliopoulos, C.S., Khan, M.R.: Identification of fingerprints using circular string approximation for mobile devices. In: PATTERNS 2016, Computer Science and Information Systems. ACSIS, vol. 13, pp. 193–197 (2016). https://doi.org/10.15439/2017f3. ISSN 2300-5963
3. Landau, G.M., Vishkin, U.: Fast string matching with k differences*. J. Comput. Syst. Sci. **37**, 63–78 (1998)
4. Sebastian, S.: Literature survey on automated person identification techniques. Inter. J. Comput. Sci. Mobile Comput. **2**(5), 232–237 (2013)
5. Unar, J., Seng, W.C., Abbasi, A.: A review of biometric technology along with trends and prospects. Pattern Recogn. **47**(8), 2673–2688 (2014)
6. Alshammary, M.H., Alanezi, F.A.: A review of recent developments in NOMA and SCMA schemes for 5G technology. In: IEEE Communications, October 2017
7. Tan, X., Bhanu, B.: Fingerprint matching by genetic algorithms. Pattern Recogn. **39**(3), 465–477 (2006)
8. Jain, A.K., Hong, L., Pankanti, S., Bolle, R.: An identity-authentication system using fingerprints. Proc. IEEE **85**(9), 1365–1388 (1997)
9. Kovacs-Vajna, Z.M.: A fingerprint verification system based on triangular matching and dynamic time warping. IEEE Trans. Pattern Anal. Mach. Intel. **22**(11), 1266–1276 (2000)
10. Tan, X., Bhanu, B.: Robust fingerprint identification. In: International Conference on Image Processing, vol. 1, pp. 1–277. IEEE (2002)
11. Kai, C., Xin, Y., Xinjian, C., Yali, Z., Jimin, L., Jie, T.: A novel ant colony optimization algorithm for large-distorted fingerprint matching. Pattern Recogn. **45**(1), 151–161 (2012)

Mining and Analysis of Air Quality Data to Aid Climate Change

Lakshmi Babu Saheer$^{(\boxtimes)}$, Mohamed Shahawy, and Javad Zarrin

Anglia Ruskin University, Cambridge, UK
{lakshmi.babu-saheer,javad.zarrin}@aru.ac.uk,
mohamed.shahawy@student.aru.ac.uk

Abstract. The data science and AI community has gathered around the world to support tackling the climate change problem in different domains. This research aims to work on the air quality through emissions and pollutant concentration data along with vegetation information. Authorities especially in urban cities like London have been very vigilant in monitoring these different aspects of air quality and reliable sources of big data are available in this domain. This study aims to mine and collate this information spread all over the place in different formats into usable knowledge base on which further data analysis and powerful Machine Learning approaches can be built to extract strong evidences useful in building better policies around climate change.

Keywords: Data mining and analysis · Data pre-processing · Air quality · Climate change · Urban planning and machine learning · Geographic information systems

1 Introduction

Climate change is the main challenge that humanity is facing today, threatening the existence of life on earth. Awareness campaigns and drastic steps towards bringing the situation under control have been initiated in every nook and corner of the world. Both developed and under developed countries are working hard to tackle this problem. Data Analysis, Data Science and Artificial Intelligence have big potential to help mankind where ever (big) data is available to help build models and make predictions or provide prescriptive solutions. Such models for emissions, resources, energy consumption, etc., have already been statistically worked out by specialist groups around the world to tackle climate change [10]. ClimateChangeAI [8] is a classic example of such an initiative.

1.1 Motivation

There are sources of big data available in the fields of energy consumption, transport, building & cities, carbon footprint, farming, climate change and prediction etc [21]. It is really hard to mine all this data in a reasonable time to get useful

© IFIP International Federation for Information Processing 2020
Published by Springer Nature Switzerland AG 2020
I. Maglogiannis et al. (Eds.): AIAI 2020 Workshops, IFIP AICT 585, pp. 232–243, 2020.
https://doi.org/10.1007/978-3-030-49190-1_21

resources with mathematical models. The approach for our research would be to first identify the most useful and informative data for the identified topics of climate change and start to build machine learning models and methodologies to extract useful and relevant information in the form of predictions or prescriptions. Even though a lot of data is available for every field, it is very difficult to gather the majority of these information in a structured useful format.

1.2   Research Objective

The research presented in this work is to look at the parallel data on pollutant concentrations, road traffic emissions and vegetation specifically around city like London. "Parallel" in this scenario refers to different datasets collected in close timelines and physical locations. London is chosen as the city to look at mainly because there is a lot of publicly available data for this city from various sources. This can directly help us plan our cities and traffic routes or even come up with laws to keep our carbon footprint under control. Further, our hypothesis (evidenced by initial experiments and literature) is that one of the major factors affecting the concentration of pollutants in atmosphere is the vegetation. This research aims to find traffic and air quality or emissions monitoring datasets along with the information of vegetation around the area to analyse the importance and effectiveness of vegetation in urban planning.

2   Background

There have been several studies to understand the potential benefits of vegetation in mitigating urban air pollution problems [4,11,19]. Bealey et al. [3] states that trees have been widely quoted as effective scavengers of both gaseous and particulate pollutants from the atmosphere. Further, effect of tree planting strategies on dispersion and deposition of airborne urban aerosol concentrations onto woodland is suggested to be considered in the planning process. Several studies have suggested the importance of including the vegetation in urban road planning [1,2]. It is even suggested that vegetation in urban settings can provide benefits beyond improvements in air quality—these include carbon sequestration, temperature and storm water regulation, noise reduction, aesthetic improvements, and opportunities for physical exercise and the experience of nature.

Most of these research use expert knowledge and postulations to predict these impacts. In this modern age, scientists should work on big data and deductions from the proofs evidenced from data. To this end, this research will collate data from different sources dispersed all over internet regarding emissions (like $CO_2, NO_x, PM_{2.5}, PM_{10}$), concentration of gaseous and particulate matter (like $NO_2, NO_x, PM_{2.5}, PM_{10}$), road transport, and vegetation details into useful parallel information base. This pool of information could help us model different Machine learning systems to understand the relations between and impact of each of these factors on the overall quality of air. The main aim of this research is finding the links between vegetation, transport and other factors on pollutant concentration. This should help us validate the earlier suggestions on urban vegetation planning. Further, this project should help in building a proposal system to the local authorities on the type and form of vegetation to be planted around our cities to help control the effects of emissions.

There has been other efforts in the area of data analysis of air quality using advanced Machine Learning techniques for data imputation [14]. Junninena et al. [14] looks at only recreating missing pollutant values in a specific air quality dataset. The other studies mentioned earlier [3,4,11,19] approach the problem as a data collection exercise as a validation of their theoretical hypothesis. It seems like our research is the first systematic effort combining the different aspects like emissions, concentration and vegetation by collating existing big data collected from different sources to perform a detailed data analysis. This in turn leads to several challenges in data pre-processing as discussed in Sect. 3.

2.1 Data Mining Approach

The first steps in this work is to identify parallel data from different sources for road transport information including number and type of vehicles, emissions in the air with different types of pollutants, pollutant concentrations, vegetation type and extend. Parallel in this scenario, as mentioned earlier, refers to both same geographical location and similar or same time scales. The idea is to build such an open source parallel database with different levels of geographic and timescale granularity. The geographic information could be as coarse as starting from big cities, to different regions in a city (boroughs), to finally narrowing down to road level details. Similarly, time scales could vary from seasons (especially where the difference would be evident with leaf shedding in trees) to peak traffic timings in the day. Time scale granularity is left as a future exercise due to unavailability of reliable resources. For the sake of simplicity, the location granularity is also taken to be at a region or borough level. Hence, the task is to find the parallel data for air pollutants in terms of concentration and emission along with data on vegetation at borough level. Later on, this information could be made more granular in terms of location and time.

This huge knowledge base once ready is expected to provide a wealth of information for the research community to study the interactions between these factors and how these learning can be combined to form useful environmental policies. Some of the main challenges in this work is mainly around finding parallel compatible information including the formats of the information is discussed in detail in the next section. The main hypothesis in this work is that Vegetation has a positive effect in reducing the concentration of the pollutants despite the emission rates. The aim of this research is to prove if the data available can support this hypothesis.

3   Research Challenges

As mentioned earlier, the UK city of London is chosen as the first city to target our study merely due to the availability of good quality data from various reliable sources. For this particular study, different public domain datasets available through government and public authorities are considered. The traffic monitoring data in UK is available with different authorities like: Cambridgeshire county council: [5], Highways England data: [13] and Traffic for London: [25].

Similarly, air quality datasets in the form of emissions and pollutant concentration monitoring data in London is available with authorities like: London Air: [16], UK Government Monitoring: [9,17], Traffic for London: [25]. Particularly for London, the local authorities have also kept track record of Vegetation information around London [18].

The challenge would be to map these different sources to come up with parallel data to extract useful information through machine learning approaches like SVMs or Neural Networks [12,15,20,26]. Traffic for London seems to have usable parallel data for traffic and emissions and is known to publicly share this information to support research. This again validates London to be a good starting point for this research, later on extending to other cities or more resources for further information.

There are several challenges even with these available datasets for London. The data available is only partially aligned with varied features between the measured concentrations and emissions. The Table 1 clearly shows the misalignment between the concentrations or emissions features, which limits the correlation analysis and the amount of useful information that could be inferred from the data. Next section presents how some of these challenges are dealt with in this study in order to perform further data analysis.

3.1 Technical Challenges

The London Atmospheric Emissions [17] dataset, collected by the Greater London (GLA) and Transport for London [24], is chosen as the primary source of data in the following analysis. While the dataset provides a vital and invaluable source of geographic information, it also has its drawbacks regarding formatting and data-types. The varied types of geographic references (as shown in the Table 1) pose an issue with both the granularity of the entire analysis (limited to London boroughs at the highest-level), as well as finding means of converting the reference types for uniformity purposes.

The first challenge was to find the data related to each borough in London. Due to the lack of support for Ordinance Survey National Grid coordinates converters, especially all-numeric grid references, a supplementary OSGB36 or WGS84 python library (PyBNG) was developed and open-sourced on GitHub and PyPi [23] as an outcome of this research. Using PyBNG, OSGB36 coordinates were converted to latitude and longitude, which can be used to find the corresponding London boroughs. The large volume of the concentration dataset, however, poses an issue with the London borough-search using APIs. Nevertheless, a GeoJSON dataset (open-sourced by Ordnance Survey) containing geographic polygonal boundaries of all the London boroughs could be used to find the encapsulated coordinates and ultimately generate the required missing data.

Table 1. Dataset format details

Data	File-type	Geographic reference	Available data	Unit
Transportation	XLSB (multi-sheet)	London borough-level, main motorways, ArcGIS project	Emissions/ vehicle type	Tonnes/ year
Concentration	CSV	All-numberic, OSGB36 coordinates	NO_2, NO_x, PM_{10} and $PM_{2.5}$	μ g/m^3
Emission	XLSB (multi-sheet)	London borough-level, ArcGIS project	CO_2, NO_x, PM_{10} and $PM_{2.5}$	Tonnes/ year
Trees	CSV	London borough-level, OSGB36 coordinates, WGS84 coordinates	Species name	N/A

Fig. 1. Greater London Boroughs' geo-spatial boundaries

In order to synthesize or validate the *boroughs* feature in some of the datasets mentioned, the ray-cast algorithm was used. This algorithm is used to determine whether or not the corresponding longitude & latitude coordinates are encapsulated within the boundaries of a geo-polygon of the corresponding London borough (Fig. 1).

Another challenge was to check for wrong or inconsistent data. Whilst verifying some of the trees dataset, it became apparent that the boroughs were incorrectly entered; the coordinates given for some rows do not correspond to the boroughs provided. To validate the entries, PyBNG was used to convert easting/northing to latitude and longitude coordinates, which were then used to infer and ultimately validate the borough for every entry. Another hurdle encountered was the varying invalid entries like the tree species names ("Failed Planting Site", "Unknown Conifer", "Zz Tree Missing", etc). Manually filtering the valid species names was a painstaking task given the fact that there are thousands of different species in the dataset. Alternative techniques for filtering using crawlers may be pursued in future to expand this data.

Sample output dataset after pre-processing and collation is shown in Table 2. Given that the data pre-processing and aggregation proved to be a challenging task, the finalized dataset will be released publicly in the near future to assist with other potential climate change solutions.

Table 2. Processed dataset sample

Borough names	Tree count numbers	Road emissions (tonnes/yr)				Concentrations (μg/m^3)			
		CO_2	NO_x	$PM_{2.5}$	PM_{10}	NO_2	NO_x	$PM_{2.5}$	PM_{10}
City	1361	52817.85	220.46	9.33	15.57	54.04	126.96	16.02	27.41
Ealing	42082	285274.47	934.35	51.08	95.17	36.35	65.51	13.17	21.79
...	...	...	...	...	...	...	...	...	

4   Data Analysis

The data-analysis process heavily relied on the aggregation of the datasets given the high volume of features. The goal was to extract the useful trends out of thousands of features whilst minimizing the loss of data and maintaining uniformity of geographic level. This was achieved by pre-processing subsets of data individually and guaranteeing uniformity prior to collating all the subsets together (essentially a divide-and-conquer data pre-processing approach). A more abstract level of the data was ensured in the end to be consistent.

The pollutants monitored for air quality can be categorised into two classes - gaseous (CO_2, SO_2, NO_x, NO_2) and particulate matter (PM_{10}, $PM_{2.5}$). It could be postulated that the trees help absorbing only gaseous pollutants. But, there have been reports on certain types or species of trees that could help absorb the particulate matter as well [3,6]. Data analysis is performed separately on the effects on gaseous and particulate matter. Unfortunately, this study has not yet looked into the species of trees in the dataset. This may be included in the future extensions of this research. Again, the particulate matter may seem to have more effect on the general health rather than climate change. But, it is known that the particulate matter has fractions of elementary carbon [7] which results in global warming and hence, affecting climate change directly. These types of pollutants also need to be included in this study.

Another limitation with the current emissions and pollutant concentration datasets is that the type of pollutants monitored are not the same. The emissions data has CO_2, NO_x, $PM_{2.5}$ and PM_{10} and the concentration data has NO_x, NO_2, $PM_{2.5}$ and PM_{10}. It is unfortunate that there is only NO_x, $PM_{2.5}$ and PM_{10} that are aligned and could be studied in parallel. Efforts are underway to gather more information from the authorities on other pollutants like CO_2 monitored as pollutant concentration. At this stage of the research, focus is only on these 3 pollutants to study the direct relations between emissions and concentration. It has to be also noted that there is difference in metrics of representation for concentration as $\mu g/m^3$ and emissions as tonnes/year. This time granularity for the data is annual values and hence concentrations are aggregated to mean concentrations per year as well.

Once the parallel data for emissions, pollutant concentration and vegetation (as number of trees) at borough level is obtained, the next step is to look for correlations between these features. The correlations between these three features are first plotted as graphs and heatmap. A negative correlation is expected between the number of trees and pollutant concentration. The values in the graph should be representing each borough in London. A closer look at the number of trees against mean values of concentrations of gaseous and particulate matter distributions for each borough could be plotted separately. Finally, number of trees, emissions and concentrations should be looked at separately for the three common pollutants viz., $NO_x, PM_{2.5}$ and PM_{10}. Next section visualizes and analyzes these plots in detail.

5 Results and Discussion

It is quite evident even from the initial analysis that the existence of trees has a negative correlation with the mean concentrations of both gaseous and particulate matter as shown in Fig. 2. Figure 3 shows a heatmap of correlation between the emissions, concentration and trees. As expected, there is a negative correlation between trees and concentrations. Also, there is a negative correlation between emissions and concentration which could be the effect of trees. This could be further investigated by looking at the boroughs with lower tree counts.

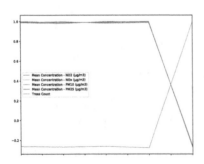

Fig. 2. Trees-concentration correlations

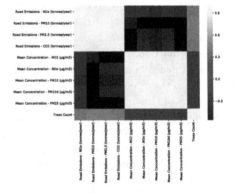

Fig. 3. Correlation: emissions, concentration and trees

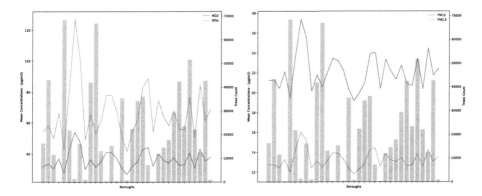

Fig. 4. Trees: effect on mean gas concentrations

Fig. 5. Trees: effect on mean PM concentrations

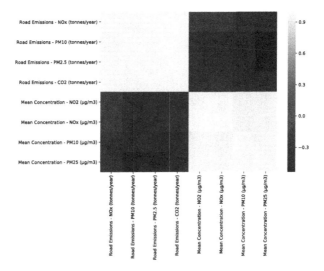

Fig. 6. Trees > 20000: correlation of emissions vs concentrations

Looking at each borough in detail, Fig. 5 shows the relation of number of trees with the particulate matter concentrations. Similarly, Fig. 4 shows the effect of trees on gaseous pollutants. It can be observed that most of the boroughs with a low volume of vegetation have relatively higher pollutant concentration means, while those with a higher volume of vegetation have low pollutant concentration. Each point or bar in the graph represents a borough. The difference in y-axis scales of these two graphs needs to be noted which suggests that there is lower variation in the particulate matter and more variation in the gaseous matter. There is no doubt that all types of trees would help in CO_2 absorption. Not all trees are particularly known to absorb nitrous oxide which could explain some discrepancies here, again, suggesting a deeper look into the species of the trees.

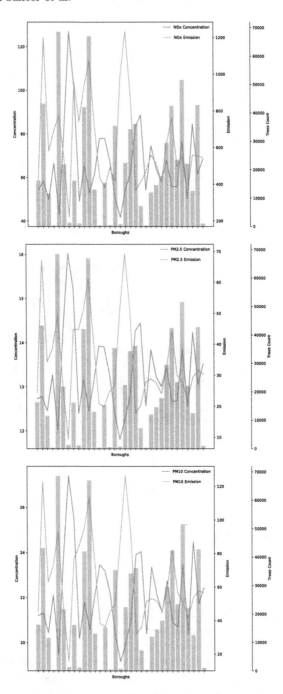

Fig. 7. Comparison: emission with concentration and trees for NO_x, $PM_{2.5}$ and PM_{10}

A statistical concern that arose was the potential collinearity (negative correlation) between the emissions and the number of trees per borough. The initial hypothesis can be contested by claiming that the concentrations measured are lower than expected due to low emissions in the area rather than it being the vegetation's effect. Separate plots for each of the three parallel pollutant in both datasets have been presented in Fig. 7. These figures further prove the hypothesis that concentration is low with even high emissions where there are more trees. It needs to be clarified that the emissions in the dataset includes only the transport or road emissions and hence in some cases, it is observed that concentrations are much higher than emissions. This again is a future work to look into. For the sake of sanity, if we look at boroughs with more than 20000 trees, it is seen that the there is a strong negative correlation between concentration and emissions as shown in Fig. 6. Hence the results of our data analysis supports and proves our hypothesis.

6   Conclusion

More and more climate data from different sources are being collected now than ever before. Analysing such big data can offer unprecedented opportunities to create innovative climate solutions and influence decision-making on a global level. This research initiates the study of influence of AI on tackling climate change with regards to air quality data. The various sources of big data that could contribute to a knowledge base facilitating a detailed data analysis (prior to applying Machine Learning algorithms) are being collated. The challenges faced during this process is briefly outlined to gauge the efforts needed in this research. The initial aim was to build borough level information for London city in order to perform data analysis. The initial analysis of this parallel data at borough level confirms the hypothesis that the vegetation is negatively correlated to the pollutant concentration. This motivates further detailed analysis on this topic to look at better granularity in time and location and impact of other factors like transport emissions, types of trees, weather etc.

7   Future Work

As mentioned in the earlier sections, there are a number of details to be figured out in the existing datasets extending the quality, quantity and granularity of information. This paves way for further data mining and data processing. Examples of these extensions include looking at tree species, more types of pollutants, more granularity of information in location and time, etc. Authorities like TFL will be contacted along with searching for other (online) resources. Finally, the research is intended to progress as a data gathering project to acquire good quality first hand information to implement the machine learning approaches derived from the initial studies.

To further eliminate any potential collinearity that might be biasing the measured concentrations and hence disproving the deductions made, other sources of emissions must be taken into account. Seeing as road transportation constitute roughly 25% to 35% of the total emissions in the Greater London region [17] and the concentrations of pollutants are measured regardless of the source, the total emissions produced should be considered.

Using AI for climate change control through efforts like the traffic-emissions control could be a major step forward to build upon strategies for tackling climate change based on big data available in various fields to build a sustainable future. Once this big data knowledge base is available, different data analysis techniques could be worked on to understand the correlations, Machine learning techniques like standard regression models (linear and non-linear) have already been used to predict the air quality [27]. Another review [22] shows that air quality estimation problems tend to implement Ensemble Learning and Regressions, whereas forecasting makes use of Neural Networks and Support Vector Machines. Since different factors are at play, it might be worth identifying correlated information using unsupervised clustering algorithms and later on use expert systems with some Bayesian prior probabilities to take into consideration several related factors.

Due to the multi-aspect nature of the problem and its internal dynamism, Multi-Perspective Machine Learning (MPML) and Classifier Ensemble can also be considered to investigate various parallel aspects and co-factors involved in the scenario. Furthermore, it is possible to enrich weak datasets through leveraging open source data and using automated approaches for harvesting and integration of publicly available online data.

References

1. Al-Dabbous, A.N., Kumar, P.: The influence of roadside vegetation barriers on airborne nanoparticles and pedestrians exposure under varying wind conditions. Atmos. Environ. **90**, 113–124 (2014)
2. Baldauf, R., et al.: Integrating vegetation and green infrastructure into sustainable transportation planning. Transp. News **288**(5), 14–18 (2013)
3. Bealey, W., et al.: Estimating the reduction of urban PM10 concentrations by trees within an environmental information system for planners. J. Environ. Manag. **85**(1), 44–58 (2007)
4. Benjamin, M.T., Winer, A.M.: Estimating the ozone-forming potential of urban trees and shrubs. Atmos. Environ. **32**(1), 53–68 (1998). Conference on the Benefits of the Urban Forest
5. Cambridge County Council (2019). https://www.cambridgeshire.gov.uk/residents/travel-roads-and-parking/roads-and-pathways/road-traffic-data/
6. Chen, L., Liu, C., Zhang, L., Zou, R., Zhang, Z.: Variation in tree species ability to capture and retain airborne fine particulate matter. Sci. Rep. **7**(1), 3206 (2017)
7. Chernyshev, V., et al.: Morphological and chemical composition of particulate matter in buses exhaust. Toxicol. Rep. **6**, 120–125 (2019)
8. Climate Change AI (2019). https://www.climatechange.ai/
9. Defra (2019). https://uk-air.defra.gov.uk/data/
10. Energy models at the UCL Energy Institute (2019). https://www.ucl.ac.uk/energy-models/

11. Fares, S., et al.: Particle deposition in a peri-urban Mediterranean forest. Environ. Pollut. **218**, 1278–1286 (2016)
12. Gastaldi, M., Rossi, R., Gecchele, G., Della Lucia, L.: Annual average daily traffic estimation from seasonal traffic counts. Procedia-Soc. Behav. Sci. **87**, 279–291 (2013)
13. Highway England (2019). http://webtris.highwaysengland.co.uk/
14. Junninena, H., Niskaa, H., Tuppurainenc, K., Ruuskanena, J., Kolehmainena, M.: Methods for imputation of missing values in air quality data sets. Atmos. Environ. **38**(18), 2895–2907 (2004)
15. Krile, R., Todt, F., Schroeder, J., Jessberger, S.: Assessing roadway traffic count duration and frequency impacts on annual average daily traffic estimation: assessing accuracy issues related to annual factoring. Technical report, United States. Federal Highway Administration (2016)
16. London Air Quality Network (2019). http://www.londonair.org.uk/LondonAir/
17. London Atmospheric Emissions (LAEI) (2016). https://data.london.gov.uk/dataset/london-atmospheric-emissions-inventory-laei-2016
18. London Local Authority Maintained Trees (2019). https://data.london.gov.uk/dataset/local-authority-maintained-trees
19. Monks, P., Allan, J., Carruthers, D., Carslaw, D., Dore, C., Fuller, G.: Air quality expert group: impacts of vegetation on urban air pollution. UK Air Quality Reports (2018)
20. Mundhenk, T.N., Konjevod, G., Sakla, W.A., Boakye, K.: A large contextual dataset for classification, detection and counting of cars with deep learning. In: Leibe, B., Matas, J., Sebe, N., Welling, M. (eds.) ECCV 2016. LNCS, vol. 9907, pp. 785–800. Springer, Cham (2016). https://doi.org/10.1007/978-3-319-46487-9_48
21. Rolnick, D., et al.: Tackling climate change with machine learning. CoRR abs/1906.05433 (2019). http://arxiv.org/abs/1906.05433
22. Rybarczyk, Y., Zalakeviciute, R.: Machine learning approaches for outdoor air quality modelling: a systematic review. Appl. Sci. **8**, 2570 (2018)
23. Shahawy, M.: PyBNG (2019). https://pypi.org/project/PyBNG/
24. Traffic for London (2019). https://tfl.gov.uk/corporate/publications-and-reports/travel-in-london-reports
25. Transport for London, London Air Quality (2019). https://tfl.gov.uk/corporate/about-tfl/air-quality
26. Tsapakis, I., Schneider, W.H.: Use of support vector machines to assign short-term counts to seasonal adjustment factor groups. Transp. Res. Rec. **2527**(1), 8–17 (2015)
27. Zhu, D., Cai, C., Yang, T., Zhou, X.: A machine learning approach for air quality prediction: model regularization and optimization. Big Data Cogn. Comput. **2**, 5 (2018)

Author Index

Printed in the United States
by Baker & Taylor Publisher Services

Author Index

Printed in the United States
by Baker & Taylor Publisher Services